FIRST LECTURE

BERLIN MARCH 24, 1905

Because I will begin by discussing elementary aspects of the fourth dimension, what you hear today may disappoint you, but dealing with these issues in greater depth would require a thorough knowledge of the concepts of higher mathematics. I would first like to provide you with very general and elementary concepts. We must distinguish between the reality of four-dimensional space and the possibility of thinking about it. Four-dimensional space deals with a reality that goes far beyond ordinary sense-perceptible reality. When we enter that realm, we must transform our thinking and become familiar with the way in which mathematicians think.

We must realize that at each step — mathematicians take, they must account for its impact on their entire line of reasoning. When we concern ourselves with mathematics, however, we also must realize that even mathematicians cannot take a single step into four-dimensional reality. [They can arrive at conclusions only from what can and cannot be thought.]. The subjects we will deal with are initially simple but become more complicated as we approach the concept of the fourth dimension. We first must be clear about what we mean by dimensions. The best way to gain clarity is to check the dimensionality of various geometrical objects, which then will lead us to considerations that were first tackled in the nineteenth century by such great mathematicians as Bòlyai, Gauss, and Riemann.[1]

The simplest geometrical object is the point. It has no size; it can only be imagined. It fixes a location in space. It has a dimension which equals zero. The first dimension is given by a line. A straight line has one dimension, — length. When we move a line, which has no thickness, it leaves the first dimension and becomes a plane. A plane has two dimensions,—length and breadth. When we move a plane, it leaves these two dimensions. The result is a solid body with three dimensions—height, breadth, and depth (Figure 1).

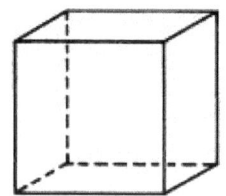

Figure 1

When you move a solid body (such as a cube) around in space, however, the result is still only a three-dimensional body. You cannot make it leave three-dimensional space by moving it.

There are still a few more concepts we need to look at. Consider a straight line segment. It has two boundaries, two endpoints—point A and point B (Figure 2).

Figure 2

Suppose we want to make point A and point B meet. To do this, we must bend the straight line segment. What happens then? It is impossible to make points A and B coincide if you stay within the [one-dimensional] straight line. To unite these two points, we must leave the straight line—that is, the first dimension—and enter the second dimension, the plane. When we make its endpoints coincide, the straight line segment becomes a closed curve, that is, in the simplest instance, a circle (Figure 3).

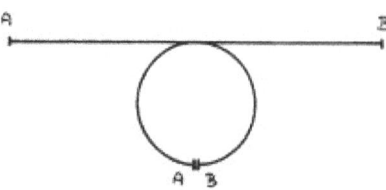

Figure 3

A line segment can be transformed into a circle only by leaving the first dimension. You can duplicate this process with a rectangular surface, but only if you do not remain in two dimensions. To transform the rectangle into a cylinder or tube, you must enter the third dimension. This operation is performed in exactly the same way as the preceding one, in which we brought two points together by leaving the first dimension. In the case of a rectangle, which lies in a plane, we must move into the third dimension in order to make two of its boundaries coincide (Figure 4).

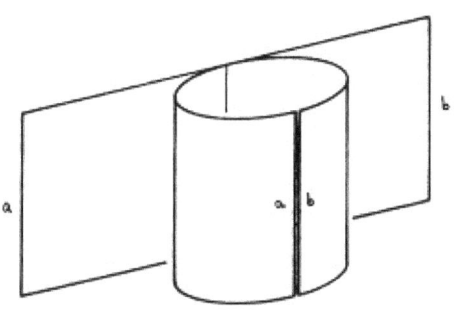

Figure 4

Is it conceivable to carry out a similar operation with an object that already has three dimensions? Think of two congruent cubes as the boundaries of a three-dimensional rectangular solid. You can slide one of these cubes into the other. Now imagine that one cube is red on one side and blue on the opposite side. The only way to make this cube coincide with the other one, which is geometrically identical but whose red and blue sides are reversed, would be to turn one of the cubes around and then slide them together (Figure 5).

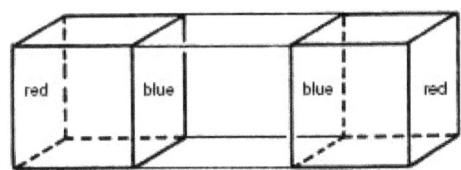

Figure 5

Let's consider another three-dimensional object. You cannot put a left-handed glove onto your right hand. But if you imagine a pair of gloves, which are symmetrical mirror images of each other and then you consider the straight line segment with its endpoints A and B, you can see how the gloves belong together. They form a single three-dimensional figure with a boundary, (the mirroring plane), in the middle. The same is true of the two symmetrical halves of a person's outer skin.[2] How can two three-dimensional objects that are mirror images of each other be made to coincide? only by leaving the third dimension, just as we left the first and second dimensions in the previous examples. A right- or left-handed glove can be pulled over the left or right hand, respectively, by going through four-dimensional space.[3] In building up depth, the third dimension of perceived space, we pull the image from our right eye over the image from our left eye, that is, we fuse the two images.[4]

Now let's consider one of Zöllners examples.[5] Here we have a circle and, outside it, a point P (Figure 6). How can we bring point P into the circle without cutting the circumference? We cannot do this if we remain within the plane. Just as we need to leave the second dimension and enter the third in order to make the transition from a square to a cube, we must also leave the second dimension in this example. Similarly, in the case of a sphere, it is impossible to get to the interior without either piercing the sphere's surface or leaving the third dimension.[6]

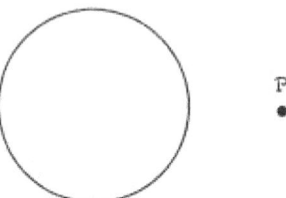

Figure 6

These are conceptual possibilities, but they are of immediate practical significance to epistemology, especially with regard to the epistemological problem of the objectivity of the contents of perception. We first must understand clearly how we actually perceive. How do we acquire knowledge about objects through our senses? We see a color. Without eyes we would not perceive it. Physicists tell us that what is out there in space is not color but purely spatial movement patterns that enter the eye and are then picked up by the visual nerve and conveyed to the brain, where the perception of the color red, for example, comes about. Next, we may wonder whether the color red is present when sensation is not.

We could not perceive red if we had no eyes or the sound of bells ringing if we had no ears. All of our sensations depend on movement patterns that are transformed by our psycho-physical apparatus. The issue becomes even more complicated, however, when we ask where that unique quality "red" is located—

is it on the object we perceive, or is it a vibrational process? A set of movements that originates outside us enters the eye and continues into the brain itself. Wherever you look, you find vibrational processes and nerve processes, but not the color red. You also will not find it by studying the eye itself. It is neither outside us nor in the brain. Red exists only when we ourselves, as subjects, intercept these movements. Is it impossible then to talk about how red comes to meet the eye or C-sharp the ear?

The questions are, what is an internal mental image of this sort, and where does it arise? These questions pervade all of nineteenth-century philosophy. Schopenhauer proposed the definition "The world is our mental image."[7] But in this case, what is left for the external object? Just as a mental image of color can be "created" by movement, so, too, the perception of movement can come about within us as a result of something that is not moving. Suppose we glue twelve snapshots of a horse in motion to the inner surface of a cylinder equipped with twelve narrow slits between the images. When we look sideways at the turning cylinder, we get the impression that we are always seeing the same horse and that its feet are moving.[8] Our bodily organization can induce the impression of movement when the object in question is really not moving at all. In this way, what we call movement dissolves into nothing.

In that case, what is matter? If we strip matter of color, movement, shape, and all other qualities conveyed through sensory perception, nothing is left. If "subjective" sensations, such as color, sound, warmth, taste, and smell, which arise in the consciousness of individuals as a result of environmental stimuli, must be sought within ourselves, so, too, must the primary, "objective" sensations of shape and movement. The outer world vanishes completely. This state of affairs causes grave difficulties for epistemology.[9]

Assuming that all qualities of objects exist outside us, how do they enter us? Where is the point at which the outer is transformed into the inner? If we strip the outer world of all the contents of sensory perception, it no longer exists. Epistemology begins to look like Münchhausen trying to pull himself up by his bootstraps.[10] To explain sensations that arise within us, we must assume that the outer world exists, but how do aspects of this outer world get inside us and appear in the form of mental images?

This question needs to be formulated differently. Let's consider several analogies that are necessary for discovering the connection between the outer world and internal sensation. Let's go back to the straight line segment with its endpoints A and B. To make these endpoints coincide, we must move beyond the first dimension and bend the line (Figure 7).

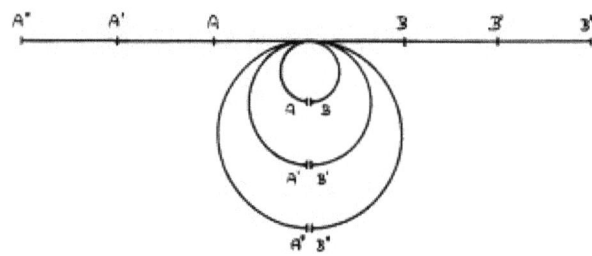

Figure 7

Now imagine that we make the left endpoint A of this straight line segment coincide with the right endpoint B in such a way that they meet below the original line. We can then pass through the overlapping endpoints and return to our starting point. If the original line segment is short, the resulting circle is small, but if I bend ever longer line segments into circles, the point where their endpoints meet moves farther and farther away from the original line until it is infinitely distant. The curvature becomes increasingly slight, until finally the naked eye can no longer distinguish the circumference of the circle from the straight line (Figure 8).

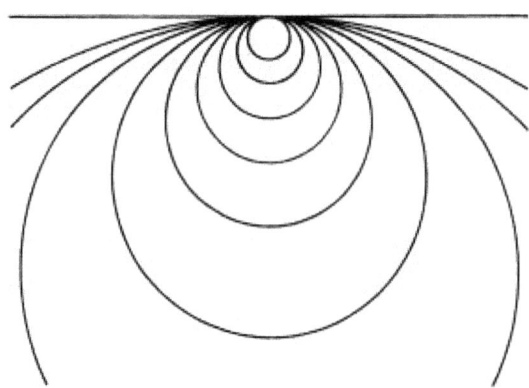

Figure 8

Similarly, when we walk on the Earth, it appears to be a straight, flat surface, though it is actually round. When we imagine the two halves of the straight line segment extended to infinity, the circle really does coincide with the straight line.[11] Thus a straight line can be interpreted as a circle whose diameter is infinitely large. Now we can imagine that if we move ever farther along the straight line, we will eventually pass through infinity and come back from the other side.

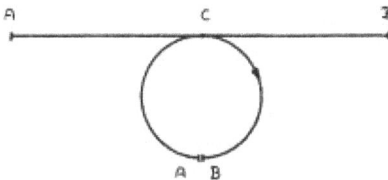

Figure 9

Instead of a geometric line, envision a situation that we can associate with reality. Let's imagine that point C becomes progressively cooler as it moves along the circumference of the circle and becomes increasingly distant from its starting point. When it passes the lower boundary A, B and begins the return trip on the other side, the temperature starts to rise (Figure 9). Thus, on its return trip, point C encounters conditions that are opposite to the ones it encountered on the first half of its journey. The warming trend continues until the original temperature is reached. This process remains the same no matter how large the circle; warmth initially decreases and then increases again. With regard to a line that stretches to infinity, the temperature decreases on one side and increases on the other. This is an example of how we bring life and movement into the world and begin to understand the world in a higher sense. Here we have two mutually dependent activities. As far as sensory observation is concerned, the process that moves to the right has nothing to do with the process that returns from the left, and yet the two are mutually dependent.[12]

Now let's relate the objects of the outer world to the cooling stage and our internal sensations to the warming stage. Although the outer world and our internal sensations are not linked directly by anything perceptible to the senses, they are interrelated and interdependent in the same way as the processes I just described. In support of their interrelationship, we also can apply the metaphor of seal and sealing wax. The seal leaves an exact impression, or copy, of itself in the sealing wax even though it does not remain in contact with the wax and there is no transfer of substance between them. The sealing wax retains a faithful impression of the seal. The connection between the outer world and our internal sensations is similar. only the essential aspect is transmitted. one set of circumstances determines the other, but no transfer of substance occurs.[13]

Viewing the connection between the outer world and our own impressions in this way, we realize that geometric mirror images in space are like right-and left-handed gloves. To make them coincide directly with a continuous motion, we need the help of a new dimension of space. If the relationship between the outer world and an internal impression is analogous to the relationship between figures that are geometric mirror images, the outer world and the internal impression also can be made to coincide directly only by means of an additional dimension. To establish a connection between the outer world and internal impressions, we must pass through a fourth dimension where we are still in the third. only there, where we are united with the outer world and inner impressions, can we discover their commonalties. We can imagine mirror images floating in a sea in which they can be made to coincide. Thus we arrive, though initially purely on the level of thinking, at something that is real but transcends three-dimensional space. To do this, we need to enliven our ideas of space.

Oskar Simony attempted to use models to depict enlivened spatial formations.[14] As we have seen, we can move step by step from considering zero dimension to imagining four-dimensional space. Four-dimensional space can be recognized most easily with the help of mirror-image figures or symmetrical relationships. Knotted curves and two-dimensional strips offer another method of studying the unique qualities of empirical, three-dimensional space as it relates to four-dimensional space. What do we mean by symmetrical relationships? When we interlink spatial figures, certain complications arise. These complications are unique to three-dimensional space; they do not occur in four-dimensional space.[15]

Let's try a few practical thought exercises. When we cut along the middle of a cylindrical ring, we get two such rings. If we give a strip a 180° twist before gluing its ends, cutting it down the middle results in a single twisted ring that will not come apart. If we give the strip a 360° twist before gluing its ends, the ring falls apart into two twisted, interlocking rings when we cut it. And finally, if we give the strip a 720° twist, cutting it results in a knot.[16] Anyone who thinks about natural processes knows that such twists occur in nature. In reality, all such twisted spatial formations possess specific forces. Take, for example, the movement of the Earth around the Sun and then the movement of the Moon around the Earth. We say that the Moon describes a circle around the Earth, but, if we look more closely, we realize that it actually describes a line that is twisted around the circle of the Earth's orbit—that is, a spiral around a circle. And then we also have the Sun, which moves so quickly through space that the Moon makes an additional spiral movement around it. Thus, the forcelines extending through space are very complex. We must realize that we are dealing with complicated spatial concepts that we can understand only if we do not try to pin them down but instead allow them to remain fluid.

Let's review what we discussed today. Zero dimension is the point, the first dimension is the line, the second dimension is the surface, and the third dimension is the solid body. How do these spatial concepts relate to one another? Imagine that you are a being who can move only along a straight line. What kind of spatial images do one-dimensional beings have? Such beings would be able to perceive only points, and not their own one-dimensionality, because when we attempt to draw something within a line, points are the only option. A two-dimensional being would be able to encounter lines and thus to distinguish one-dimensional beings. A three-dimensional being, such as a cube, would perceive two-dimensional beings. Human beings, however, can perceive three dimensions. If we draw the right conclusions, we must say that just as a one-dimensional being can perceive only points, a two-dimensional being only one dimension, and a three-dimensional being only two dimensions, a being that perceives three dimensions must be a four-dimensional being. Because we can delineate external beings in three dimensions and manipulate three-dimensional spaces, we must be four-dimensional beings.[17] Just as a cube can perceive only two dimensions and not its own third dimension, it is also true that we human beings cannot perceive the fourth dimension in which we live.

Second Lecture

BERLIN MARCH 31, 1905

Today I will discuss elementary aspects of the idea of multidimensional space, with particular reference to the thoughts of Charles Hinton, a very wise man.[18] As you recall, last time we began by considering the zero dimension and moved on to multidimensional space. Let me briefly reiterate the ideas we developed about two-and three-dimensional space.

What do we mean by a symmetrical relationship? How do I make two plane figures that are mirror images of each other, such as this red figure and this blue one, coincide?

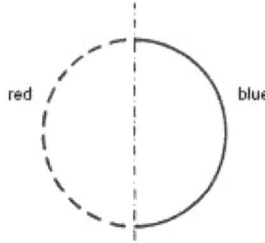

Figure 10

This is relatively easy to do with two half circles. I simply insert the red one into the blue one by rotating it (Figure 10). This is not so easy with the mirror-image symmetry below (Figure 11). No matter how I try to insert the red part into the blue part, I cannot make them coincide if I remain within the plane. There is a way to accomplish this, however, if we leave the board—that is, the second dimension—and use the third dimension; in other words, if we lay the blue figure on top of the red by rotating it through space around the axis of reflection.

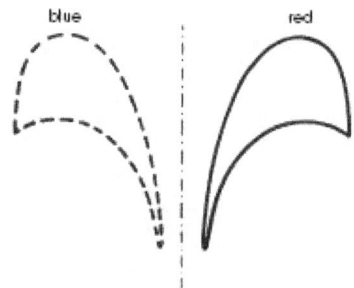

Figure 11

The situation is similar with a pair of gloves. We cannot make the one coincide with the other without leaving three-dimensional space. We have to go through the fourth dimension.

Last time I said that if we want to acquire an idea of the fourth dimension, we must allow relationships in space to remain fluid in order to produce circumstances similar to those present when we make the transition from the second to the third dimension. We created interlocking spatial figures from strips of paper and saw that interlocking brings about certain complications. This is not just a game, because such interlocking occurs everywhere in nature, especially in the intertwined motions of material objects. These motions include forces, so the forces also are intertwined. Take the Earth's movement around the Sun in connection with the Moon's movement around the Earth. The Moon describes a circle that winds around the Earth's orbit around the Sun, that is, the Moon describes a spiral around a circle. Because of the Sun's own movement, however, the Moon makes an additional spiral around it, resulting in very complicated lines of force that extend throughout space.

The relationships of the heavenly bodies resemble Simony's twisted strips of paper, which we looked at last time. We must realize, as I said earlier, that we are dealing with complicated spatial concepts that we can understand only if we do not allow them to become fixed. If we want to understand the nature of space, we will have to conceive of it as immobile, initially, but then allow it to become fluid again. It is like going all the way to zero, where we find the living essence of a point.

Let's visualize again how the dimensions are built up. A point is zero dimensional, a line is one dimensional, a surface two dimensional, and a solid object is three dimensional. Thus, a cube has three dimensions: height, width, and depth. How do spatial figures of different dimensions relate to one another? Imagine being a straight line. You have only one dimension and can move only along a line. If such one-dimensional beings existed, what would their idea of space be? They would not be able to perceive their one-dimensionality. Wherever they went, they would be able to imagine only points, because points are all we can draw while remaining within a straight line. A two-dimensional being would encounter only lines, that is, it would perceive only one-dimensional beings. A three-dimensional being, such as a cube, would perceive two-dimensional beings but not its own three dimensions.

Human beings, however, can perceive their own three dimensions. If we draw the correct conclusion, we must realize that if a one-dimensional being can perceive only points, a two-dimensional being only straight lines, and a three-dimensional being only surfaces, a being who perceives three dimensions must be four dimensional. The fact that we can delineate external beings in three dimensions and manipulate three-dimensional spaces means that we ourselves must be four-dimensional. Just as a cube would be able to perceive only two dimensions and not its own third dimension, it is clear that we cannot perceive the fourth dimension in which we ourselves live. Thus you see that human beings must be four-dimensional beings. We float in the sea of the fourth dimension like ice in water.

Let's return to our discussion of mirror images (Figure 11). This vertical line represents a cross-section formed by a mirror. The mirror reflects an image of the figure on the left side. The reflection process points beyond the second dimension into the third. In order to understand the direct, uninterrupted relationship of the mirror image to the original, we must assume that a third dimension exists in addition to the first and second.

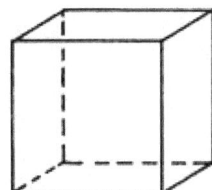

Figure 12

Now let's consider the relationship between external space and internal perception. A cube outside me appears as a perception inside me (Figure 12). My idea of the cube relates to the cube itself as a mirror image relates to the original. our sensory apparatus develops a mental image of the cube. If we want to make this image coincide with the original cube, we must pass through the fourth dimension. Just as a two-dimensional mirroring process must pass through the third dimension, our sensory apparatus must be four-dimensional to be able to bring about a direct connection between a mental image and an outer object. [19] If you were to visualize in two dimensions only, you would confront merely a dream image. You would have no idea that an actual object exists in the outer world. When we visualize an object, we spread our capacity for mental pictures directly over outer objects by means of four-dimensional space.

In the astral state during earlier periods of human evolution, human beings were only dreamers. The only images arising in their consciousness were dream images.[20] Later, humans made the transition from the astral state to physical space. Having said this, we have defined the transition from astral to physical, material existence in mathematical terms: before this transition, astral humans were three-dimensional beings, therefore, they could not extend their two-dimensional mental images to the objective, three-dimensional, physical, material world. When human beings themselves became physical, material beings, they acquired the fourth dimension and therefore also could experience life in three dimensions.

The unique structure of our sensory apparatus enables us to make our mental images coincide with outer objects. By relating our mental images to outer things, we pass through four-dimensional space, putting the mental image over the outer object. How would things look from the other side, if we could get inside them and see them from there? To do so, we would have to go through the fourth dimension. The astral world itself is not a world of four dimensions. Taken together with its reflection in the physical world, however, it is four-dimensional. When we are able to survey the astral and physical worlds simultaneously, we exist in four-dimensional space. The relationship of our physical world to the astral world is four-dimensional.

We must learn to understand the difference between a point and a sphere. In reality, a point such as the one pictured here is not passive, but radiates light in all directions (Figure 13).

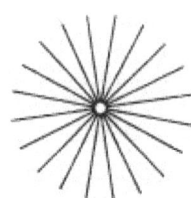

Figure 13

What would the opposite of such a point be? Just as the opposite of a line running from left to right is a line running from right to left, a point radiating light also has an opposite. Imagine a gigantic sphere, an infinitely large sphere that radiates darkness inward from all sides (Figure 14). This sphere is the opposite of a point that radiates light.

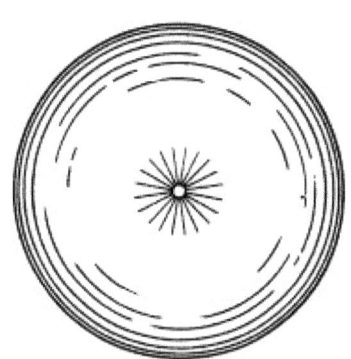

Figure 14

The true opposite of a light-radiating point is an infinite space that is not passively dark but actively floods space with darkness from all directions. The source of darkness and the source of light are opposites. We know that a straight line that vanishes into infinity returns to the same point from the other side. Similarly, when a point radiates light in all directions, the light returns from infinity as its opposite, as darkness.

Now let's consider the opposite case. Take the point as a source of darkness. Its opposite is then a space that radiates light inward from all directions. As I explained in the previous lecture, a point moving on a line does not vanish into infinity, it returns from the other side (Figure 15).

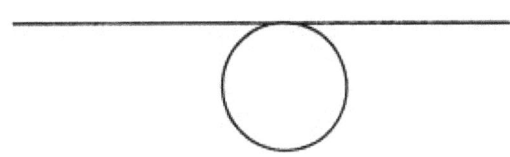

Figure 15

Analogously, a point that expands or radiates does not vanish into infinity, it returns from infinity as a sphere. The sphere is the opposite of the point. Space dwells within the point. The point is the opposite of space.

What is the opposite of a cube? Nothing less than the totality of infinite space minus the part defined by the cube. We must imagine the total cube as infinite space plus its opposite. We cannot get by without polarities when we attempt to imagine the world in terms of dynamic forces. only polarities give us access to the life inherent in objects.

When occultists visualize a red cube, the rest of space is green, because red is the complementary color of green. occultists do not have simple, self-contained mental images. Their mental images are alive rather than abstract and dead. our mental images are dead, while the objects in the world are alive. When we dwell in our abstract mental images, we do not dwell in the objects themselves. When we imagine a star that radiates light, we must also imagine its opposite—that is, infinite space—in the appropriate complementary color. When we do such exercises, we can train our thinking and gain confidence in imagining dimensions.

You know that a square is a two-dimensional area. A square composed of two red and two blue smaller squares (Figure 16) is a surface that radiates in different directions in different ways. The ability to radiate in different directions is a three-dimensional ability. Thus we have here the three dimensions of length, width, and radiant ability.

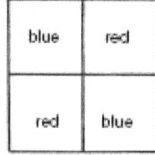

Figure 16

What we did here with a surface also can be done with a cube. Just as the square above is composed of four sub-squares, we imagine a cube composed of eight sub-cubes (Figure 17). Initially, the cube has three dimensions: height, width, and depth. In addition, we must distinguish a specific light-radiating capacity within each sub-cube. The result is another dimension, radiant ability, which must be added to height, width, and depth.

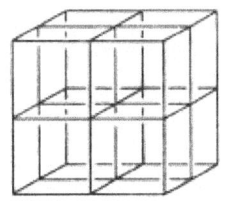

Figure 17

If every one of the eight sub-cubes has a different capacity to radiate, then, if I have just one cube with its one-sided capacity to radiate and I want to get a cube that radiates in all directions, I have to add another one in all directions, double it with its opposites — I have to compose it out of 16 cubes.[21].

Next time we meet, we will learn ways of imagining higher-dimensional space.

Third Lecture

BERLIN MAY 17, 1905

Today I will continue with the difficult subject we have undertaken to explore. We will need to refer back to the topics I mentioned in the last two lectures. After that, I would like to develop a few basic concepts so that in the two final lectures we will be able to use Mr. Schouten's models to fully grasp both the details of the geometric relationships and theosophy's interesting practical perspectives.[22]

As you know, the reason we tried to envision the possibility of four-dimensional space was to gain at least some idea of the so-called astral realm and still higher forms of existence. I have already pointed out that entering the astral world is initially quite confusing for students of esotericism. Without making a closer study of theosophy and esoteric subjects, at least on a theoretical level, it is *extremely* difficult to form any idea of the very different nature of the objects and beings that we encounter in the so-called astral world. Let me briefly sketch this difference to show you how great it is.

In the simplest example I mentioned, we have to learn to read all numbers in reverse. Esoteric students who are accustomed to reading numbers only as they are read here in the physical world will not be able to find their way through the labyrinth of the astral realm. In the astral world, a number such as 467 must be read 764. You must become used to reading each number symmetrically, as its mirror image. This is the basic prerequisite. Applying this rule to spatial figures or numbers is easy enough, but it becomes more difficult when we begin to deal with relationships in time, which also must also be interpreted symmetrically—that is, later events come first and earlier events appear later. Thus, when you observe astral events, you must be able to read them backward, from the end to the beginning. I can only suggest the character of these phenomena, which can seem totally grotesque if you have no idea of what is going on. In the astral realm, the son is there first and then the father, the egg is there first, and the chicken follows. In the physical world, the sequence is different—birth happens first, and birth means that something new emerges from something old. In the astral world, the reverse takes place. There, the old emerges from the new. In the astral realm, the fatherly or motherly element appears to engulf the son or daughter.

Greek mythologies provide a lovely allegory. The three gods Uranus, Kronos, and Zeus symbolize the three worlds. Uranus represents the heavenly world, or devachan, Kronos the astral world, and Zeus the physical world. It is said of Kronos that he devoured his children.[23] In the astral realm, offspring are not born but devoured.

The issue becomes even more complex when we consider morality on the astral plane. Morality, too, appears in reverse form, or as its own mirror image. You can imagine how greatly explanations of events there differ from our habitual explanations in the physical world. Imagine, for example, that we see a wild animal approaching us in the astral realm, and it strangles us. That is how it appears to someone who is used to interpreting external events, but we cannot interpret this event as we would in the physical world. In reality, the wild animal is an internal quality; an aspect of our own astral body is strangling us. The attacking strangler is a quality that is rooted in our own desires. If we have a vengeful thought, for example, the thought may appear in external form, tormenting us as the Angel of Death.

In reality, everything in the astral world radiates from us. We must interpret everything that seems to approach us in the astral world as radiating outward from ourselves (Figure 18). It comes back to us on all sides as if from the periphery, from infinite space. In truth, however, we are confronting only what our own astral body has given off.

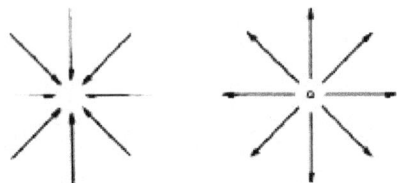

Figure 18

We interpret the astral world correctly and discover its truth only when we are able to bring the periphery into the center, to construe the periphery as the central element. The astral world appears to bear down on you from all sides, but you must envision it as actually radiating outward from you in all directions.

At this point I would like to make you aware of a concept that is very important in esoteric schooling. It appears, ghostlike, in many different works on occult research but seldom is it understood correctly. once you have achieved a certain level of esoteric development, you must learn what your karma predisposes you to find in the astral world. What joys, sorrows, pain, and so forth can you expect to encounter?

Correct theosophical thinking allows you to realize that in this day and age, your outer life and physical body are nothing more than the result, or intersection, of two streams that converge from opposite directions. Picture one stream coming from the past and one coming from the future. The result is two intermingling streams that join together at all these points (Figure 19). Imagine a red stream flowing from one direction and a blue stream flowing from the other. Now picture four different points where the streams join together. At each of these four points, the red and blue streams interact. This is an image of the interaction of four successive incarnations, in each incarnation we encounter something coming from one direction and something coming from the other. You might say that one stream always travels toward you and that you bring the other stream along with you. Each human being is the confluence of two such streams.

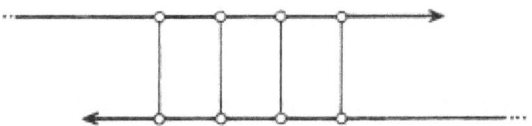

Figure 19

To gain an idea of this state of affairs, imagine in this way: As you sit here today, you have a certain sum of experiences. At the same time tomorrow, the sum of these events will be different. Now imagine that the experiences you will possess tomorrow are already there. Becoming aware of them would be like seeing a panorama of events coming toward you in space. Imagine that the stream coming toward you from the future is bringing you the experiences you will have between today and tomorrow. You are supported by the past as the future comes to meet you.

At any point in time, two streams flow together to form your life. one stream flows from the future toward the present and the other from the present toward the future, and an interface occurs wherever they meet. Anything that still remains for us to experience in our life appears in the form of astral phenomena, which make a tremendous impression on us.

Imagine that students of esotericism reach the point in their development when they are meant to see into the astral world. Their senses are opened, and they perceive all their future experiences until the end of this time period as outer phenomena surrounding them in the astral world. This sight makes a great impression on each student. An important level in esoteric schooling is reached when students experience an astral panorama of everything they have yet to encounter up to the middle of the sixth root race, which is how long our incarnations will last. The way is opened to them. Without exception, students of esotericism experience all the remaining outer phenomena they will encounter from the near future to the sixth root race.

When you reach this threshold, a question arises: Do you want to experience all this in the shortest possible time? That is the issue for initiation candidates. As you consider this question, your entire future life appears to you in a single moment in the external panorama characteristic of astral vision. Some people will decide not to set out into the astral realm, while others will feel that they must enter. At this point in esoteric development, which is known as the threshold, or moment of decision, we experience ourselves along with everything we must still live through. This phenomenon, which is known as meeting the "guardian of the threshold," is nothing more than facing our own future life. our own future lies beyond the threshold.

Another unique quality of the world of astral phenomena is initially quite impenetrable if that world is revealed suddenly, through one of life's unforeseen events. When this happens, there is nothing more confusing than this terrible sight. It is good to know about it in case the astral world suddenly breaks in on you as the result of a pathological event, such as the loosening of the connection between the physical body and ether body or between the ether body and the astral body. Such events can reveal a view of the astral world to people who are quite unprepared for it. These people then report seeing apparitions that they cannot interpret because they do not know that they must read them in reverse. For instance, they do not know that a wild animal attacking them must be interpreted as a reflection of an internal quality. In kamaloka, a person's astral forces and passions appear in a great variety of animal forms.

In kamaloka, recently disembodied individuals who still possess all their passions, drives, wishes, and desires are not a pretty sight. Such people, though they are no longer in possession of physical and etheric bodies, still retain all the astral elements that bind them to the physical world and that can be satisfied only through a physical body. Think of average, modern citizens who never amounted to much in their lives and made no particular effort to achieve religious development. They may not have rejected religion in theory, but in practice—that is, as far as their own feelings were concerned—they threw it out the window. It was not a vital element in their lives. What do such people's astral bodies contain? They contain nothing but urges that can be satisfied only through the physical organism, such as the desire to enjoy tasty food, for example. Satisfying this desire, however, would require taste buds. or the individual in question may long for other pleasures that can be satisfied only by moving the physical body. Suppose that such urges persist, living on in the astral body after the physical body is gone. We find ourselves in this situation if we die without first undergoing astral cleansing and purification. We still have the urge to enjoy tasty food and so on, but such urges are impossible to satisfy. They cause terrible torment in kamaloka, where those who die without first purifying the astral body must lay their desires aside. The astral body is freed only when it learns to relinquish the desires and wishes that can no longer be satisfied.

In the astral world, urges and passions take on animal shapes. As long as a human being is incarnated in a physical body, the shape of the astral body conforms more or less to the human physical body. When the material body is gone, however, the animal nature of urges, desires, and passions is revealed in the forms they assume. In the astral world, therefore, an individual is a reflection of his or her urges and passions. Because these astral beings can also make use of other bodies, it is dangerous to allow mediums to go into a trance without the presence of a clairvoyant who can ward off evil. In the physical world, the form of a lion expresses certain passions, while a tiger expresses other passions and a cat still others. It is interesting to realize that each animal form is the expression of a specific passion or urge.

In the astral world, in kamaloka, we approximate the nature of animals through our passions. This fact is the source of a common misunderstanding with regard to the doctrine of transmigration of souls taught by Egyptian and Indian priests and teachers of wisdom. This doctrine, which teaches that we should live in ways that do not cause us to incarnate as animals, does not apply to physical life but only to higher life. It is intended only to encourage people to live their earthly lives in ways that will not require them to assume animal forms after death, in kamaloka. For example, someone who cultivates the character of a cat during earthly life appears in the form of a cat in kamaloka. To allow individuals to appear in human form in kamaloka is the goal of the doctrine of transmigration of souls. Scholars who fail to understand the true teachings have only an absurd idea of this doctrine.

We saw that when we enter the astral realm of numbers, time, and morality, we are dealing with a complete mirror image of everything we customarily think and do here on the physical plane. We must acquire the habit of reading in reverse, a skill we will need when we enter the astral realm. Learning to read in reverse is easiest when we take up elementary mathematical ideas such as those suggested in the previous lecture. In the discussions that follow, we will become more and more familiar with these ideas. I would like to begin with a very simple one, namely, the idea of a square. Picture a square as you are accustomed to seeing it (Figure 20). I will draw each of its four sides in a different color.

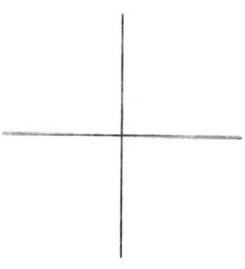

Figure 20

This is what a square looks like in the physical world. Now I will draw a square as it looks in devachan. It is impossible to draw this figure precisely, but I want to give you at least an idea of what a square would look like on the mental plane. The mental equivalent [of a square] is something approximating a cross (Figure 21).

Figure 21

Its main features are two intersecting perpendicular axes—or, if you will, two lines that cross each other. The physical counterpart is constructed by drawing lines perpendicular to each of these axes. The physical counterpart of a mental square can best be imagined as a stoppage in two intersecting streams. Let's imagine these perpendicular axes as streams or forces working outward from their point of intersection, with counter tendencies working in from the opposite direction, from the outside inward (Figure 22). A square arises in the physical world when we imagine that these two types of streams or forces—one coming from within and one coming from outside—meet and hold each other at bay. Boundaries develop where a stoppage occurs in the streams of force.

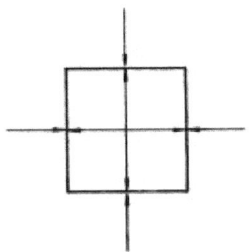

Figure 22

This image describes how everything on the mental plane relates to everything on the physical plane. You can construct the mental counterpart of any physical object in the same way. This square is only the simplest possible example. If, for any given physical object, you could construct a correlate that relates to that object in the same way that two intersecting perpendicular lines relate to a square, the result would be the image of the physical object in devachan, on the mental level. With objects other than a square, this process is much more complicated, of course.

Now instead of the square, imagine a cube. A cube is very similar to a square. A cube is a figure bounded by six squares. Mr. Schouten has made an extra model showing the six squares that delineate a cube. Instead of the four boundary lines in a square, imagine six surfaces forming the boundaries. Imagine that the boundary of the stopped forces consists of perpendicular surfaces instead of perpendicular lines and assume that you have three instead of two perpendicular axes. You have just defined a cube. At this point, you probably also can imagine a cube's correlate on the mental level. Again we have two figures that complement each other. A cube has three perpendicular axes and three different directions to its surfaces. We must imagine that stoppage occurs in these three surface directions (Figure 23). The three directions of the axes and the six surfaces, like the square's two axes (directions) and four lines, can be imagined only as opposites of a particular sort.

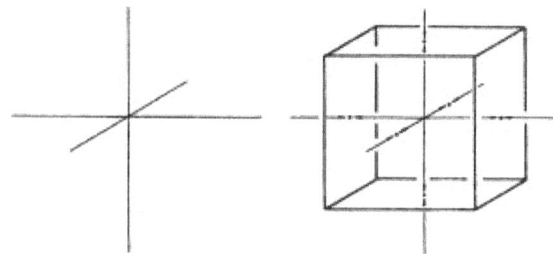

Figure 23

Anyone who thinks about this subject at all must conclude that in order to imagine these figures, we must first arrive at a concept of opposites that contrast activity and counter-activity, or stoppage. This concept of opposites must enter into our considerations. The examples we used are simple, but by practicing with geometric concepts, we will learn how to construct the mental counterparts of more complicated objects properly; this activity will show us the way to higher knowledge to a certain extent. You already can imagine the monumental complexity of trying to find the mental counterpart of some other figures. Far greater complications emerge. Just imagine thinking about a human form and its mental counterpart with all its different shapes and activity. You can conceive what a complicated mental structure this would be. My book *Theosophy* gives approximations of how mental counterparts would look.[24]

In the case of a cube, we have three extensions, or three axes. Two planes, one on each side, are perpendicular to each axis. At this point you need to understand clearly that each surface of a cube, like the human life I described earlier, comes about as the meeting of two streams. You can picture streams moving outward from the midpoint. Imagine one of these axial directions. Space streams outward from the midpoint in one direction and toward the midpoint from the other direction, from infinity. Now envision these streams in two different colors, one red and one blue. At the moment of their meeting, they flow together to create a surface. Thus, we can see the surface of a cube as the meeting of two opposing streams in a surface. This visualization gives us a living idea of the nature of a cube.

A cube is a section of three interacting streams. When you think of the totality of their interaction, you are dealing with six directions rather than three: backward/forward, up/down, and right/left. There are actually six directions. The issue is complicated further by the existence of two types of streams, one moving outward from a point and another moving inward from infinity. This will give you a perspective on the practical applications of higher, theoretical theosophy. Any direction in space must be interpreted as two opposing streams, and any physical shape must be imagined as their result. Let's call these six streams, or directions, *a, b, c, d, e,* and *f*. If you could visualize these six directions—and next time we will talk about how to cultivate such mental images—and then eliminate the first and last, *a* and *f*, four would remain. Please note that these remaining four are the ones you can perceive when you see only the astral world.

I have attempted to provide you with some idea of the three ordinary dimensions and of three additional and opposite dimensions. Physical forms arise as a result of the opposing action of these dimensions. If you remove one dimension on the physical level and one on the mental level, however, you are left with the four dimensions that represent the astral world, which exists between the physical and mental worlds.

The theosophical worldview must work with a higher geometry that transcends ordinary geometry. ordinary geometrists describe a cube as delineated by six squares. We must conceive of a cube as the result of six interpenetrating streams—that is, as the result of a movement and its opposite or as the consequence of interacting opposing forces.

I would still like to give you an example from the natural world of a concept that embodies such a pair of opposites and shows us one of the profound mysteries of the world's evolution. In his *The Green Snake and the Beautiful lily*, Goethe speaks of the 'revealed mystery,' one of the truest and wisest phrases ever formulated.[25] Nature does indeed contain unseen but quite tangible mysteries, including many inversion processes. Let me describe one of them.

Let's compare a human being to a plant. This is not a game, though it looks like one. It points to a profound mystery. Which part of the plant is in the ground? It is the root. Up top, the plant develops stems, leaves, flowers, and fruit. The plant's 'head,' its root, is in the ground, and its organs of reproduction develop above ground, closer to the sun. This can be called the chaste method of reproduction. Picture the whole plant inverted, with its root becoming the human head. There you have the human being,—with the head above and the reproductive organs below,—as the inverse of a plant. The animal occupies the middle and represents an interface. The result of inverting a plant is a human being. Esotericists throughout the ages have used three lines to symbolize this phenomenon (Figure 24).

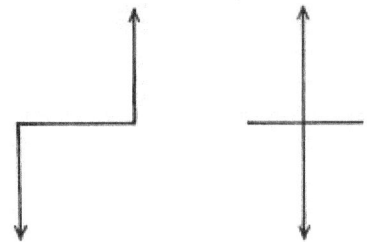

Figure 24

One line symbolizes the plant, another represents the human being, and a third opposing line corresponds to the animal-three lines that together form a cross. The animal occupies the horizontal position—that is, it crosses what we humans have in common with plants.

As you know, Plato speaks of a universal soul that is crucified on the body of the Earth, bound to the cross of the Earth.[26] If you envision the world soul as plant, animal, and human being, the result is the cross. since it lives in these three kingdoms, the world soul is bound to the cross they form. Here you find an extension of the concept of interfaced forces. The plant and the human being represent two complementary, and divergent, but intersecting streams, while the animal, which actually interjects itself into an upward and a downward stream, represents the interface that arises between them. similarly, kamaloka, or the astral sphere, stands between devachan and the physical world. Between these two worlds, whose relationship is that of mirror images, an interface arises—the world of kamaloka—whose outer expression is the animal kingdom.

Strength is required to perceive this world, but those who already have the appropriate organs of perception will recognize what we see in the interrelationship of these three kingdoms. if you interpret the animal kingdom as emerging from an interface, you will discover the relationship between the plant and animal kingdoms and the animal and human kingdoms. The animal stands perpendicular to the direction of the two other kingdoms, which are complementary, interpenetrating streams. Each lower kingdom serves the next higher one as food. This fact sheds light on the difference between the human-plant relationship and the animal-human relationship. Human beings who eat animals develop a relationship to a condition of interfacing. The real activity consists in the meeting of opposing streams. in making this statement, I am initiating a train of thought that will reappear later in a strange and very different guise.

In summary, we have seen that a square comes about when two axes are cut by lines. A cube comes about when three axes are cut by surfaces. Can you imagine four axes being cut by something? The cube is the boundary of the spatial figure that comes about when four axes are cut.

A square forms the boundary of a three-dimensional cube. Next time we will see what figure results when a cube forms the boundary of a four-dimensional figure.

Questions and Answers

What does it mean to imagine six streams and then eliminate two, and so on?

The six streams must be imagined as two times three: three of them work from the center outward in the directions defined by the three axes, and the other three work in the opposite directions, coming from infinity. Thus, for each axial direction there are two types,—one going outward from the interior and the other moving inward from outside. if we call these two types positive and negative, plus and minus, the result is this:

$$+a \quad -a$$
$$+b \quad -b$$
$$+c \quad -c$$

To enter the astral realm we must eliminate one entire direction of inward and outward streams—$+a$ and $-a$, for example.

Fourth Lecture

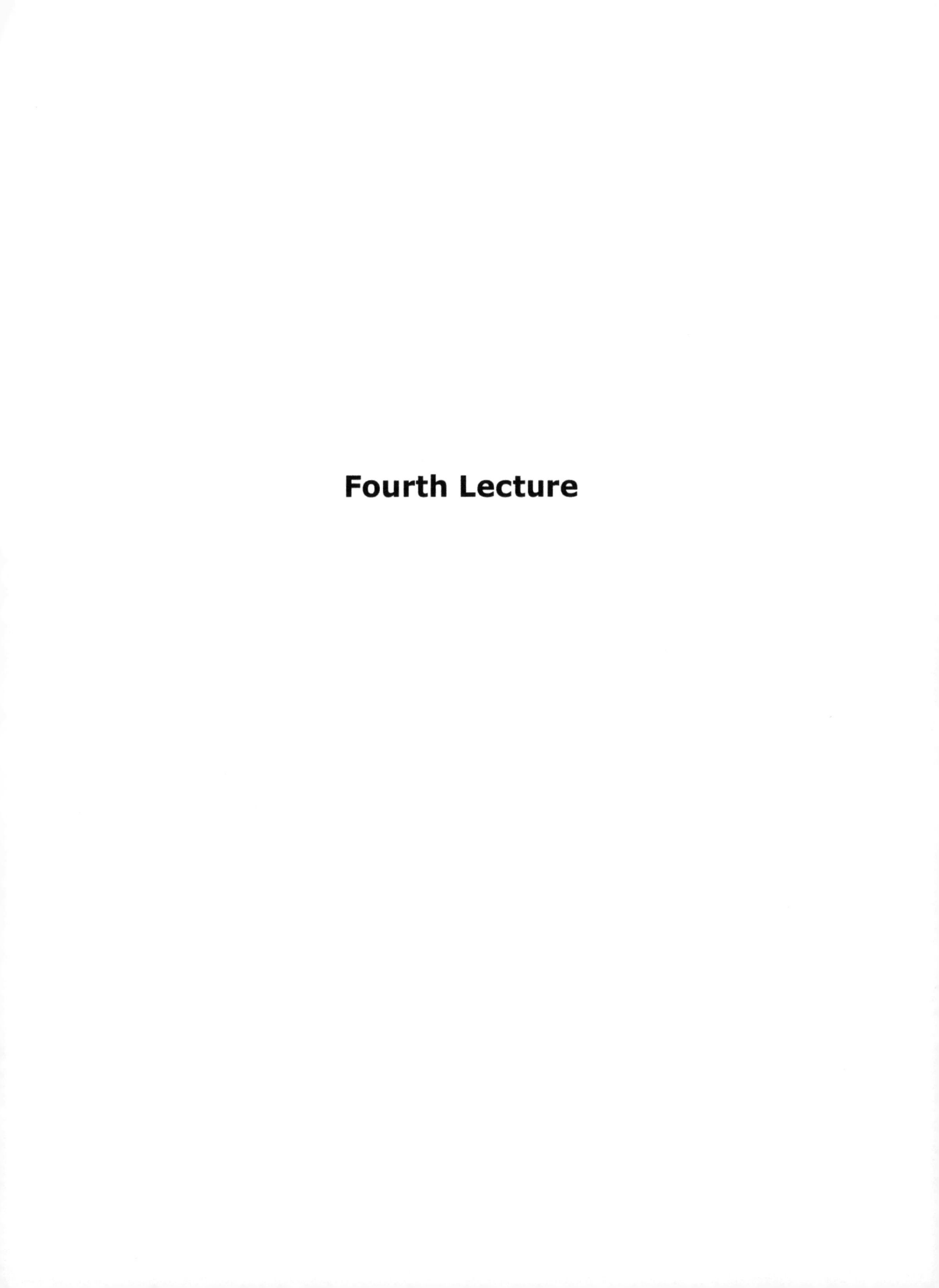

BERLIN MAY 24, 1905

In a recent lecture I attempted to develop a schematic idea of four-dimensional space, which would be very difficult to do without using an analogy of sorts. The problem that confronts us is how to indicate a four-dimensional figure here in three-dimensional space, which is the only type of space initially accessible to us. To link the unfamiliar element of four-dimensional space to something we know about, we must find ways to bring a four-dimensional object into three dimensions, just as we brought a three-dimensional object into two dimensions. I would like to use the method popularized by Mr. Hinton to demonstrate a solution to the problem of how to represent four-dimensional space in three dimensions.[27]

Let me begin by showing how three-dimensional space can be depicted in two dimensions. Our chalkboard here is a two-dimensional surface. Adding depth to its dimensions of height and width would give us a three-dimensional space. Now let's attempt to depict a three-dimensional figure here on the chalkboard.

A cube is a three-dimensional figure because it has height, width, and depth. Let's try to bring a cube into two-dimensional space—that is, into a plane. We can take a cube and unfold it so that its six square sides are spread out in a plane (Figure 25). In two dimensions, therefore, the surfaces defining a cube can be imagined as forming a cross.

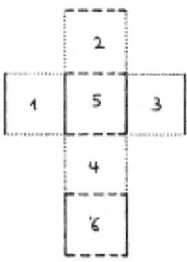

Figure 25

These six squares form a cube again when I fold them up so that squares 1 and 3 are opposite each other. Squares 2 and 4 are also opposite each other, as are 5 and 6. This is a simple way of transferring a three-dimensional figure to a plane.

We cannot use this method directly when we want to draw the fourth dimension in three-dimensional space. For that, we need a different analogy. We will need to use colors. i will color the edges of the six squares differently, so that opposite sets of squares are of the same colors. For squares 1 and 3, I will make one pair of edges red (dotted lines) and another blue (solid lines). I also will color all the horizontal edges of the other squares blue and all the verticals red (Figure 26).

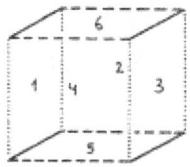

Figure 26

Look at these two squares, 1 and 3. Their two dimensions are represented by two colors, red and blue. For us, then, on the vertical board, where square 2 is flat against the board, red means height, and blue means depth.

Having consistently used red for height and blue for depth, let's add green (dashed lines) for width, the third dimension, and complete our unfolded cube. square 5 has blue and green sides, so square 6 must look the same. Now only squares 2 and 4 are left. When you imagine them unfolded, you find that their sides are red and green.

Having visualized these colored edges, you realize that we have transformed the three dimensions into three colors. instead of height, width, and depth, we now call them red (dotted), green (dashed), and blue (solid). These three colors replace and represent the three dimensions of space. Now imagine the whole cube folded up again. You can explain the addition of the third dimension by saying that the blue and red square has moved through green i.e., from left to right in Figure 26. Moving through green, or disappearing into the dimension of the third color, represents the transition through the third dimension. imagine that a green fog tints the red-and-blue squares, so that both edges (red and blue) appear colored. The blue edge becomes blue-green and the red acquires a murky tint. Both edges reappear in their own color only where the green stops. i could do the same thing with squares 2 and 4 by allowing a red-and-green square to move through a blue space. You could do the same with the two blue-and-green squares, 5 and 6, moving one of them through red. in each case, the square disappears on one side, submerging into a different color that tints it until it emerges on the other side in its original coloration. Thus, the three colors positioned at right angles to each other are a symbolic representation of our cube. We simply have used colors for the three directions. To visualize the changes the cube's three pairs of surfaces undergo, we imagine them passing through green, red, and blue, respectively.

Instead of these colored lines, imagine squares, and instead of empty space, picture squares everywhere. Then I can draw the entire figure in a still different way (Figure 27). The square through which the others pass is colored blue, and the two that pass through it—before and after they make the transition—are drawn flanking it. Here they are in red and green. In a second step, the blue-and-green squares pass through the red square, and, in a third step, the two red-and-blue squares pass through the green.

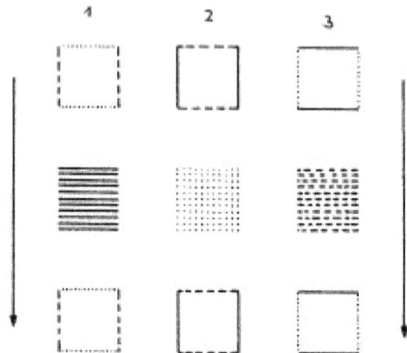

Figure 27

Here you see a different way of flattening out a cube. of the nine squares arranged here, only six—the upper and lower rows—form the boundaries of the cube itself (Figure 27). The other three squares in the middle row represent transitions; they simply signify that the other two colors disappear into a third. Thus, with regard to the movement of transition, we must always take two dimensions at once, because each of these squares in the upper and lower rows is made up of two colors and disappears into the color that does not contain it. We make these squares disappear into the third color in order to reappear on the other side. The red-and-blue squares pass through green. The red-and-green squares have no blue sides, so they disappear into blue, while the green-and-blue squares pass through red. As you see, we can thus construct our cube out of two-dimensional—that is, bicolored—squares that pass through a third dimension or color.[28]

The next obvious step is to imagine cubes in the place of squares and to visualize these cubes as being composed of squares of three colors (dimensions), just as we constructed our squares out of lines of two colors. The three colors correspond to the three dimensions of space. if we want to proceed just as we did with the squares, we must add a fourth color so that we can make each cube disappear through the color it lacks. We simply have four differently colored transition cubes—blue, white, green, and red—instead of three transition squares. Instead of squares passing through squares, we now have cubes passing through cubes. Mr. schouten's models use such colored cubes.[29]

Just as we made one square pass through a second square, we must now make one cube pass through a second cube of the remaining color. Thus the white-red-and-green cube passes through a blue one. on one side, it submerges in the fourth color; on the other side, it reappears in its original colors (Figure 28.1). Thus we have here one color or dimension that is bounded by two cubes whose surfaces are three different colors.

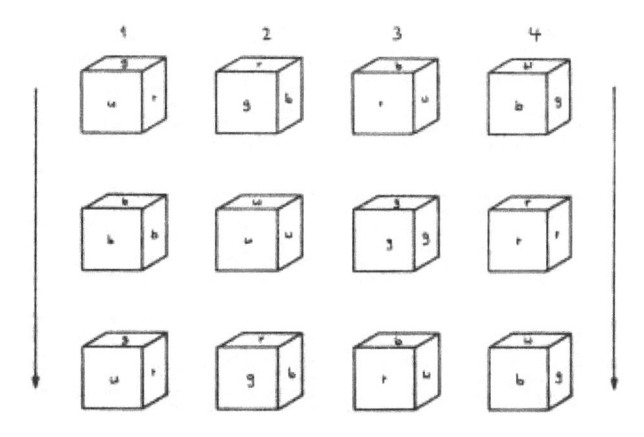

Figure 28

Similarly, we must now make the green-blue-and-red cube pass through the white cube (Figure 28.2). The blue-red-and-white cube passes through the green one (Figure 28.3), and, in the last figure (Figure 28.4), the blue-green-and-white cube has to pass through a red dimension; that is, each cube must disappear into the color it lacks and reappear on the other side in its original colors.

These four cubes relate to each other in the same way as the three squares in our previous example. We needed six squares to delineate the boundaries of a cube.[30] Similarly, we need eight cubes to form the boundaries of the analogous four-dimensional figure, the tessaract.[31] In the case of a cube, we needed three accessory squares that simply signified disappearance through the remaining dimension. A tessaract requires a total of twelve cubes, which relate to one another in the same way as the nine squares in a plane. We have now done to a cube what we did with squares in the earlier example. Each time we chose a new color, we added a new dimension. We used colors to represent the four directions incorporated by a four-dimensional figure. Each of the cubes in this figure has three colors and passes through a fourth. The point in replacing dimensions with colors is that three dimensions as such cannot be incorporated into a two-dimensional plane. using three colors makes this possible. We do the same thing with four dimensions when we use four colors to create an image in three-dimensional space. This is one way of introducing this otherwise complicated subject. Hinton used this method to solve the problem of how to represent four-dimensional figures in three dimensions.

Next I would like to unfold the cube again and lay it down in the plane. I'll draw it on the board. For the moment, disregard the bottom square in Figure 25 and imagine that you can see in two dimensions only—that is, you can see only what you can encounter on the surface of the board. In this instance, we have placed five squares so that one square is in the middle. The interior area remains invisible (Figure 29). You can go all the way around the outside, but since you can see only in two dimensions, you will never see square 5.

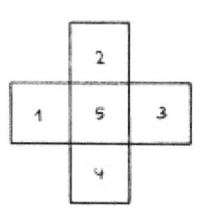

Figure 29

Now instead of taking five of the six square sides of a cube, let's do the same thing with seven of the eight cubes that form the boundaries of a tessaract, spreading our four-dimensional figure out in space. The placement of the seven cubes is analogous to that of the cube's surfaces laid down in a plane on the board, but now we have cubes instead of squares. The resulting three-dimensional figure is analogous in structure to the two-dimensional cross made of squares and is its equivalent in three-dimensional space. The seventh cube, like one of the squares, is invisible from all sides. It cannot be seen by any being capable only of three-dimensional sight (Figure 30). If we could fold up this figure, as we can do with the six unfolded squares in a cube, we could move from the third into the fourth dimension. Transitions indicated by colors show us how this process can be visualized.[32]

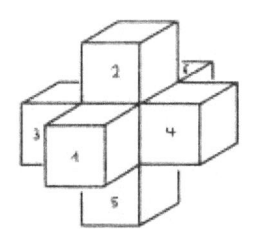

Figure 30

We have demonstrated at least how we humans can visualize four-dimensional space in spite of being able to perceive only three dimensions. At this point, since you also may wonder how we can gain an idea of real four-dimensional space, I would like to make you aware of the so-called *alchemical mystery*, because a true view of four-dimensional space is related to what the alchemists called *transformation*.

[First text variant:] if we want to acquire a true view of four-dimensional space, we must do very specific exercises. First we must cultivate a very clear and profound vision—not a mental image—of what we call water. such vision is difficult to achieve and requires lengthy meditation. We must immerse ourselves in the nature of water with great precision. We must creep inside the nature of water, so to speak. As a second exercise, we must create a vision of the nature of light. Although light is familiar to us, we know it only in the form in which we receive it from outside. By meditating, we acquire the inner counterpart of outer light. We know where and how light arises; we ourselves become able to produce something like light. Through meditation, yogis or students of esotericism acquire the ability to produce light. When we truly meditate on pure concepts, when we allow these concepts to work on our souls during meditation or sense-free thinking, light arises out of the concepts. Our entire surroundings are revealed to us as streaming light. Esoteric students must "chemically combine" the vision of water that they have cultivated with their vision of light. Water fully imbued with light is what the alchemists called *mercury*. In the language of alchemy, water plus light equals mercury. In the alchemical

tradition, however, mercury is not simply ordinary quicksilver. After we awaken our own ability to create light out of our own work with pure concepts, mercury comes about as the mingling of this light with our vision of water. We take possession of this light-imbued power of water, which is one of the elements of the astral world.

The second element arises when we cultivate a vision of air, just as we previously cultivated a vision of water. Through a spiritual process, we extract the power of air. Then, by concentrating the power of feeling in certain ways, feeling kindles fire. When you chemically combine, as it were, the power of air with the fire kindled by feeling, the result is "fire-air." As you may know, this fire-air is mentioned in Goethe's Faust.[33] It requires the inner participation of the human being. one component is extracted from an existing element, the air, while we ourselves produce the other fire or warmth. Air plus fire yields what the alchemists called *sulfur*, or shining fire-air. The presence of this fire-air in a watery element is truly what is meant when the Bible says, "And the spirit of God brooded upon the face of the waters."[34]

The third element comes about when we extract the power of the earth and combine it with the spiritual forces in sound. The result is what is called the spirit of God. it also is called thunder. The active Spirit of God is thunder,— earth plus sound. Thus, the Spirit of God hovered over astral substance. The biblical "waters" are not ordinary water but what we know as astral substance, which consists of four types of forces:—water, air, light, and fire. The sequence of these four forces is revealed to astral vision as the four dimensions of astral space. That is what they really are. Astral space looks very different from our world. Many supposedly astral phenomena are simply projections of aspects of the astral world into physical space.

As you can see, astral substance is half-subjective, that is, passively given to the subject, and half water and air. Light and feeling (fire), on the other hand, are objective, that is, made to appear by the activity of the subject. Only one part of astral substance can be found outside, given to the subject in the environment. The other part must be added by subjective means, through personal activity. conceptual and emotional forces allow us to extract the other aspect from what is given through active objectification. In the astral realm, therefore, we find subjective-objective substance. In devachan, we would find only a completely subjective element; there is no longer any objectivity at all that is simply given to the subject.

In the astral realm, therefore, we find an element that must be created by human beings. Everything we do here is simply a symbolic representation of the higher worlds, or devachan. These worlds are real, as I have explained to you in these lectures. What lies within these higher worlds can be attained only by developing new possibilities for vision. Human beings must be active in order to reach these worlds.

[Second text variant: (Vegelahn):] If we want to acquire a true view of four-dimensional space, we must do very specific exercises. First, we must cultivate a clear and profound vision of water. such vision cannot be achieved as a matter of course. We must immerse ourselves in the nature of water with great precision. We must creep inside water, so to speak. second, we must create a vision of the nature of light. Although light is familiar to us, we know it only in the form in which we receive it from outside. By meditating, we acquire the inner counterpart of outer light. We learn where light comes from, so we ourselves become able to produce light. We can do this by truly allowing these concepts to work on our souls during meditation or sense-free thinking. our entire surroundings are revealed to us as streaming light. Then we must "chemically combine" the mental image of water that we have cultivated with that of light. Water fully imbued with light is what the alchemists called *mercury*. In the language of alchemy, water plus light equals mercury. This alchemical mercury, however, is not simply ordinary quicksilver. We must first awaken our own ability to create mercury out of the concept of light. We then take possession of mercury, the light-imbued power of water, which is one element of the astral world.

The second element arises when we cultivate a vivid mental image of air and then extract the power of air through a spiritual process, combining it with feeling inside us to kindle the concept of warmth, or fire. one element is extracted, while we ourselves produce the other. These two—air plus fire—yield what the alchemists called *sulfur*, or shining fire-air. The watery element is truly the substance referred to in the biblical statement "The Spirit of God brooded upon the face of the waters."[35]

The third element is "Spirit-God," or earth combined with sound. It comes about when we extract the power of the earth and combine it with sound. The biblical "waters" are not ordinary water but what we know as astral substance, which consists of four types of forces: water, air, light, and fire. These four forces constitute the four dimensions of astral space.

As you can see, astral substance is half subjective; only one part of astral substance can be acquired from the environment. The other part is acquired through objectification from conceptual and emotional forces. In devachan, we would find only a completely subjective element; there is no objectivity there. Everything we do here is simply a symbolic representation of the world of devachan. What lies within the higher worlds can be reached only by developing in ourselves new ways of perceiving. Human beings must be active in order to reach these worlds.

FIfth Lecture

BERLIN MAY 31, 1905

Last time we attempted to visualize a four-dimensional spatial figure by reducing it to three dimensions. First we converted a three-dimensional figure into a two-dimensional one. We substituted colors for dimensions, constructing our image using three colors to represent the three dimensions of a cube. Then we unfolded the cube so that all of its surfaces lay in a plane, resulting in six squares whose differently colored edges represented the three dimensions in two-dimensional space.

We then envisioned transferring each square of the cube's surface into the third dimension as moving the square through a colored fog and allowing it to reappear on the other side. We imagined all the surface squares moving through and being tinted by transition squares. Thus, we used colors to attempt to picture a three-dimensional cube in two dimensions. To represent squares in one dimension, we used two different colors for their edge pairs; to represent a cube in two dimensions, we used three colors. Depicting a four-dimensional figure in three-dimensional space required a fourth color.

Then we imagined a cube with three different surface colors as analogous to our square with two different edge colors. Each such cube moved through a cube of the fourth color; that is, it disappeared into the fourth dimension or color. In accordance with Hinton's analogy, we made each boundary cube move through the new fourth color and reappear on the other side in its own original color.

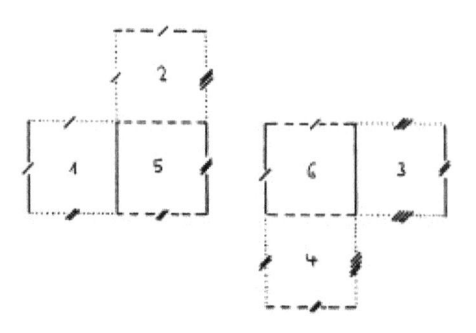

Figure 31

Now I would like to give you another analogy. We will begin once again by reducing three dimensions to two in preparation for reducing four dimensions to three. We must envision constructing our cube out of its six square sides, but instead of leaving all six squares attached when we spread them out, we will arrange them differently, as shown here (Figure 31). As you see, we have split the cube into two groups of three squares each. Both groups lie in the same plane. We must understand the location of each group when we reassemble the cube. To complete the cube, I must place one group above the other so that square 6 lies over square 5. Once square 5 is in position, I must fold squares 1 and 2 upward, while squares 3 and 4 must be folded downward (Figure 32). The corresponding pairs of line segments—that is, the ones of the same color (here, with the same number and weight of slashes as shown in Figure 31)—will then coincide. These lines that are spread out in two-dimensional space coincide when we make the transition to three-dimensional space.

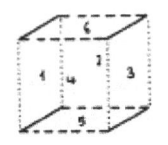

Figure 32

A square consists of four edges, a cube of six squares, and afour-dimensional figure of eight cubes.[36] Hinton calls this four-dimensional figure a tessaract. our task is not simply to put these eight cubes together into a single cube, but to do so by making each one pass through the fourth dimension. When I do to a tessaract what I just did to a cube, I must observe the same law. We must use the analogy of the relationship of a three-dimensionalfigure to its two-dimensional counterpart to discover the relationship of a four-dimensional figure to its three-dimensional counterpart. In the case of an unfolded cube, I had two groups of threesquares. Similarly, unfolding a four-dimensional tessaract in three-dimensional space results in two groups of four cubes, which looklike this (Figure 33). This eight-cube method is very ingenious.

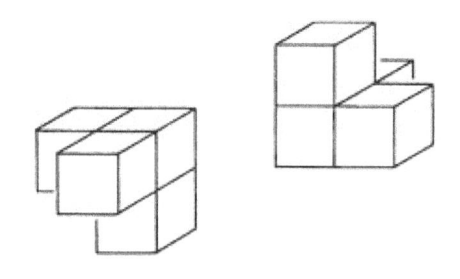

Figure 33

We must handle these four cubes in three-dimensional space exactly as we handled the squares in two-dimensional space. Look closely at what I have done here. unfolding a cube so that it lies flat in two-dimensional space results in a grouping of six squares. Performing the corresponding operation on a tessaract results in a system of eight cubes (Figure 34). We have transferred our reflections on three-dimensional space to four-dimensional space. Folding up the squares and making their edges coincide in three-dimensional space corresponds to folding up the cubes and making their surfaces coincide in four-dimensional space. Laying the cube flat in two-dimensional space resulted in corresponding lines that coincided when we reconstructed the cube. something similar happens to the surfaces of individual cubes in the tessaract. Laying out a tessaract in three-dimensional space results in corresponding surfaces that will later coincide. Thus, in a tessaract, the upper horizontal surface of cube 1 lies in the same plane as the front surface of cube 5 when we move into the fourth dimension.

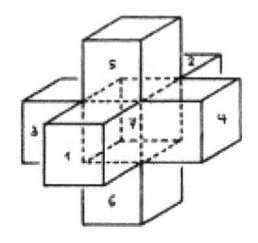

Figure 34

Similarly, the right surface of cube 1 coincides with the front surface of cube 4, the left square in cube 1 coincides with the front square in cube 3, and the lower square in cube 1 coincides with the front square in cube 6. similar correspondences exist between the remaining surfaces. When the operation is completed, the cube that remains is cube 7, the interior cube that was surrounded by the other six.[37]

As you see, we are concerned once more with finding analogies between the third and fourth dimensions. As we saw in one of the illustrations from the last lecture (Figure 29), just as a fifth square surrounded by four others remains invisible to any being who can see only in two dimensions, the same applies to the seventh cube in this instance. it remains hidden from three-dimensional vision. In a tessaract, this seventh cube corresponds to an eighth cube, its counterpart in the fourth dimension.

All of these analogies serve to prepare us for the fourth dimension, since nothing in our ordinary view of space forces us to add other dimensions to the three familiar ones. Following Hinton's example, we might also use colors here and think of cubes put together so that the corresponding colors coincide. other than through such analogies, it is almost impossible to give any guidance in how to conceive of a four-dimensional figure.

I would now like to talk about another way of representing four-dimensional bodies in three-dimensional space that may make it easier for you to understand what is actually at issue. Here we have an octahedron, which has eight triangular surfaces that meet in obtuse angles (Figure 35).

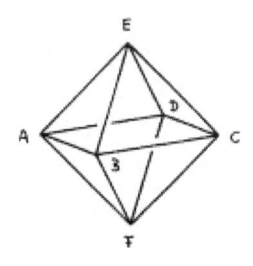

Figure 35

Please imagine this figure and then follow this train of thought with me. You see, these edges are where two surfaces intersect. Two intersect at *AB*, for example, and two at *EB*. The only difference between an octahedron and a cube is the angle at which the surfaces intersect. Whenever surfaces intersect at right angles, as they do in a cube, the figure that is formed must be a cube. But when they intersect at an obtuse angle, as they do here, an octahedron is formed. By making the surfaces intersect at different angles, we construct different geometric figures.[38]

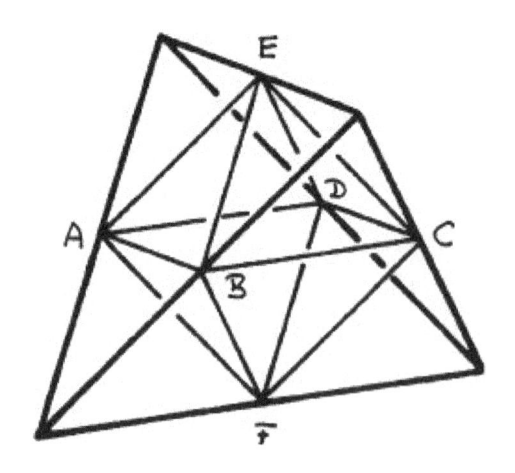

Figure 36

Next, envision a different way of making the surfaces of an octahedron intersect. Picture that one of these surfaces here, such as *AEB*, is extended on all sides and that the lower surface, *BCF*, and the surfaces *ADF* and *EDC*, at the back of the figure, are similarly extended. These extended surfaces must also intersect. There is a two-fold symmetry at this line of reflection also called "half-turn symmetry." When these surfaces are extended, the other four original surfaces of the octahedron, *ABF*, *EBC*, *EAD*, and *DCF*, are eliminated. out of eight original surfaces, four remain, and these four form a tetrahedron, which also can be called half an octahedron because it causes half of the surfaces of the octahedron to intersect. It is not half an octahedron in the sense of cutting the octahedron in half in the middle. When the other four surfaces of the octahedron are extended until they intersect, they also form a tetrahedron. The original octahedron is the intersection of these two tetrahedrons. In stereometry or geometric crystallography, what is called half a figure is the result of halving the number of surfaces rather than of dividing the original figure in two. This is very easy to visualize in the case of an octahedron.[39] If you imagine a cubed halved in the same way, by making one surface intersect with another surface, you will always get a cube. Half of a cube is always another cube. There is an important conclusion to be drawn from this phenomenon, but first I would like to use another example.[40]

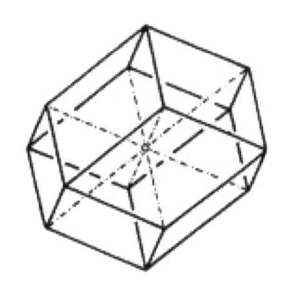

Figure 37

Here we have a rhombic dodecahedron (Figure 37). As you see, its surfaces meet at specific angles. Here we also have a system of four wires—I will call them axial wires—that run in different directions, that is, they are diagonals connecting specific opposite corners of the rhombic dodecahedron. These wires represent the system of axes in the rhombic dodecahedron, similar to the system of axes you can imagine in a cube.[41]

In a system of three perpendicular axes, a cube results when stoppage occurs in each of these axes, producing intersecting surfaces. Causing the axes to intersect at different angles results in different geometric solids. The axes of a rhombic dodecahedron, for example, intersect at angles that are not right angles. Halving a cube results in a cube.[42] This is true only of a cube. When the number of surfaces in a rhombic dodecahedron is halved, a totally different geometric figure results.[43]

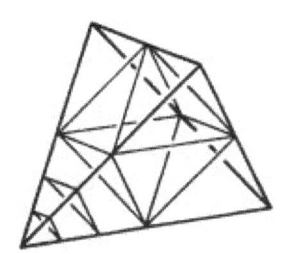

Figure 38

Now let's consider how an octahedron relates to a tetrahedron. Let me show you what I mean. The relationship is clearly apparent if we gradually transform a tetrahedron into an octahedron. For this purpose, let's take a tetrahedron and cut off its vertices, as shown here (Figure 38). We continue to cut off larger portions until the cut surfaces meet on the edges of the tetrahedron. The form that remains is an octahedron. By cutting off the vertices at the appropriate angle, we have transformed a spatial figure bounded by four planes into an eight-sided figure.

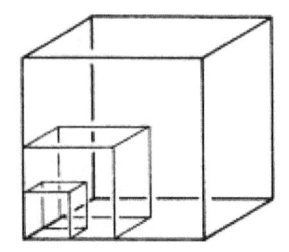

Figure 39

What I have just done to a tetrahedron cannot be done to a cube.[44] A cube is unique in that it is the counterpart of three-dimensional space. Imagine that all the space in the universe is structured by three axes that are perpendicular to each other. Inserting planes perpendicular to these three axes always produces a cube (Figure 39). Thus, whenever we use the term *cube* to mean a theoretical cube rather than a specific one, we are talking about the cube as the counterpart of three-dimensional space. Just as the tetrahedron can be shown to be the counterpart of an octahedron by extending half of the octahedron's sides until they intersect, an individual cube is also the counterpart of all of space.[45] If you imagine all of space as positive, the cube is negative. The cube is the polar opposite of space in its entirety. The physical cube is the geometric figure that actually corresponds to all of space.

Suppose that instead of a three-dimensional space bounded by two-dimensional planes, we have a space bounded by six spheres, which are three-dimensional figures. I start by defining a two-dimensional space with four intersecting circles, i.e., two-dimensional figures. Now imagine these circles growing bigger and bigger; that is, the radius grows ever longer and the midpoint becomes increasingly distant. With time, the circles will be transformed into straight lines (Figure 40). Then, instead of four circles, we have four intersecting straight lines and a square.

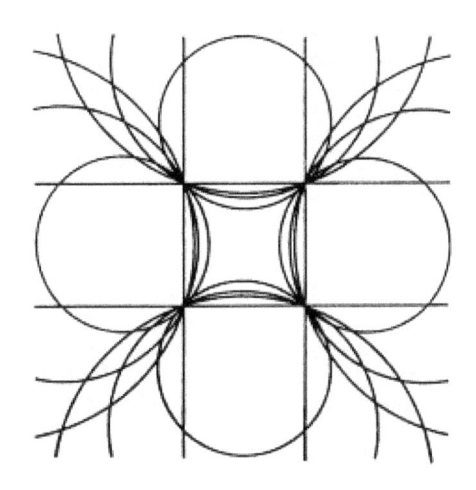

Figure 40

Now instead of circles, imagine six spheres, forming a mulberry-like shape (Figure 41). Picture the spheres growing ever larger, just as the circles did. ultimately, these spheres will become the planes defining a cube, just as the circles became the lines defining a square. This cube is the result of six spheres that have become flat. The cube, therefore, is only a special instance of the intersection of six spheres, just as the square is simply a special instance of four intersecting circles.

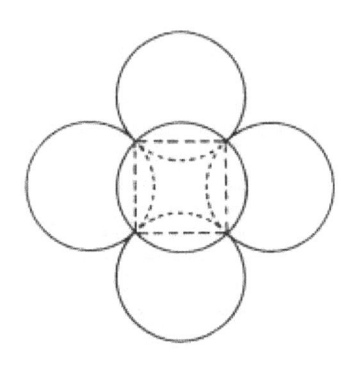

Figure 41

When you clearly realize that these six spheres flattening into planes correspond to the squares we used earlier to define a cube—that is, when you visualize a spherical figure being transformed into a flat one—the result is the simplest possible three-dimensional figure. A cube can be imagined as the result of flattening six intersecting spheres.

We can say that a point on a circle must pass through the second dimension to get to another point on the circle. But if the circle has become so large that it forms a straight line, any point on the circle can get to any other point by moving only through the first dimension. Let's consider a square that is bounded by two-dimensional figures. As long as the four figures defining a square are circles, they are two-dimensional. Once they become straight lines, however, they are one-dimensional.

The planes defining a cube develop out of three-dimensional figures (spheres) when one dimension is removed from each of the six spheres. These defining surfaces come about by being bent straight, through reducing their dimensions from three to two. They have sacrificed a dimension. They enter the second dimension by sacrificing the dimension of depth. Thus, we could say that each dimension of space comes about by sacrificing the next higher dimension.

If we have a three-dimensional form with two-dimensional boundaries, and so reduce three-dimensional forms to two dimensions, you must conclude from this that, if we consider three-dimensional space, we have to think of each direction as the flattened version of an infinite circle. Then if we move in one direction, we would ultimately return to the same point from the opposite direction. Thus each ordinary dimension of space has come about through the loss of the next higher dimension. A tri-axial system is inherent in our three-dimensional space. Each of its three perpendicular axes has sacrificed the next dimension to become straight.

In this way, we achieve three-dimensional space by straightening each of its three axial directions. Reversing the process, each element of space also could be curved again, resulting in this train of thought: When you curve a one-dimensional figure, the resulting figure is two-dimensional. A curved two-dimensional figure becomes three-dimensional. And, finally, curving a three-dimensional figure produces a four-dimensional figure. Thus, four-dimensional space can be imagined as curved three-dimensional space.[46]

At this point, we can make the transition from the dead to the living. In this bending you can find spatial figures that reveal this transition from death to life. At the transition to three-dimensionality, we find a special instance of four-dimensional space; it has become flat. To human consciousness, death is nothing more than bending three dimensions into four dimensions. With regard to the physical body taken by itself, the opposite is true: death is the flattening of four dimensions into three.

Sixth Lecture

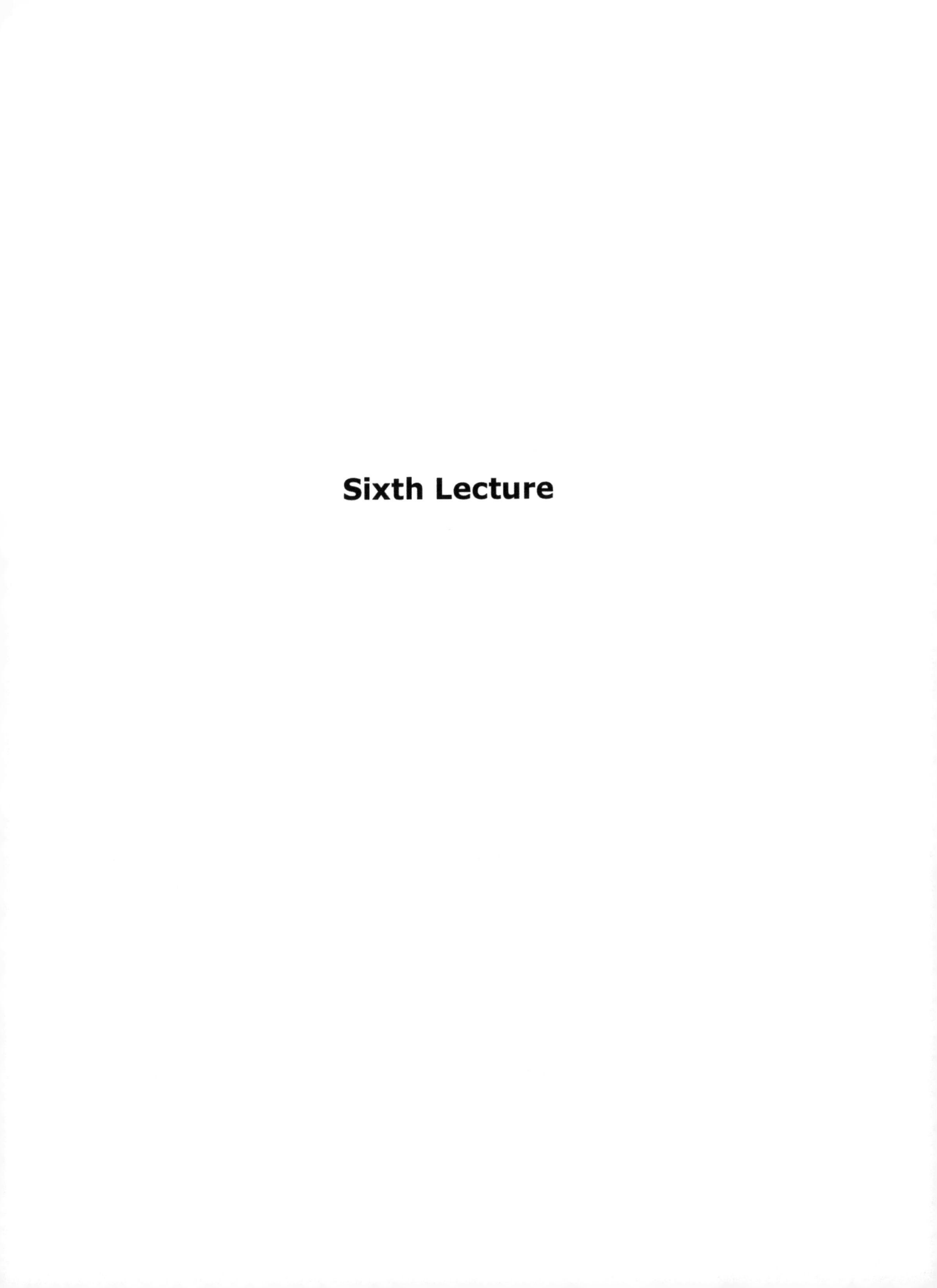

BERLIN JUNE 7, 1905

Today I must conclude these lectures on the fourth dimension of space, though I actually would like to present a complicated system in greater detail, which would require demonstrating many more of Hinton's models. All I can do is refer you to his three thorough and insightful books.[47] Of course, no one who is unwilling to use analogies such as those presented in the previous lectures will be able to acquire a mental image of four-dimensional space. A new way of developing thoughts is needed.

Now I would like to develop a real image (parallel projection) of a tessaract. We saw that a square in two-dimensional space has four edges. Its counterpart in three dimensions is the cube, which has six square sides (Figure 42).

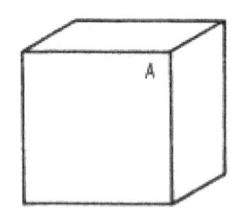

Figure 42

The four-dimensional counterpart is the tessaract, which is bounded by eight cubes. Consequently, the projection of a tessaract into three-dimensional space consists of eight interpenetrating cubes. We saw how these eight cubes can coincide in three-dimensional space. I will now construct a different projection of a tessaract.[48]

Imagine holding a cube up to the light so that it casts a shadow on the board. We can then trace the shadow with chalk (Figure 43). As you see, the result is a hexagon. If you imagine the cube as transparent, you can see that in its projection onto a plane, the three front faces coincide with the three rear faces to form the hexagonal figure.

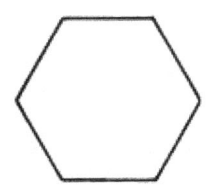

Figure 43

To get a projection that we can apply to a tessaract, please imagine that the cube in front of you is positioned so that the front point *A* exactly covers the rear point *C*. If you then eliminate the third dimension, the result is once again a hexagonal shadow. Let me draw this for you (Figure 44).

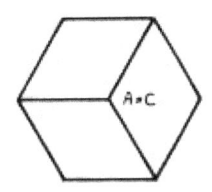

Figure 44

When you imagine the cube in this position, you see only its three front faces; the three other faces are concealed behind them. The faces of the cube appear foreshortened, and its angles no longer look like right angles. seen from this perspective, the cube looks like a regular hexagon. Thus, we have created an image of a three-dimensional cube in two-dimensional space. Because this projection shortens the edges and alters the angles, we must imagine the six square faces of the cube as rhombuses.[49]

Now let's repeat the operation of projecting a three-dimensional cube onto a plane with a four-dimensional figure that we project into three-dimensional space. We will use parallel projection to depict a tessaract, a figure composed of eight cubes, in the third dimension. Performing this operation on a cube results in three visible and three invisible edges; in reality, they jut into space and do not lie flat in the plane of projection. Now imagine a cube distorted into a rhombic parallelepiped.[50] If you take eight such figures, you can assemble the structures defining a tessaract so that they interpenetrate and doubly coincide with the rhombic cubes in a rhombic dodecahedron (Figure 45).

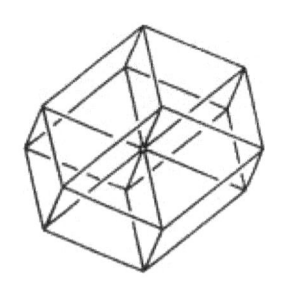

Figure 45

This figure has one more axis than a three-dimensional cube. Naturally, a four-dimensional figure has four axes. Even when its components interpenetrate, four axes remain. Thus, this projection contains eight interpenetrating cubes, shown as rhombic cubes. A rhombic dodecahedron is a symmetrical image or shadow of a tessaract projected into three-dimensional space.[51]

Although we have arrived at these relationships by analogy, the analogy is totally valid. Just as a cube can be projected onto a plane; a tessaract also can be depicted by projecting it into three-dimensional space. The resulting projection is to the tessaract as the cube's shadow is to the cube. I believe this operation is readily understandable.

I would like to link what we have just done to the wonderful image supplied by Plato and schopenhauer in the metaphor of the cave.[52] Plato asks us to imagine people chained in a cave so that they cannot turn their heads and can see only the rear wall. Behind them, other people carry various objects past the mouth of the cave. These people and objects are three dimensional, but the prisoners see only shadows cast on the wall. Everything in this room, for example, would appear only as two-dimensional shadow images on the opposite wall.

Then Plato tells us that our situation in the world is similar. We are the people chained in the cave. Although we ourselves are four-dimensional, as is everything else, all that we see appears only in the form of images in three-dimensional space.[53] According to Plato, we are dependent on seeing only the three-dimensional shadow images of things instead of their realities. I see my own hand only as a shadow image; in reality, it is four-dimensional. We see only images of four-dimensional reality, images like that of the tessaract that I showed you.

In ancient Greece, Plato attempted to explain that the bodies we know are actually four-dimensional and that we see only their shadow images in three-dimensional space. This statement is not completely arbitrary, as I will explain shortly. Initially, of course, we can say that it is mere speculation. How can we possibly imagine that there is any reality to these figures that appear on the wall? But now imagine yourselves sitting here in a row, unable to move. Suddenly, the shadows begin moving. You cannot possibly conclude that the images on the wall could move without leaving the second dimension. When an image moves on the wall, something must have caused movement of the actual object, which is not on the wall. Objects in three-dimensional space can move past each other, something their two-dimensional shadow images cannot do if you imagine them as impenetrable—that is, as consisting of substance. If we imagine these images to be substantial, they cannot move past each other without leaving the second dimension.

As long as the images on the wall remain motionless, I have no reason to conclude that anything is happening away from the wall, outside the realm of two-dimensional shadow images. As soon as they begin to move, however, I am forced to investigate the source of the movement and to conclude that the change can originate only in a movement outside the wall, in a third dimension. Thus, the change in the images has informed us that there is a third dimension in addition to the second.

Although a mere image possesses a certain reality and very specific attributes, it is essentially different from the real object. A mirror image, too, is undeniably a mere image. You see yourself in the mirror, but you are also present out here. Without the presence of a third element—that is, a being that moves—you cannot really know which one is you. The mirror image makes the same movements as the original; it has no ability to move itself but is dependent on the real object, the being. In this way, we can distinguish between an image and a being by saying that only a being can produce change or movement out of itself. I realize that the shadow images on the wall cannot make themselves move; therefore, they are not beings. I must transcend the images in order to discover the beings.

Now apply this train of thought to the world in general. The world is three-dimensional, but if you consider it by itself, grasping it in thought, you will discover that it is essentially immobile. Even if you imagine it frozen at a certain point in time, however, the world is still three-dimensional. In reality, the world is not the same at any two points in time. it changes. Now imagine the absence of these different moments—what is, remains. If there were no time, the world would never change, but even without time or changes it would still be three-dimensional. similarly, the images on the wall remain two dimensional, but the fact that they change suggests the existence of a third dimension. That the world is constantly changing but would remain three-dimensional even without change suggests that we need to look for the change in a fourth dimension. The reason for change, the cause of change, the activity of change, must be sought outside the third dimension. At this point you grasp the existence of the fourth dimension and the justification for Plato's metaphor. We can understand the entire three-dimensional world as the shadow projection of a four-dimensional world. The only question is how to grasp the reality of this fourth dimension.

Of course, we must understand that it is impossible for the fourth dimension to enter the third directly. It cannot. The fourth dimension cannot simply fall into the third dimension. Now I would like to show you how to acquire a concept of transcending the third dimension. (In one of my earlier lectures here, I attempted to awaken a similar idea in you.)[54] Imagine that we have a circle. If you picture this circle getting bigger and bigger, so that any specific segment becomes flatter and fatter, the diameter eventually becomes so large that the circle is transformed into a straight line. A line has only one dimension, but a circle has two. How do we get back into two dimensions? By bending the straight line to form a circle again.

When you imagine curving a circular surface, it first becomes a bowl and eventually, if you continue to curve it, a sphere. A curved line acquires a second dimension and a curved plane a third. And if you could still make a cube curve, it would have to curve into the fourth dimension, and the result would be a spherical tessaract.[55] A spherical surface can be considered a curved two-dimensional figure. In nature, the sphere appears in the form of the cell, the smallest living being. The boundaries of a cell are spherical. Here we have the difference between the living and the lifeless. Minerals in their crystalline form are always bounded by planes, by flat surfaces, while life is built up out of cells and bounded by spherical surfaces. Just as crystals are built up out of flattened spheres, or planes, life is built up out of cells, or abutting spheres. The difference between the living and the lifeless lies in the character of their boundaries. An octahedron is bounded by eight triangles. When we imagine its eight sides as spheres, the result is an eight-celled living thing.

When you "curve" a cube, which is a three-dimensional figure, the result is a four-dimensional figure, the spherical tessaract. But if you curve all of space, the resulting figure relates to three-dimensional space as a sphere relates to a plane.[56] As a three-dimensional object, a cube, like any crystal, is bounded by planes. The essence of a crystal is that it is constructed of flat boundary planes. The essence of life is that is constructed of curved surfaces, namely, cells, while a figure on a still higher level of existence would be bounded by four-dimensional structures. A three-dimensional figure is bounded by two-dimensional figures. A four-dimensional being—that is, a living thing—is bounded by three-dimensional beings, namely, spheres and cells. A five-dimensional being is bounded by four-dimensional beings, namely, spherical tessaracts. Thus, we see the need to move from three-dimensional beings to four-dimensional and then five-dimensional beings.

What needs to happen with a four-dimensional being?[57] A change must take place within the third dimension. In other words, when you hang pictures, which are two-dimensional, on the wall, they generally remain immobile. When you see two-dimensional images moving, you must conclude that the cause of the movement can lie only outside the surface of the wall—that is, that the third dimension of space prompts the change. When you find changes taking place within the third dimension, you must conclude that a fourth dimension has an effect on beings who experience changes within their three dimensions of space.

We have not truly recognized a plant when we know it only in its three dimensions. Plants are constantly changing. Change is an essential aspect of plants, a token of a higher form of existence. A cube remains the same; its form changes only when you break it. A plant changes shape by itself, which means that the change must be caused by some factor that exists outside the third dimension and is expressed in the fourth dimension. What is this factor?

You see, if you draw this cube at different points in time, you will find that it always remains the same. But when you draw a plant and compare the original to your copy three weeks later, the original will have changed. Our analogy, therefore, is fully valid. Every living thing points to a higher element in which its true being dwells, and time is the expression of this higher element. Time is the symptomatic expression or manifestation of life (or the fourth dimension) in the three dimensions of physical space. In other words, all beings for whom time is intrinsically meaningful are images of four-dimensional beings. After three years or six years, this cube will still be the same. A lily seedling changes, however, because time has real meaning for it. What we see in the lily is merely the three-dimensional image of the four-dimensional lily being. Time is an image or projection of the fourth dimension, of organic life, into the three spatial dimensions of the physical world.

To clarify how each successive dimension relates to the preceding one, please follow this line of thought: A cube has three dimensions. To imagine the third, you tell yourself that it is perpendicular to the second and that the second is perpendicular to the first. It is characteristic of the three dimensions that they are perpendicular to each other. We also can conceive of the third dimension as arising out of the next dimension, the fourth. Envision coloring the faces of a cube and manipulating the colors in a specific way, as Hinton did. The changes you induce correspond exactly to the change undergone by a three-dimensional being when it develops over time, thus passing into the fourth dimension. When you cut through a four-dimensional being at any point—that is, when you take away its fourth dimension—you destroy the being. Doing this to a plant is just like taking an impression of the plant and casting it in plaster. You hold it fast by destroying its fourth dimension, the time factor, and the result is a three-dimensional figure. When time, the fourth dimension, is critically important to any three-dimensional being, that being must be alive.

And now we come to the fifth dimension. You might say that this dimension must have another boundary that is perpendicular to the fourth dimension. We saw that the relationship between the fourth dimension and the third is similar to the relationship between the third and second dimensions. It is more difficult to imagine the fifth dimension, but once again we can use an analogy to give us some idea about it. How does any dimension come about? When you draw a line, no further dimensions emerge as long as the line simply continues in the same direction. Another dimension is added only when you imagine two opposing directions or forces that meet and neutralize at a point. The new dimension arises only as an expression of the neutralization of forces. We must be able to see the new dimension as the addition of a line in which two streams of forces are neutralized. We can imagine the dimension as coming either from the right or from the left, as positive in the first instance and negative in the second. Thus I grasp each independent dimension as a polar stream of forces with both a positive and a negative component. The neutralization of the polar component forces is the new dimension.

Taking this as our starting point, let's develop a mental image of the fifth dimension. We must first imagine positive and negative aspects of the fourth dimension, which we know is the expression of time. Let's picture a collision between two beings for whom time is meaningful. The result will have to be similar to the neutralization of opposing forces that we talked about earlier. When two four-dimensional beings connect, the result is their fifth dimension. The fifth dimension is the result or consequence of an exchange or neutralization of polar forces, in that two living things who influence each other produce something that they do not have in common either in the three ordinary dimensions of space or in the fourth dimension, in time. This new element has its boundaries outside these dimensions. It is what we call empathy or sensory activity, the capacity that informs one being about another. It is the recognition of the inner (soul-spiritual) aspect of another being. Without the addition of the higher, fifth dimension—that is, without entering the realm of sensory activity, — no being would ever be able to know about any aspects Of another being that lie outside time and space. of course, in this sense we understand sensory activity simply as the fifth dimension's projection or expression in the physical world.

It would be too difficult to build up the sixth dimension in the same way, so for now I will simply tell you what it is. If we continued along the same line of thinking, we would find that the expression of the sixth dimension in the three-dimensional world is self-awareness. As three-dimensional beings, we humans share our image character with other three-dimensional beings. Plants possess an additional dimension, the fourth. For this reason, you will never discover the ultimate being of the plant in the three dimensions of space. You must ascend to a fourth dimension, to the astral sphere. If you want to understand a being that possesses sensory ability, you must ascend to the fifth dimension, lower devachan or the Rupa sphere, and to understand a being with self-awareness—namely, the human being—you must ascend to the sixth dimension, upper devachan or the Arupa sphere. The human beings we encounter at present are really six-dimensional beings. What we have called sensory ability (or empathy) and self-awareness are projections of the fifth and sixth dimensions, respectively, into ordinary three-dimensional space. Albeit unconsciously for the most part, human beings extend all the way into these spiritual spheres; only there can their essential nature be recognized. As six-dimensional beings, we understand the higher worlds only when we attempt to relinquish the characteristic attributes of lower dimensions.

I cannot do more than suggest why we believe the world to be merely three-dimensional. Our view is based on seeing the world as a reflection of higher factors. The most you can see in a mirror is a mirror image of yourself. In fact, the three dimensions of our physical space are reflections, material images of three higher, causal, creative dimensions. Thus, our material world has a polar spiritual counterpart in the group of the three next higher dimensions, that is, in the fourth, fifth, and sixth. similarly, the fourth through sixth dimensions have their polar counterparts in still more distant spiritual worlds, in dimensions that remain a matter of conjecture for us.

Consider water and water that has been allowed to freeze. In both cases, the substance is the same, but water and ice are very different in form. You can imagine a similar process taking place with regard to the three higher human dimensions. When you imagine human beings as purely spiritual beings, you must envision them as possessing only the three higher dimensions of self-awareness, feeling, and time and that these dimensions are reflected in the three ordinary dimensions in the physical world.

When yogis (students of esotericism) want to ascend to knowledge of the higher worlds, they must gradually replace reflections with realities. For example, when they consider a plant, they must learn to replace the lower dimensions with the higher ones. Learning to disregard one of a plant's spatial dimensions and substitute the corresponding higher dimension—namely, time—enables them to understand a two-dimensional being that is moving. What must students of esotericism do to make this being correspond to reality rather than remaining a mere image? If they were simply to disregard the third dimension and add the fourth, the result would be something imaginary. The following thought will help us move toward an answer: By filming a living being, even though we subtract the third dimension from events that were originally three-dimensional, the succession of images adds the dimension of time. When we then add sensory ability to this animated image, we perform an operation similar to the one I described as curving a three-dimensional figure into the fourth dimension. The result of this operation is a four-dimensional figure whose dimensions include two of our spatial dimensions and two higher ones, namely, time and sensory ability. such beings do indeed exist, and now that I have come to the real conclusion of our study of the dimensions, I would like to name them for you.

Imagine two spatial dimensions—that is, a plane—and suppose that this plane is endowed with movement. Picture it curving to become a sensate being pushing a two-dimensional surface in front of it. Such a being is very dissimilar to and acts very differently from a three-dimensional being in our space. The surface being that we have constructed is completely open in one direction. It looks two-dimensional; it comes toward you, and you cannot get around it. This being is a radiant being; it is nothing other than openness in a particular direction. Through such a being, initiates then become familiar with other beings whom they describe as divine messengers approaching them in flames of fire. The description of Moses receiving the Ten Commandments on Mount Sinai shows simply that he was approached by such a being and could perceive its dimensions.[58] This being, which resembled a human being minus the third dimension, was active in sensation and time.

The abstract images in religious documents are more than mere outer symbols. They are mighty realities that we can learn about by taking possession of what we have been attempting to understand through analogies. The more diligently and energetically you ponder such analogies, the more eagerly you submerse yourself in them, the more they work on your spirit to release higher capacities. This applies, for example, to the explanation of the analogy between the relationship of a cube to a hexagon and that of a tessaract to a rhombic dodecahedron. The latter is the projection of a tessaract into the three-dimensional physical world. By visualizing these figures as if they possessed independent life—that is, by allowing a cube to grow out of its projection, the hexagon, and the tessaract to develop out of its projection, the rhombic dodecahedron—your lower mental body learns to grasp the beings I just described. When you not only have followed my suggestions but also have made this operation come alive as esoteric students do, in full waking consciousness, you will notice that four-dimensional figures begin to appear in your dreams. At that point, you no longer have far to go to be able to bring them into your waking consciousness. You then will be able to see the fourth dimension in every four-dimensional being.

*

The astral sphere is the fourth dimension.
Devachan up to Rupa is the fifth dimension.
Devachan up to Arupa is the sixth dimension.[59]

These three worlds—physical, astral, and heavenly (devachan)—encompass six dimensions. The still higher worlds are the polar opposites of these dimensions.

	Mineral	Plant	Animal	Human
Arupa	self-awareness			
Rupa	sensory ability	self-awareness		
Astral plane	life	sensory ability	self-awareness	
Physical plane	form	life	sensory ability	self-awareness
		form	life	sensory ability
			form	life
				form

Four-Dimensional Space

BERLIN NOVEMBER 7, 1905

Our ordinary space has three dimensions—length, width, and height. A line has only one dimension, length. This blackboard is a plane, that is, it has two dimensions, length and width. A solid object encompasses three dimensions. How does a three-dimensional figure arise?

Imagine a figure with no dimensionality at all, namely, the point. It has zero dimensions. When a point moves in a constant direction, a straight line, or one-dimensional figure, results. Now visualize the line moving. The result is a plane, which has length and width. And, finally, a moving plane describes a three-dimensional figure. We cannot continue this process, however. We cannot use movement to create a four-dimensional figure or a fourth dimension from a three-dimensional object. How can we use images to develop a concept of the fourth dimension? some mathematicians and scientists—Zöllner, for example—have felt tempted to bring the spiritual world into harmony with our sense-perceptible world by assuming that the spiritual world exists in four-dimensional space.[60]

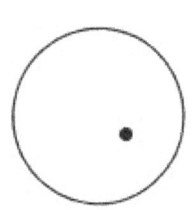

Figure 46

Imagine a circle, a completely closed figure lying in a plane. suppose that someone asks us to move a coin into the circle from outside. We must either cross the circumference of the circle (Figure 46) or—if we are not allowed to touch the circumference—pick up the coin, lift it into space, and place it inside the circle, which requires leaving the second dimension and entering the third. To move a coin magically into a cube or a sphere, we must leave the third dimension and pass through the fourth.[61] In this lifetime, I first began to grasp the nature of space when I began to study modern synthetic, projective geometry and understood the significance of transforming a circle into a line ([Figure 47](#)). The world is revealed in the soul's subtlest thoughts.[62]

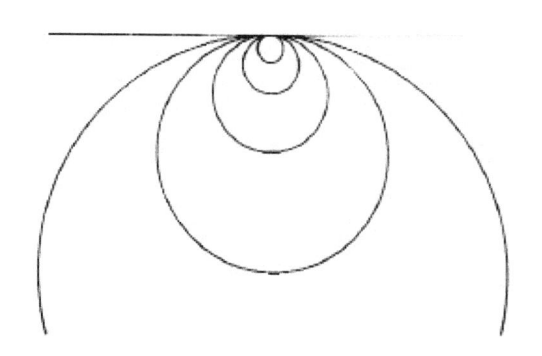

Figure 47

Now let's imagine a circle. We can trace its circumference all the way around and return to our original starting point. Let's picture the circle growing bigger and bigger while a tangent line remains constant. since the circle is growing increasingly flat, it will eventually become a straight line. When I trace these successively larger circles, I always go down on one side and come back up on the other before returning to my starting point. Ultimately, I move in one direction—let's say to the right—until I reach infinity. Thus, I must return from infinity on the other side, from the left, since the sequence of points in a straight line behaves just like a circle. so we see that space has no end, just as a straight line has no end, since its points are arranged just like those in a closed circle. Correspondingly, we must imagine the infinite expanse of space as self-contained, like the surface of a sphere. We have now depicted infinite space in terms of circles or spheres. This concept will help us conceive the reality of space.[63]

Instead of imagining ourselves proceeding mindlessly toward infinity and returning unchanged from the other direction, let's imagine that we carry a light. As seen from a constant point on the line, this light becomes ever weaker as we carry it away and ever stronger as we return with it from infinity. If we then picture the changes in the intensity of the light as positive and negative, we have positive on one side, where the light grows stronger, and negative on the other. We find these two poles, which are simply the opposite effects of space, in all effects in the natural world. This thought leads to the concept of space as possessing force; the forces at work in space are simply manifestations of force itself. We will no longer doubt the possibility of discovering a force that works from within in three-dimensional space, and we will realize that all spatial phenomena are based on actual relationships in space.

One such relationship is the intertwining of two dimensions. To make two closed rings interlock, you must open one of them in order to insert the other. I will now convince myself of the inherent manifoldness of space by twisting this figure, a rectangular strip of paper, twice—that is, I secure one end while rotating the other end 360°. I then hold the two ends together, securing the strip with pins. Cutting this twisted ring in half lengthwise results in two interlocking rings that cannot be separated without breaking one of them. simply twisting the strip made it possible to perform an operation in three dimensions that can otherwise be carried out only by entering the fourth dimension.[64] This is not just a game; it is cosmic reality. Here we have the sun, the Earth's orbit around the sun, and the Moon's orbit around the Earth (Figure 48). Because the Earth moves around the sun, the orbits of the Moon and Earth are just as intertwined (as our two rings of paper). In the course of Earth's evolution, the Moon broke away from the Earth. This separation occurred in the same way as the interlocking of our two rings of paper. When we look at space in this way, it becomes inherently alive.

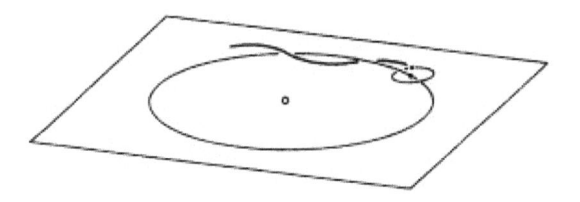

Figure 48

Next, consider a square. imagine it moving through space until a cube has been described. The square's movement must be perpendicular to its original location. A cube consists of six squares that form its surface. To give you an overview of a cube, I can lay the six squares down beside each other in a plane (Figure 49). I can reconstruct the cube by folding these squares upward, moving them into the third dimension. The sixth cube lies on top. To form this cross-shaped figure, I broke the cube down into two dimensions. Unfolding a three-dimensional figure transforms it into a two-dimensional figure.

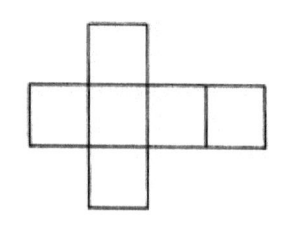

Figure 49

As you see, the boundaries of a cube are squares. A three-dimensional cube is always bounded by two-dimensional squares. Let's look at a single square. It is two-dimensional and bounded by four one-dimensional line segments. I can lay these four line segments out in single dimension (Figure 50). The edges defining one of the square's dimensions are colored red solid lines, and the other dimension is colored blue dotted lines. instead of saying length and width, I can talk about the red and blue dimensions.

Figure 50

I can reconstruct a cube from six squares. That is, I go beyond the number four (the number of line segments forming the edges of a square) to the number six (the number of planes forming the sides of a cube). Taking this process one step further, I move from six to eight (the number of cubes forming the "sides" of a four-dimensional figure). I arrange the eight cubes to form the three-dimensional counterpart of the earlier figure, which consisted of six squares, in the two-dimensional plane (Figure 51).

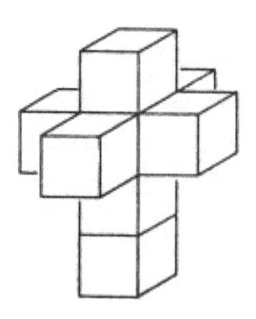

Figure 51

Now, imagine that I can turn this figure inside out, fold it up, and put it together so that the eighth cube closes off the entire figure. I use eight cubes to create a four-dimensional figure in four-dimensional space. Hinton calls this figure a tessaract. Its boundaries consist of eight cubes, just as the boundaries of an ordinary cube consist of six squares. Thus, a four-dimensional tessaract is bounded by eight three-dimensional cubes.

Envision a being that can see only in two dimensions. When this being looks at the unfolded squares of a cube, it sees only squares 1, 2, 3, 4, and 6, but never square 5, the shaded square in the middle (Figure 52). Something similar is true when you yourself look at an unfolded four-dimensional object. Since you can see only three-dimensional objects, you can never see the hidden cube in the middle.

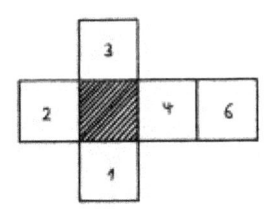

Figure 52

Picture drawing a cube on the board like this, so that the outline of a regular hexagon appears. The rest of it is hidden behind. What you see is a shadow image of sorts, a projection of the three-dimensional cube into two-dimensional space (Figure 53). The cube's two-dimensional shadow image consists of rhombuses or equilateral parallelepipeds. If you imagine the cube made of wire, you can also see the rhombuses in the back. This projection shows six overlapping rhombuses. In this way, you can project the entire cube into two-dimensional space.

Figure 53

Now imagine our tessaract in four-dimensional space. Projecting this figure into three-dimensional space must yield four oblique cubes (parallelepipeds) that do not interpenetrate. One of these rhombic oblique cubes would be drawn like this (Figure 54).

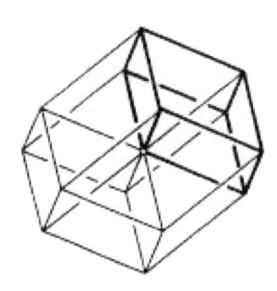

Figure 54

Eight such oblique rhombic cubes, however, must interpenetrate in order to yield a complete three-dimensional image of a four-dimensional tessaract in three-dimensional space. We can depict the complete three-dimensional shadow of a tessaract with the help of eight suitably interpenetrating rhombic cubes. The resulting spatial figure is a rhombic dodecahedron with four diagonals (Figure 55). In our rhombic projection of a cube, three adjacent rhombuses coincide with the other three so that only three of the six surface cubes are visible. Similarly, in the rhombic dodecahedron projection of a tessaract, only four non-interpenetrating rhombic cubes are visible as the projections of the tessaract's eight boundary cubes, since four adjacent rhombic cubes completely cover the remaining four.[65]

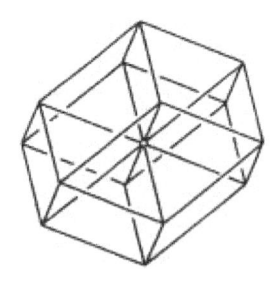

Figure 55

Thus we can construct a tessaract's three-dimensional shadow, though not the four-dimensional object itself. Similarly, we ourselves are shadows of four-dimensional beings. When we move from the physical to the astral plane, we must cultivate our capacity to form mental images. Picture a two-dimensional being repeatedly attempting to imagine vividly such a three-dimensional shadow image. Mentally constructing the relationship of the third dimension to the fourth fosters inner forces that will permit you to see into real, not mathematical, four-dimensional space.

We will always remain powerless in the higher world if we do not develop faculties that permit us to see in the higher world here, in the world of ordinary consciousness. The eyes we use for seeing in the physical, sense-perceptible world develop when we are still in the womb. Similarly, we must develop supersensory organs when we are still in the womb of the Earth so that we can be born into the higher world as seers. The development of physical eyes in utero is an example that illuminates this process.

A cube must be constructed by using the dimensions of length, width, and height. A tessaract must be constructed by using the same dimensions with the addition of a fourth. Because it grows, a plant breaks out of three-dimensional space. Any being that lives in time frees itself from the three ordinary dimensions. Time is the fourth dimension. It remains invisible within the three dimensions of ordinary space and can be perceived only with clairvoyant powers. A moving point creates a line, a moving line creates a plane, and a moving plane creates a three-dimensional figure. When three-dimensional space moves, the result is growth and development. There we have four-dimensional space, or time, projected into three-dimensional space as movement, growth, and development.

You will find that our geometric thoughts on building up the three ordinary dimensions continue into real life. Time is perpendicular to the three dimensions and constitutes the fourth dimension. It grows. When time is enlivened within a being, sensory ability arises. When time is multiplied internally within a being so that self-movement takes place, the result is a sensate animal being. In reality, such a being has five dimensions, while a human being has six. We have four dimensions in the ether realm (astral plane), five dimensions in the astral realm (lower devachan), and six dimensions in upper devachan. Thus, the various manifestations of the spirit emerge in you. When devachan casts its shadow into astral space, the result is our astral body. When the astral realm casts its shadow into etheric space, the result is our ether body, and so on.[66]

The natural world dies when time moves in one direction and is re-enlivened when it moves in the other. The two points where these streams meet are birth and death. The future is constantly coming to meet us. If life moved in one direction only, nothing new would ever arise. Human beings also possess genius —that is, their future, their intuitions, streaming toward them. The past that has been worked on is the stream coming from the other side; it determines the being as it has evolved up to the present time.

*

On Higher-Dimensional Space

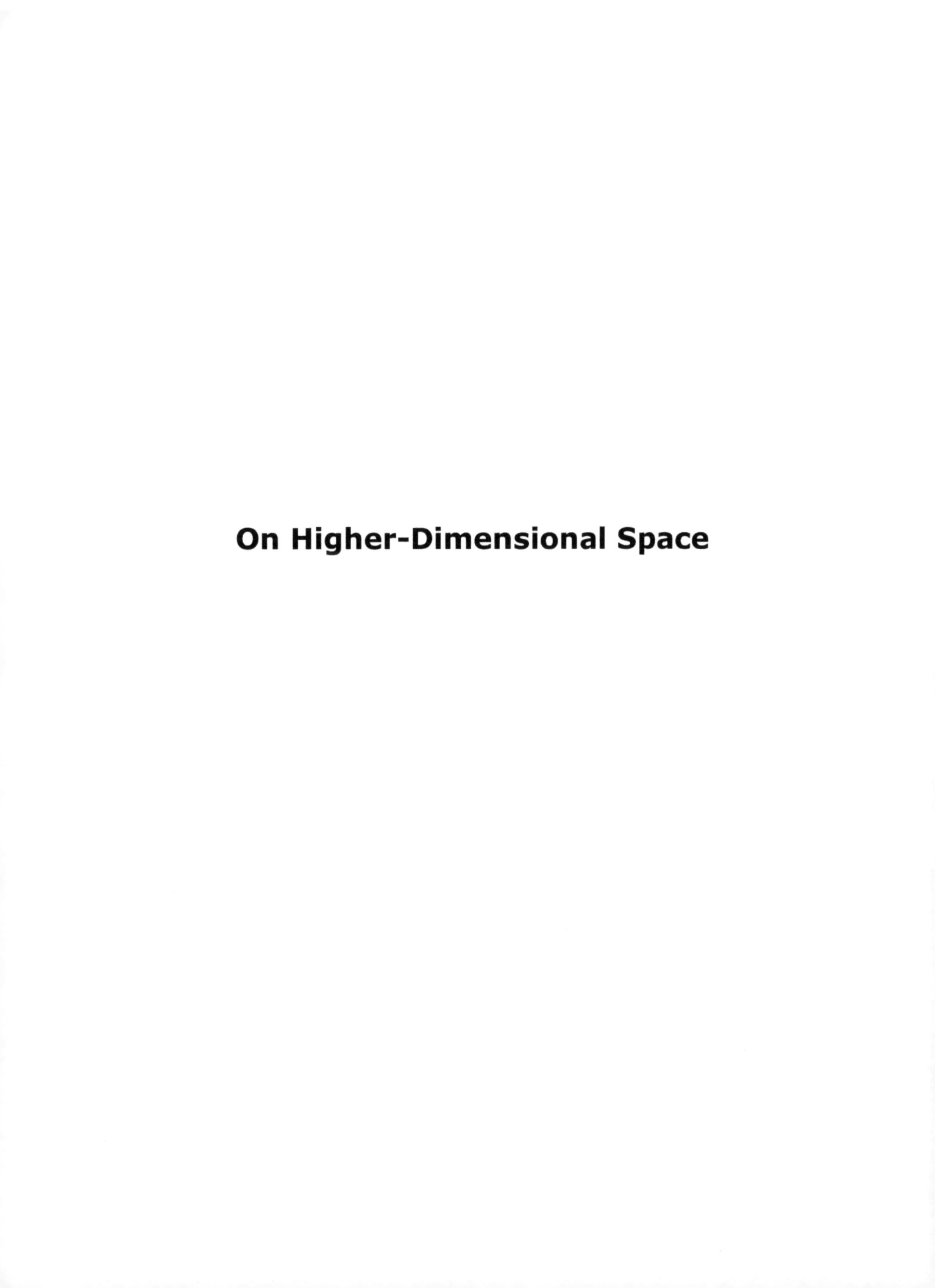

BERLIN OCTOBER 22, 1908

Today's subject will present us with a variety of difficulties, and this lecture you requested must be seen as one in a series. A profound understanding of the subject, even on a merely formal level, requires previous mathematical knowledge. Grasping the reality of the subject, however, requires deeper insight into esotericism. We will be able to address this aspect only very superficially today, providing stimulus for further thought.

It is very difficult to talk about higher dimensions at all, because in order to picture any dimensions beyond the ordinary three, we must enter abstract realms, where we fall into an abyss if our concepts are not very precisely and strictly formulated. This has been the fate of many people we know, both friends and foes. The concept of higher-dimensional space is not as foreign to mathematics as we generally believe.[67] Mathematicians are already performing calculations involving higher-dimensional operations. Of course, mathematicians can speak about higher-dimensional space only to a very limited extent; essentially, they can discuss only the possibility that it exists. Determining whether or not such space is real must be left to those who actually can see into it. Here we are dealing with pure concepts that, if precisely formulated, will truly clarify our concept of space.

What is space? We usually say that space is all around us, that we walk around in space, and so on. To gain a clearer idea of space, we must accept a higher level of abstraction. We call the space we move around in *three-dimensional*. It extends upward and downward, to the right and to the left, and forward and backward. It has length, width, and height. When we look at objects, we see them as occupying three-dimensional space, that is, as possessing a certain length, width, and height. We must deal with the details of the concept of space, however, if we wish to achieve greater clarity. Let's look at the simplest solid shape, the cube, as the clearest example of length, width, and height. The length and width of a cube's lower surface are equal. When we raise this lower surface until its height above its original location is the same as its length or width, we get a cube, that is, a three-dimensional figure. When we examine the boundaries of a cube, we find that they consist of plane surfaces, which are bounded in turn by sides of equal length. A cube has six such plane surfaces.

What is a plane surface? At this point, those incapable of very keen abstractions will begin to go astray. For example, it is impossible to cut off one of the boundaries of a wax cube in the form of a very thin layer of wax, because we would always get a layer with a certain thickness—that is, a solid object. We can never arrive at the boundary of the cube in this way. Its real boundary has only length and width, but no height—that is, no thickness. Thus, we arrive at a formula: a plane surface is one boundary of a three-dimensional figure and has one less dimension. Then what is the boundary of a plane surface such as a square? Again, the definition requires a high degree of abstraction. The boundary of a plane figure is a line, which has only one dimension, length. Width has been eliminated. What is the boundary of a line segment? It is a point, which has zero dimensions. Thus we always eliminate one dimension to find the boundary of a geometric figure.

Let's follow the train of thought of many mathematicians, including Riemann, who has done exceptionally good work.[68] Let's consider a point, which has zero dimensions; a line, which has one; a plane, which has two; and a solid object, which has three. On a purely technical level, mathematicians ask whether it is possible to add a fourth dimension. If so, the boundary of a four-dimensional figure would have to be a three-dimensional figure, just as a plane is the boundary of a solid body, a line the boundary of a plane, and a point the boundary of a line segment. Of course, mathematicians can then proceed to consider figures with five, six, seven, or even n dimensions, where n is a positive integer.

At this point a certain lack of clarity enters in, when we say that a point has zero dimensions, a line one, a plane two, and a solid object three. We can make solid objects, such as cubes, out of any number of materials—wax, silver, gold, and so on. Their materials are different, but if we make them all the same size, each one occupies the same amount of space. If we then eliminate all the matter these cubes contain, we are left with only specific segments of space, the spatial images of the cubes. These segments of space are the same size for all the cubes, regardless of the material of which they were made, and they all have length, width, and height. We can imagine such cubical spaces extending to infinity, resulting in an infinite three-dimensional space. The material object is only a segment of this space.

The next question is, Can we extend our conceptual considerations, which took space as their point of departure, to higher realities? For mathematicians, such considerations include only calculations involving numbers. Is this permissible? As I will now show you, using numbers to calculate the size of spaces results in great confusion. Why is this so? A single example will suffice. Imagine you have a square figure. This plane figure can be made broader and broader on both sides, until eventually we have a plane figure that extends to infinity between two lines (Figure 56)

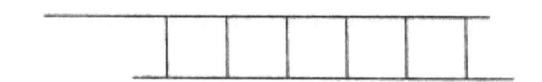

Figure 56

Because this plane figure is infinitely wide, its size is infinity (∞). Now suppose other people hear that the area between these two lines is infinitely large. Naturally, these people think of infinity. But if you mention infinity, they may get a totally incorrect idea of what you mean. suppose I add another square to each of the existing ones, that is, a second row of infinitely many squares. The result is again infinity, but a different infinity that is exactly twice as great as the first (Figure 57). Consequently, ∞ = 2∞.

In the same way, I could also arrive at ∞ = 3∞ In calculating with numbers, infinity can be used just as easily as any finite number. It is true in the first case that the space is infinite, but it is just as true in the latter instances that it is 2∞, 3∞, and so on. That's what happens when we calculate using numbers.

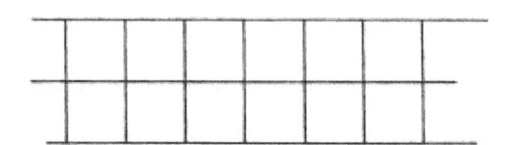

Figure 57

You see, as long as the concept of infinite space is linked to a numerical reckoning, it makes it impossible to penetrate more deeply into higher realities. Numbers actually have no relationship to space. Like peas or any other objects, numbers are totally neutral with regard to space. As you know, numerical calculations in no way change the reality of the situation. If we have three peas, multiplication cannot change that fact, even if we multiply correctly. Calculating that 3 × 3 = 9 will not produce nine peas. Merely thinking about something changes nothing in such cases, and numerical calculations are mere thinking. We are left with three peas, not nine, even if we performed the multiplication correctly. similarly, although mathematicians perform calculations pertaining to two, three, four, or five dimensions, the space that confronts us is still three-dimensional. I'm sure you can experience the temptation of such mathematical considerations, but they prove only that it is possible to perform calculations concerning higher-dimensional space. Mathematics cannot prove that higher-dimensional space actually exists; it cannot prove that the concept is valid in reality. We must be rigorously clear on this point.

Let's consider some of the other very astute thoughts mathematicians have had on this subject. We human beings think, hear, feel, and so on in three-dimensional space. Let's imagine beings capable of perceiving only in two-dimensional space. Their bodily organization would force them to remain in a plane, so they would be unable to leave the second dimension. They would be able to move and perceive only to the right and left and forward and backward. They would have no idea of anything that exists above or below them.[69]

Our situation in three-dimensional space, however, may be similar. Our bodily organization may be so adapted to three dimensions that we cannot perceive the fourth dimension but can only deduce it, just as two-dimensional beings would have to deduce the existence of the third dimension. Mathematicians say that it is indeed possible to think of human beings as being limited in this particular way. Of course, it is certainly possible to say that even though this conclusion might be true, it might also simply be a misinterpretation. Here again, a more exact approach is required, though the issue is not as simple as the first example, where we tried to use numbers to understand the infinity of space. I will deliberately restrict myself to simple explanations today.

The situation with this conclusion is not the same as with the first, purely technical arithmetical line of reasoning. In this instance, there is really something to take hold of. It is true enough that a being might exist who could perceive only objects that move in a plane. Such a being would be totally unaware of anything existing above or below. Imagine that a point within the plane becomes visible to the being. Of course, the point is visible only because it lies within the plane. As long as the point moves within the plane, it remains visible, but as soon as it moves out of the plane, it becomes invisible. It disappears as far as the plane-being is concerned. Now let's suppose that the point appears later somewhere else. It becomes visible again, disappears again, and so on. When the point moves out of the plane, the plane-being cannot follow it but may say, "In the meantime, the point is somewhere where I cannot see it." Let's slip into the mind of the plane-being and consider its two options. On the one hand, it might say, "There is a third dimension, and that object disappeared into it and later reappeared." Or it could also say, "Only stupid beings talk about a third dimension. The object simply disappeared, and each time it reappeared, it was created anew." In the latter case, we would have to say that the plane-being violates the laws of reason. If it does not want to assume that the object repeatedly disintegrates and is recreated, it must acknowledge that the object disappears into a space that plane-beings cannot see. When a comet disappears, it passes through four-dimensional space.[70]

Now we see what must be added in a mathematical consideration of this issue. We would have to find something in our field of observation that repeatedly appears and disappears. No clairvoyant abilities are needed. If the plane-being were clairvoyant, it would know from experience that there is a third dimension and would not have to deduce its existence. something similar is true of human beings. Anyone who is not clairvoyant is forced to say, "I myself am restricted to three dimensions, but as soon as I observe something that disappears and reappears periodically, I am justified in saying that a fourth dimension is involved."

Everything that has been said thus far is completely incontestable, and its confirmation is so simple that it is unlikely to occur to us in our modern state of blindness. The answer to the question, "Does something exist that repeatedly disappears and reappears?" is very easy. Just think of the pleasure that sometimes rises in you and then disappears again, so that no one who is not clairvoyant can still perceive it. Then the same feeling reappears because of some other event. In this case, you, like the plane-being, can behave in one of two ways. Either you can say that the feeling has disappeared into a space where you cannot follow it, or you can insist that the feeling vanishes and is created anew each time it reappears.

It is true, however, that any thought that disappears into the unconscious is evidence of something that can disappear and then reappear. If this idea seems plausible to you, the next step is to attempt to formulate all the possible objections that could be raised from the materialistic viewpoint. I will mention the most pertinent objection now; all the others are very easy to refute. People may claim to explain this phenomenon in purely materialistic terms. I want to give you an example of something that disappears and reappears in the context of material processes. Imagine a steam piston in action. As long as force is applied to the piston, we perceive its motion. Now suppose we counteract its motion with an identical piston working in the opposite direction. The movement stops and the machines are motionless. The movement disappears.

Similarly, people might claim that the sensation of pleasure is nothing more than molecules moving in the brain. As long as the molecules are moving, I experience pleasure. Let's assume that some other factor causes an opposite movement of molecules. The pleasure disappears. Anyone who does not pursue this line of thought very far might indeed find it a very significant argument against the ideas presented earlier, but let's take a closer look at this objection. Just as the movement of a piston disappears as a result of an opposite movement, a feeling that is based on molecular movement is said to be eliminated by an opposing molecular movement. What happens when one piston movement counteracts another? Both the first and the second movement disappear. The second movement cannot eliminate the first without eliminating itself, too. The result is a total absence of movement; no movement remains. Thus, no feeling that exists in my consciousness could ever eliminate another without also eliminating itself. The assumption that one feeling can eliminate another is therefore totally false. In that case, no feeling would be left, and a total absence of feeling would result. The most that can still be said is that the first feeling might drive the second into the subconscious. Having said this, however, we admit the existence of something that persists yet evades our direct observation.

Today we have been speaking only about purely mathematical ideas, without considering clairvoyant perception at all. Now that we have admitted the possibility that a four-dimensional world exists, we may wonder whether we can observe a four-dimensional object without being clairvoyant. A projection of sorts allows us to do so. We can turn a plane figure until the shadow it casts is a line. Similarly, the shadow of a line can be a point, and the shadow image of a solid three-dimensional object is a two-dimensional plane figure. Thus, once we are convinced of the existence of a fourth dimension, it is only natural to say that three-dimensional figures are the shadow images of four-dimensional figures.

Figure 58

This is one purely geometric way of imagining four-dimensional space. But there is also a different way of visualizing it with the help of geometry. Imagine a square, which has two dimensions. Now picture the four line segments that form its boundaries straightened out to form a single line. You have just straightened out the boundaries of a two-dimensional figure so that they lie in one dimension (Figure 58). Let's take this process one step further. Imagine a line segment. We proceed just as we did with the square, (removing one dimension) so that the boundaries of the figure fall in two points. We have just depicted the boundaries of a one-dimensional figure in zero dimensions. We can also unfold a cube, flattening it into six squares (Figure 59). We unfold the boundaries of a cube so that it lies in a plane. In this way, we can say that a line can be depicted as two points, a square as four line segments, and a cube as six squares. Note the sequence of numbers: two, four, six.

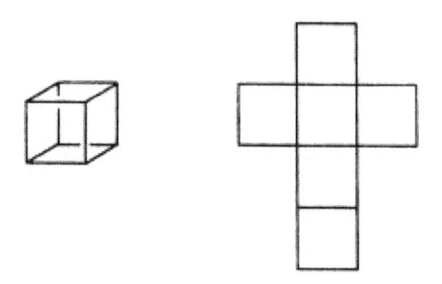

Figure 59

Next we take eight cubes. Just as the previous examples consist of the unfolded boundaries of geometric figures, the eight cubes form the boundaries of a four-dimensional figure (Figure 60). Laying them out results in a double cross that represents the boundaries of a regular four-dimensional figure. Hinton calls this four-dimensional cube a tessaract.

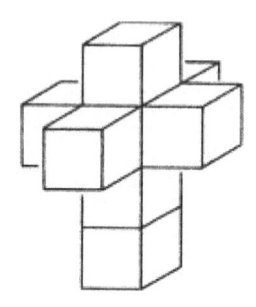

Figure 60

This exercise gives us a mental image of the boundaries of a tessaract. Our idea of this four-dimensional figure is comparable to the idea of a cube that two-dimensional beings can develop by flattening a cube's boundaries, that is, by unfolding them.

PART II

Questions And Answers

1904–1922

Editor's Note:
In the original German publication the first question and answer is from 1904 in Berlin.[1] There is no recorded question, only that it was asked by Mr. Schouten[2] and the answer is simply a reply from Steiner that he would be giving a lecture shortly on the fourth dimension.

STUTTGART SEPTEMBER 2, 1906

A question about the work of the "I."

The "I" works on the astral body, the ether body, and the physical body. All human beings work on the astral body through moral self-education. But even when a person begins the process of initiation or esoteric schooling, much work remains to be done on the astral body. Initiation marks the beginning of more intensive work on the ether body through the cultivation of aesthetic taste and religion. Initiates work consciously on the ether body.

In a certain respect, astral consciousness is four-dimensional. To give you an approximate idea of it, let me say that anything dead tends to remain within the three ordinary dimensions, while anything living constantly transcends them. Through its movement, any growing thing incorporates the fourth dimension within the three. If we move in a circle that is growing ever larger, we eventually arrive at a straight line (Figure 61). If we continue moving along this line, however, we will no longer be able to return to our starting point, because our space is three-dimensional. In astral space, which is closed off on all sides, we would return. In astral space, it is impossible to continue to infinity.[4] Physical space is open to the fourth dimension. Height and width are two dimensions, and the third dimension is the lifting out and entering into the fourth dimension.[5] A different geometry prevails in astral space.

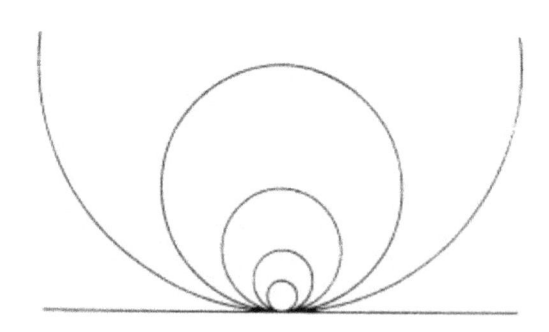

Figure 61

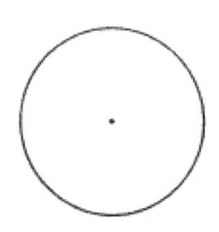

Figure 62

NüRNBERG JUNE 28, 1908

QUESTION: Since time had a beginning, it is obvious to assume that space also has limits. What is the reality of the situation?

That's a very difficult question, because the faculties needed to understand the answer cannot be developed by most people of today. For now, you will have to simply take the answer at face value, but a time will come when it will be understood completely. The physical world's space with its three dimensions, as we human beings conceive of it, is a very illusory concept. We usually think that space either must reach to infinity or have boundaries where it is somehow boarded up and comes to an end. Kant put forward these two concepts of the infinity and the finiteness or limitedness of space and showed that there is something to be said for and against both of them.[7]

We cannot judge the issue so simply, however. Since all matter exists in space and all matter is a condensed part of spirit, it becomes evident that we can achieve clarity on the question of space only by ascending from the ordinary physical world to the astral world. Our non-clairvoyant mathematicians already have sensed the existence of a strange and related phenomenon. When we imagine a straight line, it seems to reach to infinity in both directions in our ordinary space. But when we follow the same line in astral space, we see that it is curved. When we move along it in one direction, we eventually return from the other side, as if we were moving around the circumference of a circle.[8]

As a circle becomes larger, the time needed to go around it grows longer. Ultimately, the circle becomes so huge that any given section seems almost like a straight line because there is so little difference between the circle's very slightly curved circumference and a straight line. On the physical plane, it is impossible to return from the other side as we would do on the astral plane. While the directions of space are straight in the physical world, space is curved in the astral world. When we enter the astral realm, we must deal with totally different spatial relationships.[9] Consequently, we can say that space is not the illusory structure we think it to be but a self-contained sphere. And what appears to human beings as physical space is only an imprint or copy of self-contained space.[10] Although we cannot say that space has limits where it is boarded up, we can say that space is self-contained, because we always return to our starting point.

DüSSELDORF APRIL 21, 1909

QUESTION: *Does the concept of three-dimensionality apply to the spiritual hierarchies, since we speak of their "areas" of dominion?*

We can say that a human being's essence is realized in space. Space itself, however, from the esoteric perspective, must be seen as something produced as a result of creative activity. Its creation precedes the work and activity of the highest hierarchies, so we can presuppose the existence of space. We should not imagine the highest Trinity in spatial terms, however, because space is a creation of the Trinity. We must imagine spiritual beings without space, because space is a creation. The effects of the hierarchies within our world, however, have spatial limits, as do those of human beings. The other hierarchies move within space.

QUESTION: *Does time apply to spiritual processes?*

Certainly, but the highest spiritual processes in the human being lead to the concept that they run their course timelessly. The activities of the hierarchies are timeless. It is difficult to talk about how time came about because the concept of time is implicit in the words to come about. Instead, we would have to talk about the essence or being of time, which is not easy to discuss. No time would exist if all beings were at the same level of development. Time arises through the interaction between a number of higher beings and a number of lower beings. In timelessness, various levels of development are possible, but their interaction makes time possible.

QUESTION: *What is space?*

We must imagine the Trinity without space, because space is a creation of the Trinity. As such, space is a creation and belongs to our world. Space is significant only for beings that develop within earthly existence. Between birth and death human beings are cut off from the spirit in space and time in the same way that a worm lives beneath the Earth's surface. As for time, the highest states accessible to human beings are timeless. Because of the subtleties that come into play, it is not easy to speak about the concept of time coming into existence or about the essence or being of time. Time has had meaning only since the separation of the ancient Moon from the Sun. Everything external exists in space, and everything internal runs its course in time. We are circumscribed by both space and time.

There would be no time if all beings of the universe were at the same level of development. In timelessness, we can imagine evolutionary levels that are equivalent. The concept of time emerges when these levels begin to differ and to interact. Even the divinity evolves. As evolution continues, even the concept of evolution itself evolves.

DüSSELDORF APRIL 22, 1909

(The wording of the question has not been preserved.)

We are able to visualize three-dimensional space. An important theorem of the Platonic school is "God geometrizes."[12] Basic geometric concepts awaken clairvoyant abilities.[13] Positional geometry proves that the same point is everywhere on the circumference—the infinitely distant point on the right is the same as the starting point on the left. Thus, ultimately, the universe is a sphere, and we return to our starting point.[14] Whenever I use geometric theorems, they turn into concepts at the borderline of normal conceptuality.[15] Here, three-dimensional space returns us to our starting point. That is how in astral space, point A can work on point B without any connection between them.[16]

We introduce materialism into theosophy when we make the mistake of assuming that matter becomes increasingly less dense as we move toward the spirit. This kind of thinking does not lead to the spirit, but ideas about the connection between point A and point B allow us to visualize the fourth dimension. As an example, we can think of the narrow waist of the gall wasp (Figure 63).[17] ᴮWhat if the physical connection in the middle were absent and the two parts moved around together, connected only by astral activity? Now extend this concept to many spheres of activity (Figure 64) in higher-dimensional space.

Figure 63–64

BERLIN NOVEMBER 2, 1910
(The wording of the question has not been preserved.)
Plants have four dimensions. In the direction of the fourth dimension, a force works from below upward, counteracting the force of gravity so that the sap can flow upward. This rising direction, in conjunction with the fact that the two horizontal directions are unimportant to the leaves, results in the spiral arrangement of the leaves. In plants, therefore, the downward direction, or the direction of gravity, is nullified by the fourth dimension. As a result, plants can move freely in one direction in space.

Animals have five dimensions. Their fourth and fifth dimensions counteract two of the other dimensions. Because two dimensions are nullified in animals, animals can move freely in two directions. Human beings are six-dimensional beings. Dimensions four through six counteract the other three dimensions. Consequently, three dimensions are nullified in humans. As a result, human beings possess three spatial dimensions and can move in three directions.[19]

BASEL OCTOBER 1, 1911

QUESTION: What is electricity?

Electricity is light in the submaterial state, light compressed to the greatest possible extent. We must also attribute inwardness to light; light is itself at every point. Warmth can expand into space in three directions, but in the case of light we must speak of a fourth direction. It expands in four directions, with inwardness as the fourth.

MUNICH NOVEMBER 25, 1912

QUESTION: Has spiritual science achieved anything with regard to the fourth and higher dimensions?

It is not easy to make the answer to your question understandable. We human beings start from what we know from the physical, sense-perceptible world, where space has three dimensions. At least on a theoretical level, mathematicians formulate ideas about a fourth dimension and higher dimensions by analytically expanding their ideas on three-dimensional space through variables. At least in the context of mathematical thought, therefore, it is possible to speak of higher manifolds.[22] For those familiar with these issues—that is, for those who put heart and soul into the question and also have the necessary mathematical knowledge—many things come to light. Let me mention Simony in Vienna as an example.[23]

Initially, higher dimensions exist only in ideas. Actually seeing them begins when we enter the spiritual world, where we are immediately forced to come to grips with more than three dimensions. There, any image presented to us—that is, anything that still possesses intrinsic characteristics of three-dimensionality—is nothing more than a reflection of our own soul processes. In the higher worlds, very different spatial relationships prevail, if indeed we still want to call them spatial relationships.

The same is true with regard to time. There are always many people who argue, How can we be sure that all your claims are not based on hallucinations? Such people need to consider the situation with regard to time, because they disregard the fact that the field of spiritual science works with phenomena that are totally different from hallucinations. Your question provides an opportunity to supplement what I said in the lecture, because it is never possible to say everything, and today's lecture was very long. Let me still point out the changes that take place with regard to time and space when we enter the spiritual world.

The return of the images that we have banished to Hades, as it were, makes sense only when approached in terms of higher dimensions. There, however, this is just as natural and self-evident as three-dimensionality is in the sense-perceptible world. That is why ordinary geometry is a poor match for the beings and events of the spiritual world. On behalf of mathematicians, it must be said that their speculations about the fourth dimension acquire real value when we enter the spiritual world. Usually, however, their conclusions about higher-dimensional space are only generalizations based on Euclidean three-dimensional perceived space rather than on reality, to which their conclusions do not fully correspond. We would need still better mathematics in order to perform calculations regarding the beings and events that spiritual researchers investigate.

And yet the answer to your question is "yes." Correlations to a suprasensible world, and also mathematical ideas about infinity, become a reality, especially certain subjects from the fringes of mathematics. Here is an example that I myself experienced many years ago. I know that I had a sudden flash of insight into an extremely important attribute of astral space when I was studying modern synthetic projective geometry and analytical mechanics at the university.[24]

There is a relationship here to the concept that, on a straight line extending to infinity, the infinitely distant point on the left is identical to the infinitely distant point on the right. That a straight line, with regard to the arrangements of its points, is really a circle; if we do not get winded and continue in a straight line long enough, we return from the other side.[25] We may understand this, but we should not draw conclusions from it, since conclusions lead nowhere in spiritual research. Instead, allowing phenomena to work on us leads to knowledge of the suprasensible world.

It is important not to overestimate mathematics when dealing with the suprasensible world. Mathematics is useful only on a purely formal level. It cannot possibly grasp the reality of the situation. Like spiritual science, however, mathematics can be understood by means of forces inherent in the soul itself and is equally true for everyone. That is what mathematics and spiritual science have in common.

BERLIN FEBRUARY 13, 1913

QUESTION: *Is the Golden Section based on occult laws?*

Because it is founded upon the effect of what exists in space, the Golden Section is indeed based on an occult law. Goethe said of this law that what is most hidden is most revealed and vice versa—namely, the law that is intimately related to our human constitution, the law of repetition and varied repetition.[27,28] If you look at the Buddha's talks, for example, you find that the same content is always repeated with slight variations that must not be omitted, because the content is not the only important factor.[29]

The golden section is not simply a matter of repetition. We repeatedly discover the same proportion, since there are actually only three components.[30] The self-contained character of a repetition, which, however, is not self-formed, is what makes the golden section so appealing to us.

BERLIN NOVEMBER 27, 1913

QUESTION: Do human beings between death and rebirth have the same perception of time as those incarnated in bodies?

My lecture on March 19, 1914 on the human being between death and rebirth will supply more information on this subject.[32] For today, let me just say that life after death means leaving the relationships of the sense-perceptible, physical world and entering totally different relationships of space and time. With the theory of relativity, we are beginning to develop different concepts of time.[33] We can make the transition from the factors in the formula for movement into the circumstances of the spiritual world only when we use these factors in the form $c = s / t$, because s and t as we know them belong to the sense-perceptible world, while c (or v for velocity) actually belongs to the domain of inner experience, even with regard to an inorganic object. Thus when we want to understand time in the spiritual world, we must first speak of the quantum of speed that the being in question has; then, through comparison, we as outsiders can determine something about temporal relationships. Through a comparison of sorts, for example, we can discover that speed is three times as great in life in kamaloka. Such investigations give us an impression of the relationship between time in spiritual life and time in the life of the senses. In the spiritual world, different principles of time prevail. In comparison with those of the sense-perceptible world, these principles are internalized and variable. Because the time we experience there is dependent on inner developmental processes, it cannot be compared in clear mathematical terms with periods of time in the physical world.

STUTTGART 1919

(The wording of the question has not been preserved.)

Mathematics is an abstraction of the sum total of forces working in space. When we say that mathematical theorems are valid *a priori*, this statement is based on the fact that human beings exist within the same lines of force as other beings and that we are able to abstract this from everything not belonging to the *pattern* of space, *etc.*

STUTTGART MARCH 7, 1920

FIRST QUESTION: Is the law of the absolute propagation of light correct?

SECOND QUESTION: Is there any reality to the relativity of time assumed by Einstein?

I assume that your first question deals with whether light in absolute space travels at a constant speed. As you know, we cannot really talk about the propagation of light in absolute space because absolute space does not exist. What basis do we actually have for talking about absolute space? You said, and rightly so, that you assume the propagation of light is infinitely great and that light derives its actual propagation from the resistance of the medium. Now I ask you, in your view is it altogether possible to speak of the speed of light in the same sense that we speak of the speed at which any other body travels?

HERMANN VON BARAVALLE: Absolutely not.

If we do not hypothetically equate light with any other body, we cannot measure its speed in the same way as that of any other body. Let's assume that an ordinary body, a material object, is flying through space at a certain speed. This object is at a specific place at a specific moment in time, and our entire method of measuring speed depends on considering the difference in the object's location from its point of departure at two different times. This method of measurement remains possible only if the moving material body completely leaves the points on the line in which it is moving. Let's assume that it does not leave these points but leaves traces behind. Applying this method of measurement immediately becomes impossible if the object moving through a given space does not leave that space but continues to occupy the line of movement, not because we cannot measure the differences but because the propelling speed constantly modifies the propelled object. I cannot apply my ordinary method of measurement when, instead of dealing with matter that leaves the space empty behind it, I am dealing with an entity that does not completely vacate the space but leaves traces behind. Thus, we cannot speak of a constant speed of light in the same sense that we speak of the speed of a material object, because we cannot formulate an equation based on differences in location, which, of course, provide a basis for calculating speed.

Thus, when we are dealing with the propagation of light, we find ourselves compelled to speak only about the speed of the outer propagation of light. But if we speak about the speed of the propagation of light, we would be obliged to go back constantly to the source of the spreading light in order to measure its speed. In the case of the Sun, for example, we would be obliged to go back to the origin of the spreading light. We would have to begin measuring where the spread of light began, and we would have to assume hypothetically that the light continues to replicate indefinitely. This assumption is not justified, however, because the frontal plane in which the light is spreading, instead of always simply growing larger, becomes subject to a certain law of elasticity and reverses direction when it achieves a certain size. At that point we are no longer dealing simply with spreading light but with returning light, with light retracing the same path in reverse. On an ongoing basis, therefore, I am not dealing with a single location that I assume to exist in light-filled space—that is, with something that is spreading from one point to another—but with an encounter between two entities, one of which is coming from the center and the other from the periphery. Thus, I cannot avoid asking the fundamental question, are we really dealing with speeds in the ordinary sense when we consider the transmission of light?

I don't know whether or not I have made myself understood. I am not dealing with speed of propagation in the ordinary sense, and when I take the step from ordinary speeds to speeds of light, I must find formulas based on formulas for elasticity. If I may use the image of material movement, such formulas must reflect how elastically related portions of space behave in a closed elastic system with a fixed sphere as its boundary.[36] Therefore, I cannot use an ordinary formula when I shift to describing the behavior of light. For this reason I see a fundamental error in Einstein's work, namely, that he applies ordinary mechanical formulas—for that is what they are—to the spreading of light and assumes hypothetically that light can be measured in the same way as any material body flying through space.[37] He does not take into account that spreading light does not consist of material cosmic particles speeding away. Light is an event in space that leaves a radiant trace behind, so that when I measure it (reference to drawing that has not been preserved), I cannot simply measure as if the object comes this far and leaves nothing behind. When light is transmitted, however, there is always a trace here, and I cannot say that it is transmitted at a specific speed. Only the frontal plane is transmitted. That is the main point. I am dealing with a specific entity in space that has been subsumed by the spreading element.

And then I see a second error that has to do with the first, namely, that Einstein applies principles to the whole cosmos that actually apply to mechanical systems of points that approach each other, thus disregarding the fact that the cosmos as a whole system cannot be merely a summation of mechanical processes. For example, if the cosmos were an organism, we could not assume that its processes are mechanical. When a mechanical process takes place in my hand, it is not essentially determined merely by the closed, mechanical system because my entire body begins to react. Is it is acceptable to apply a formula for other movements to the movement of light, or is the reaction of the entire cosmos involved? A universe without light is even more difficult to imagine without the reaction of the entire universe, and this reaction works very differently from speeds in a closed, mechanical system.[38]

It seems to me that these are Einstein's two principal errors. I have studied his theory only briefly, and we all know that mathematical derivations can indeed coincide with empirical results. The fact that starlight that has passed the Sun, for example, coincides with theoretical predictions does not verify Einstein's theory once and for all.[39]

These two principal underlying factors are why Einstein's way of thinking is always so paradoxical and abstract. The situation here is somewhat similar to the example from Wilhelm Busch that you used earlier, where an arm is raised forcefully and you almost have the feeling that you are going to be slapped on the face. It's a bit like that when Einstein draws conclusions from what would happen if a clock sped away at the speed of light and then returned.[40] I ask you, is there any reality to this notion? I absolutely cannot complete the thought, because I am forced to wonder what happens to the clock. If you are accustomed to restricting your thoughts to reality, you cannot carry thoughts such as this through to completion.[41] The passages where Einstein presents such thoughts show that his conclusions are based on fundamental errors such as the one I just mentioned.

That was my first comment. On the subject of time, we would need to begin basing our thoughts on elastic formulas rather than ordinary mechanical formulas. We would need to borrow from the theory of elasticity. By extension, any distribution or spreading that forms a frontal plane cannot be imagined as an entity that continues to spread out to infinity. It always reaches a certain sphere where it turns back in on itself. If we want to address the reality of the situation, we cannot say that the Sun radiates light that vanishes into infinity. That is never the case. There is always a boundary where the spreading force of elasticity is exhausted and turns back in on itself. There is no such thing as an infinite system that meets the criteria of spreading out and disappearing into nothingness. Any spreading entity reaches a boundary where it turns around, somewhat as if it were obeying the law that governs elastic bodies. When we speak of light, we are never dealing with something that continues to spread indefinitely in all directions. Instead, we always find a situation comparable to standing waves. *That* is where we must look for the formulas, not in ordinary mechanics.[42]

Then there is still the question of time itself. In fact, time does not go through all these transformations, does it? Here in the realm of mechanics time as such is not a reality. Take the very simplest formula, $s = c \times t$. According to the ordinary law of multiplication, s must be essentially identical to c; otherwise the space s would be identical to the time, which is impossible. In this formula, I can think of space only as somehow mathematically identical to c.

We cannot multiply apples and pears, can we? We have to put one in terms of the other. In mathematical formulas, time can only be a number, which, however, does not mean that the reality of time is a number. We can write the formula like this only when we assume that we are dealing with an unnamed number.[43]

The formula $c = s/t$ is a different matter. Here we have a space s of a certain size as it relates to the size of the number t. The result is the speed c. This is the reality of the situation regardless of whether I imagine atoms, molecules, or matter that occupies a specific, perceivable amount of space. I must imagine that anything I confront empirically has a specific speed. Any further conclusions are just abstractions. Time is something that I derive from the divisor and the distance traveled is something I derive from the dividend, but these are abstractions. The reality—and this applies only to mechanical systems—is the immanent speed of each body. For example, when physicists accept atomic theory for other reasons, they must not assume that atoms exist without immanent speed. Speed is a true reality.[44] Thus we must say that we abstract time as such from events and processes. It is actually an abstraction from events. Only the speeds of what we encounter can be seen as realities.

When we understand this completely, we can no longer avoid concluding that what I call time appears as a result of phenomena. It plays a collaborative role in phenomena, and we must not disregard it as a relative.[45] The collaboration of this abstracted factor yields a specific real and fundamental concept of an organism's life span, for example. The life span of an organism cannot be measured externally; its course is immanent. Any given organism has a specific, inherent life span that is integrated into and results from all the processes taking place in the organism. The same is true of an organism's size. It is intrinsic to the organism and is not to be measured in relationship to anything else. The fitting conclusion is that such concepts of life span and size are not valid in the same way that we ordinarily assume.

Human beings are a specific size. Now let me hypothetically assume that very small human beings exist in our ordinary universe. For all other purposes, the size of human beings relative to other objects is not important. Their typical size is important to human beings, however, because this size is intrinsic. This point is important. Imagining that human beings can be arbitrarily larger or smaller is an offense against the entire universe. For example, certain scientific thinkers wonder what life would be like in a solar system that is infinitely large or small compared with ours. This question is nonsense. Both the sizes and the life spans of the real entities we encounter are matters of inner necessity.

At this point I must state that any entity that can be considered a totality essentially carries its own time within it. I can look at a piece of an inorganic object independent of anything else, but I cannot do the same with a leaf because its continued existence depends on the tree. Thus, I must consider whether or not the entity I am observing is a totality, a whole, self-contained system. Any totality that I observe, however, incorporates time as an immanent factor. Consequently, I do not think much of the idea of an abstract time that exists outside objects and in addition to the time that is inherent in each object or event. Looking at time that is supposed to run from beginning to end is a bit like developing the abstract concept *horse* on the basis of individual horses. Individual horses exist in the external reality of space, but the concept requires something more. The same is true of time. Whether time is inherently changeable or not is essentially an empty question because each total system in its own immanent existence has its own time and its own speed. The speed of any inorganic or vital process points back to this immanent time.

For this reason, instead of a theory of relativity that always assumes we can relate one axial coordinate system to another, I would prefer to establish a theory of absolutes to discover where total systems exist that can be addressed in the same way we address an organism as a totality. We cannot talk about the totality of the Silurian period in the Earth's evolution, for example, because the Silurian period must be united with other evolutionary periods to form a system that is a totality. It is equally impossible to speak about the human head as a totality, because the rest of the body belongs with it.

We describe geologic periods independently of each other, as if that were the reality of the situation. It is not. One period is a reality only in connection with the entire evolution of the Earth, just as a living organism is a reality from which nothing can be removed. Instead of relating our processes to coordinate systems, it would be much more pertinent to relate them to their own inherent reality, so that we could see the whole systems, or totalities. At that point, we would have to return to a certain type of monadism. We would overcome the theory of relativity and arrive at a theory of absolutes.

We would then truly see that Einstein's theory is the last expression of the striving for abstraction. Einstein functions in abstractions that sometimes become intolerable when his assumptions are applied to very elementary matters. For example, how does sound work when I myself am moving at the speed of sound? If I do that, of course I never hear real sounds, because the sound is traveling with me. To anyone who thinks in real terms, in terms of totalities, such a concept cannot be implemented, because any being that can hear would fall apart if it moved at the speed of sound. Such concepts are not rooted in observations of the real world.[46]

The same is true when I ask whether time is inherently changeable. Of course, it is impossible to confirm any changes in abstract or absolute time, which must be imagined *a priori*. When we talk about changes in time, however, we must grasp the reality of time, which we cannot do without considering how temporal processes are intrinsically linked to total systems that exist in the world.

STUTTGART MARCH 7, 1920

QUESTION: *According to Einsteins theory, there is a tremendous amount of energy stored in one kilogram of matter. Is it possible to tap a new source of energy by breaking matter apart—that is, by spiritualizing it?*

The issues you raise are not related directly to the part of Einstein's theory that we discussed today.[48] It certainly would be possible to release energy through the fission of matter. The theoretical aspects present no particular difficulties. The only question is whether we have the technology to utilize this energy. Would we be able to put to use the gigantic forces that would be released? We would not, if they destroy the motor they are meant to run. We first would have to develop mechanical systems capable of harnessing this energy. From a purely theoretical perspective, releasing large amounts of radiant energy for use in a mechanical system requires a substance that can resist the energy. Releasing the energy is quite possible and much easier than utilizing it.

QUESTION: *Would it be possible to eliminate matter altogether, so that only energy or radiation is left?*[49]

In a certain respect, matter is eliminated as in what happens in vacuum tubes. Only a flow of electricity remains. Only speed remains and speed is the determining factor in the mathematical formulas that refer to this phenomena.[50] The question is, Does the formula ($E = mc^2$), in which energy and mass appear at the same time, sufficiently consider the fact that mass as such is different from energy? Or, when I write this formula, am I very abstractly separating two things that are actually one and the same? Is this formula justifiable?[51] It is justifiable only for potential energy, in which case Einstein's formula ($E = mc^2$) is simply the old formula for potential energy in a new disguise.[52]

QUESTION: *Cant we take p × s as our starting point?*[53]

A difficulty arises here simply because when I relate two members of one system of magnitude to something that belongs to another system—for example, if I relate the time it takes two people to do a certain job to a factor supplied by the Sun's setting—the process in the whole system (because it can truly be applied to all members of the system) very easily assumes the character of something that does not belong to any system but can stand on its own. You must not assume that an abstraction, such as a year, that is derived from the solar system is also valid in another system. For example, if you confirm how much a human heart changes in five years, you can then describe the condition of a person's heart as it was five years ago in comparison to what it is now. But by simply continuing the same arithmetical process, you also can ask what that person's heart was like a hundred and fifty years ago or what it will be like three hundred years from now.

This is what astronomers do when they start from the present state of the Earth. They neatly calculate changes over periods of time that make as little sense with regard to present conditions on Earth as our calculations about the state of a human heart in three hundred years. We always forget that a conclusion that is valid with regard to the immanent time of a process ceases to have meaning when the process comes to an end. Thus I cannot transcend the organism as a currently living total system. The total system allows me to keep my concepts within the system, and I immediately violate the system when I step outside its bounds. The appearance of validity is evoked because we are accustomed to relating to systems of magnitude in the sense of total systems and then make absolutes out of factors that apply only within such systems of magnitude.

STUTTGART MARCH 11, 1920

FIRST QUESTION: Does my attempt to define the hyperimaginary through relationships of points on curved surfaces, or manifolds, correspond to reality?

SECOND QUESTION: Is it possible to acquire an enlivened view of the realm of imaginary numbers, and do actual entities underlie this realm?

THIRD QUESTION: Which aspects of modern mathematics, and which formal aspects in particular, need to be developed further along spiritual scientific lines?

Let me begin with your second question. The answer is not easy to formulate because in order to do so, we must leave the realm of visualization to a very great extent. When I answered Dr. Müller's question several days ago,[55] you saw that in order to provide a concrete correlate for a mathematical case, I had to turn to the transition from long bones to head bones, and yet the graphic example was still valid.[56] At least in that case we were still able to visualize the objects and hence the transition from one to another.

When we attempt to look at the domain of imaginary numbers as a spiritual reality,.[57] we find that we need to shift from positive to negative, as I recently demonstrated in these lectures on physics.[58] This shift makes our ideas true to reality when we attempt to understand certain relationships between so-called ponderable matter and so-called imponderables. But even when we visualize very ordinary domains, we can see the need to transcend customary ways of illustrating them. Let me mention just one example. On a plane drawing of the ordinary spectrum, we can draw a straight line from red through green to violet.[59] Such a drawing, however, does not symbolize all the relevant aspects, which are encompassed only when we draw a curve, more or less in this plane (reference to a drawing that has not been preserved), to symbolize the red. Then, to depict the violet, we go to the board and behind the board, so that the red, as seen from above, lies in front of the violet. I would have to move out of the plane for the red and back into it for the violet in order to characterize the violet as moving inward toward chemical activity and the red as moving outward toward warmth.[60] Thus, I am forced to expand the straight line here and to see my ordinary drawing as a projection of what I actually ought to draw.

To achieve clarity concerning certain phenomena of higher reality, it is not enough to shift from the positive material aspect to the negative. That is just as unsatisfactory as moving in a straight line from red through green to violet. When we move from the spatial realm to the non-spatial (as symbolized by positive and negative, respectively), we must shift to a higher form of spatial and non-spatial. This process is like moving along a spiral, instead of moving around a circle and returning to our starting point.

Just as elsewhere two different types may be summed up in a union that contains both, we also can imagine the existence of something that is both spatial and non-spatial. We must seek this third element. In the domain of higher reality, if we describe physical reality as positive, we are obliged to describe the etheric realm, where we leave space and begin to enter spirit, as negative.[61] When we take the step into the astral realm, however, space and negative space are no longer enough. We must turn to a third element that relates to positive and negative space in exactly the same way that imaginary numbers relate to positive and negative numbers in formal mathematics. And if we then take the step from the astral realm to the true being of the "I," we need a concept that is hyperimaginary in relationship to the imaginary. For this reason, I have never been happy with academic antipathy to the concept of hyperimaginary numbers, because this concept is truly needed when we ascend to the level of the "I" and cannot be omitted unless we want our mathematical formulations to leave the realm of reality.[62] The issue is simply how to use the concept correctly in purely formal mathematics.

Someone I met today discussed the problem of probability, a question that very clearly demonstrates the great difficulty of relating a mathematical procedure to reality. Insurance companies can calculate when a person is likely to die, and their figures are very accurate when applied to groups. It is impossible, however, to conclude from actuarial figures that any individual is going to die exactly in the year that is predicted. Consequently, these calculations lack reality.

The results of calculations are often correct in a formal respect yet do not correspond to reality. We also might have to rectify the formal aspects of mathematics in some instances to accord with such results of hyperempirical reality. For example, is it correct to state that $a \times b = 0$ is true only when one of the factors is zero? When either a or b is equal to zero, their product certainly is zero. But is it possible for the product to equal zero when neither of the two factors is zero? Indeed, this might be possible if the reality of the situation forced us to turn to hyperimaginary numbers, which are the correlates of hyperempirical reality.[63] We must indeed attempt to clarify the relationship of real to imaginary numbers and the relationship of hyperimaginary numbers to imaginary and real numbers, but we also may have to modify the rules governing calculations.[64]

With regard to your first question, in the human being we can distinguish only what lies above a certain level and below a certain level. I explain this to almost everyone I think will be able to understand it. To anyone who looks at the wooden sculpture in Dornach of Christ in the center as the representative of humanity, with Ahriman and Lucifer on either side, I explain that we truly must imagine the human beings we encounter as existing in a state of balance. On one side is the suprasensible, on the other the subsensible. Each human being always represents only the state of balance between the suprasensible and the subsensible.

Of course, the human being is a microcosm of sorts and as such is related to the macrocosm. Therefore, we must be able to express the connection between each detail of the human being and a corresponding phenomenon in the macrocosm. Let me illustrate it like this: If this is the plane of balance (reference to a drawing that has not been preserved) and I imagine the subsensible element in the human being as a closed curve and the suprasensible element, or what human beings have in their consciousness, as an open curve, the resulting form is knotted below and opens outward above. This also represents how the human being is incorporated into the macrocosm. This lower, knoblike area pulls us out of the macrocosm, while the open curve of this upper surface incorporates us into the macrocosm. Here is the approximate location of freely willed human decisions. Above the level of free will, human forces are allowed to move out into the macrocosm. Everything below this level encloses macrocosmic forces so that we can assume a specific form.

Within the plane figures formed by this curve, let's note a series of data that I will call x, representing the cosmic thoughts that we can survey. Here we have the cosmic forces that can be surveyed and here the cosmic movements. If I formulate a function involving these numbers up here, the result corresponds to what is down here in the human being. We need a function of factors x, y, and z.

When I attempt to find numbers that express this relationship, however, I cannot find them in the domain of the number system that is available on this plane. In order to connect the suprasensible and the subsensible human being, I must resort to equations containing numbers that belong to systems lying on curved surfaces. These surfaces can be more precisely defined as the surfaces lying on paraboloids of revolution, surfaces that emerge when cones rotate in such a way that each rotating point constantly changes speed.[65] There are also more complicated rotational paraboloids whose points, instead of maintaining fixed relationships among each other, are able to change within the limits of certain laws. Thus, the surfaces that serve my purpose are enlivened rotational paraboloids.

The relationship I am describing is extremely difficult. To date, certain individuals have imagined it, and the need for it has been discovered, but formal calculations will become possible only once esoteric or spiritual science is able to collaborate with mathematics. The path you have outlined for us today constitutes a beginning, a possible initial response to the challenge to discover what corresponds to the association of related functions that refer to number systems on the surfaces of two rotational paraboloids (one that is closed below and one that is open above) whose vertices meet in one point. As I have described, we would simply need to find the numbers lying on these surfaces, which do indeed correspond to a real situation.

With regard to the future development of formal mathematics, I must admit that it seems that much remains to be done and that much is possible. My next comment may do formal mathematics an injustice, since I have been less able to keep up with it in recent years. It has been a long time since I was fully aware of what is going on in this field, and things may have changed. Before the turn of the century, however, I always had the feeling that the papers published in the field of formal mathematics were terribly unconcerned about whether their calculations and operations were actually possible at all, or whether they would need to be modified at a certain point in accordance with some real situation. For example, we can ask what happens when we multiply a one-dimensional manifold by a two-dimensional manifold. Although it is possible to answer such questions, we must nonetheless wonder whether an operation like this corresponds to any reality at all or even to anything we can imagine. In order to get somewhere, it may be necessary to define clearly the concept of "only calculable."

As an example, a long time ago I attempted to prove the Pythagorean theorem in purely numerical terms, without resorting to visual aids.[66] It will be important to formulate the purely arithmetical element so strictly that we do not unwittingly stray into geometry. When we calculate with numbers—as long as we stay with ordinary numbers—they are just numbers, and there is no need to talk about number systems in specific domains of space. When we talk about other numbers, however—imaginary numbers, complex numbers, hypercomplex numbers, hyperimaginary numbers—we do have to talk about a higher domain of space. You have seen that this is possible, but we have to leave our ordinary space. That is why I feel that before purely formal mathematics sets up numbers that can only be symbolized—and in a certain sense, applying additional corresponding points to specific domains of space is symbolization—we must investigate how such higher numbers can be imagined without the help of geometry,[67] that is, in the sense that I can represent a linear function through a series of numbers.

We would have to answer the question of how to imagine the relationship of positive and negative numbers on a purely elementary level. Although I cannot provide a definitive answer, because I have not concerned myself with the subject and do not know enough about it, Gauss's solution—namely, to assume that the difference between positive and negative is purely conceptual—seems inadequate to me.[68] Dühring's interpretation of negative numbers as nothing more than subtraction without the minuend seems equally inadequate.[69] Dühring accounts for the imaginary number $\sqrt{-1}$ in a similar way, but this number is nothing more than an attempt to perform an operation that cannot be carried out in reality, though the notation for it exists.[70] If I have 3 and nothing I can subtract from it, 3 remains. The notation for the operation exists, but nothing changes. In Dühring's view, the differential quotient is only a notated operation that does not correspond to anything else.[71] To me, Dühring's approach also seems one-sided, and the solution probably lies in the middle. We will get nowhere in formal mathematics, however, until these problems are solved.

STUTTGART MARCH 11, 1920

FIRST QUESTION: The question is, does such an understanding correspond to reality? Since what we did in simple geometry also would have to be possible in all domains of mathematics, could understanding mathematical objects as intermediary links between archetype and physical image perhaps serve as a foundation for the types of calculations needed to support the physics presented in this lecture?

SECOND QUESTION: Might this be a path to the so-called hyperempirical realm that we reach by controlling and enhancing our thinking?

If I understand your first question correctly, you are asking whether we can approach the realm of mathematics as an intermediary stage between archetype and physical image.[73] Let's look at the domains of mathematics from a purely spiritual and empirical perspective. What are the spatial and geometric domains of mathematics? Or were you thinking of arithmetic as well?

ALEXANDER STRAKOSCH: I was thinking of geometry.

During this lecture series, I have already suggested parenthetically how we arrive at ordinary geometric figures.[74] We do not discover them by abstracting from empirical ideas. Initially, mathematical and geometric figures are an intuition of sorts. They are derived from the will nature of the human being, so we can say that when we experience mathematical figures, it is always possible for us to be active and to relate to reality in the mathematical domain. Thus, such figures, even on an empirical level, already represent a type of intermediate state between external realities (which we can possess only in image form) and the direct contents of being (which we experience inwardly). A spiritually empirical perspective would show that when we understand geometry, we grasp an intermediate stage between archetype and physical image.

However, there is something we must still do in order to verify this train of thought. If geometric and mathematical figures are indeed intermediate states between archetype and image, they must have a certain nonmaterial ideal attribute that images do not have, though it only becomes so nonmaterial in the sphere of images.

An image also can be a combination; it does not necessarily correspond to its archetype. Any mere image that we confront need not correspond to an archetype. But if we have an intermediate state that incorporates a certain amount of reality, we need to be able to discover a corresponding specific field of reality, and we cannot combine such domains arbitrarily. We can never combine archetypes in a living way, we must seek them out in their own domains, where they are present as distinct experiences. Thus, in order to grasp this middle domain in the right way, what you called the domain of the perceived lawfulness of mathematical objects, we also must understand its construction as an intermediate state between absolute, fixed archetypes and a boundless number of images. That is, we would have to interpret all of mathematics, and especially geometry, as inherently mobile, as existing at least in latent form in all of reality. For example, we could not imagine a triangle as immobile but would have to visualize the full scope of the concept. What is a triangle? A triangle is an area bounded by straight lines, and the sum of its angles is 180°. We would have to imagine the lengths of its three sides as being infinitely variable, and our definition would yield an infinite number of triangles, or a triangle in flux. This way of looking at things would result in a fluid geometry.[75] We would have to be able to prove that this fluid geometry has some significance for the natural kingdom—that it corresponds to an aspect of the law of crystallization, for example. So the answer to your question is yes, this view is indeed based on an idea that corresponds to reality, but a great deal remains to be done to make the entire concept clear.

I must still touch on another subject that plays into all this. You see, in recent times people have made a habit of taking refuge in higher dimensions when they want to enter higher domains of reality. That was not always the case in the formalism that formed the basis of our conceptions of the occult. In earlier times, people said that while we must conceive of ordinary physical figures as three dimensional, figures belonging to astral space must be seen in the context of a two-dimensional plane. Note that I am now talking about the spheres or planes of existence, and therefore the term *astral* is used in a sense different from the one I used when talking with Mr. Blümel and describing the steps between the physical body and the "I." We must imagine the next level, the Rupa plane, as one-dimensional in scope, and when we imagine the Arupa plane, we arrive at a point.[76]

In this way we can say that as we move toward more spiritual ideas, the number of dimensions must decrease rather than increase. We are subject to this phenomenon when we move from above to below, as we do, for example, when we attempt the following train of thought. We can distinguish quite well among spirit, soul, and body. But what is the spiritual element in a human being walking around on Earth? We must say that this spiritual element is present in an extremely filtered form. We humans owe our abstract thinking to the spirit; it is the spiritual element in us. On its own, it tends to perceive only sense-perceptible objects and events, but the means of perceiving is spiritual. When we trace the spirituality of thinking down into the bodily element, we find that it has an expression in the human physical body, while the more comprehensive spiritual element has no such expression. Crudely speaking, one-third of the spiritual world in which we humans take part has an expression in the physical human body.

Moving on to the soul, two-thirds of the spiritual world in which humans take part achieve expression in the physical human body. And when we move on to the physical body, three-thirds has achieved expression. As we move from above to below, we must imagine that in the progression from the archetype to its image, the archetype easily leaves aspects of its being behind, and this phenomenon provides the essential characteristic of our physical aspect. In contrast, as we move upward, we discover new elements that have not been incorporated into the image. As we move downward, however, what we encounter is not merely an image; reality plays into it. It is not true that at night when the physical and ether bodies are lying in bed, the astral body and "I" simply pull out of the body and leave it empty. Higher forces enter the physical and ether bodies and enliven them while the astral body and "I" are gone. Similarly, an image contains elements that do not originate only in its archetype. These elements enter when the image becomes an image, when it belongs to the entity.

Then the interesting question arises, How does a merely imaginatively combined image become a real image? That is when the other subject I mentioned enters in. Let me still comment that when we consider two dimensions, our initial train of thought leads directly to a second that can illuminate the first. All two-dimensional figures can be drawn in two dimensions, but figures that occupy three-dimensional space cannot. Suppose, however, that I begin to sketch a picture using colors instead of drawing in perspective or the like—that is, I copy colors, I supply images of colors. Anyone will admit that I am then incorporating space directly into the plane to form the image. At this point I may ask, Does what expresses color in this image lie in any of the three dimensions of space? Is it possible to use colors to suggest something that can replace the three dimensions? Once we have an overview of the element of color, we can arrange colors in a specific way that creates an image of three-dimensionality in two dimensions. Anyone can see that all blues tend to recede, while reds and yellows advance. Thus, simply by supplying color, we express three dimensions. By using the intensive aspect of color to express the extensive aspect of three-dimensionality, we can compress three-dimensionality into two dimensions.

By linking other thoughts to this train of thought, we arrive at fluid geometry. And we may indeed be able to expand geometry to incorporate considerations such as this: In mathematics, we can construct congruent triangles A and B, but could we not also discover an expanded mathematical connection between red and blue triangles drawn in a plane? Is it really permissible for me simply to draw the simple lines that form a red triangle in the same way that I draw a blue triangle? Would I not have to state expressly that when I draw a red triangle and a blue one in the same plane, the red one would have to be small just because it is to represent red, while the blue one would have to be large simply because it is blue?

Now the question arises, Is it possible to incorporate an intensity factor into our geometry, so that we can perform calculations with intensities? This would reveal the full significance of how our right and left eyes work together. Stereoscopic vision depends on both eyes working together. In the domain of optics, this phenomenon is the same as grasping my left hand with the right. A being that could never touch one part of its body with another would be physically incapable of conceiving of the "I." This conception depends on being able to touch one part of my being with another. I can experience myself as an "I" in space only because of a phenomenon that is slightly hidden by ordinary empiricism, namely, the fact that my right and left vision crosses. This fact, though it does not encompass the reality of the "I," allows us to form a correct conception of the "I."

Now imagine how our physical ability to conceive of the "I" would be affected if our eyes were strongly asymmetrical instead of more or less symmetrical. What if your left eye, for example, was significantly smaller than the right, making your left and right stereoscopic images very different? Your left eye would produce a smaller image that it would constantly attempt to enlarge, while your right eye would have to attempt the opposite, namely, to reduce the size of its image. These efforts would add an enlivened form of vision to your static stereoscopic vision.

Real enlivened vision, however, must be achieved as soon as you even begin to approach imaginative perception. This perception results from constantly having to adapt asymmetrical elements to each other. The central figure in the Dornach sculpture had to be depicted as strongly asymmetrical in order to show that it is ascending to the spirit. It also suggests that every aspect of the human being—for example, our stereoscopic vision—is basically a state of balance that constantly deviates toward one or the other pole. We are human because we must continually create a state of balance between above and below, forward and back, and left and right.

DORNACH MARCH 30, 1920

QUESTION: *How will anthroposophy affect the further evolution of chemistry?*

Assuming that we undertake the type of phenomenology described by Dr. Kolisko, this question is so all-encompassing that the answer can only be hinted at. First and foremost, we must realize that we would have to develop an appropriate phenomenology. Phenomenology is not simply an arbitrary assemblage of phenomena or experimental results. Real phenomenology is a systematization of phenomena, such as that attempted by Goethe in his theory of color.[78] It derives the complicated from the simple, leading back to the foundations where the basic elements or phenomena appear.

Of course, I am quite aware that some truly intelligent people will argue that a sophisticated presentation of the connection between qualitative phenomena and archetypal phenomena is not comparable to the way in which complicated geometric relationships are mathematically derived from axioms. This is because geometric relationships are systematized on the basis of intrinsic structure. We experience the further development of mathematics from these axioms as an inherently necessary continuation of the mathematical process, while, on the other hand, we must depend on observing a physical state of affairs when we systematize phenomena and archetypal phenomena.

This argument, though it enjoys widespread support, is not valid and is simply the result of an incorrect epistemology, specifically, a confused mingling of the concept of experience with other concepts. This confusion results in part from failure to consider that human subjects shape their own experience. It is impossible to develop a concept of experience without imagining the connection of an object to a human subject. Suppose I confront a Goethean archetypal image. When I make it more complicated, the result is a derivative phenomenon, and I seem to depend on outer experience to support my conclusion. Is there any difference, in principle, between this subject-object relationship and what happens when I demonstrate mathematically that the sum of the three angles in a triangle is 180° or when I prove the Pythagorean theorem empirically? Is there really any difference?

In fact, there is no difference, as became evident from studies by very gifted nineteenth-and twentieth-century mathematicians who realized that mathematics ultimately also rests on experience in the sense in which the so-called empirical sciences use the term. These mathematicians developed non-Euclidean geometries that initially merely supplemented Euclidean geometry.[79] Theoretically, the geometric thought that the three angles of a triangle add up to 380° is indeed possible, though admittedly we must presuppose that space has a different rate of curvature.[80] Our ordinary space has regular Euclidean measurements/dimensions and a rate of curvature of zero. Simply by imagining that space curves more, that is, that its rate of curvature is greater than 1, we arrive at statements such as: The sum of the three angles of a triangle is greater than 180°.

Interesting experiments have been conducted in this field, such as those of Oskar Simony, who has studied the subject in greater detail.[81] Such efforts show that from a certain perspective, it is already necessary to say that conclusions we state in mathematical or geometric theorems need empirical verification as much as any phenomenological conclusions.

DORNACH MARCH 31, 1920

QUESTION: Ordinary mathematics encompasses the forms, surfaces, and lines of force of solids, liquids, and gases. How would you imagine a mathematics of the domains of warmth, chemistry, and life?

First of all, the field of mathematics as such would need to be appropriately expanded if we want to describe higher realms in a way that is analogous—but no more than analogous—to mathematics. As you may know, the need to expand mathematics became evident already in the nineteenth century. Let me just mention a point I have discussed on other occasions—including yesterday, I believe.[83] In the late nineteenth century, it became apparent that a non-Euclidean geometry was needed to supplement Euclidean geometry and to make it possible to carry out calculations involving higher dimensions. Mathematicians of that time were suggesting that mathematics needed to be expanded.[84] In contrast, as long as we are considering ordinary, ponderable matter, there is no appropriate use for dimensions other than the three ordinary Euclidean dimensions.

Mathematicians today, however, are so disinclined to explore appropriate views of the domains of warmth, chemical effects, and the elements of life that extending mathematical thinking into these areas is really very problematic.[85] The views mathematicians propound today certainly do not create a counterbalance to the professed inability of physics to grasp the essential nature of matter. And to be consistent, physicists would have to admit that physics does not deal with the essential nature of light but only with what Goethe calls the image of light. Of course, sensible physicists will refuse to delve into the essential nature of things in the pursuit of their profession. Admittedly, the result is an unfortunate state of affairs: Physicists refuse to deal with the essential nature of things on any level. And those who concoct philosophies from the conventional, material views of physics not only refuse to inquire into the essential nature of things but even claim that it is impossible to do so. As a result, our view of the Earth today is very one-sided, because, in fact, physics is never simply a matter of geology but deals with the sum total of what such a specialized field can yield for general knowledge. Thus, we face the adverse consequences of the mechanistic, non-mathematical worldview that physics has developed over time.

What Goethe meant when he said that we should not talk about the being or nature of light but rather should attempt to become familiar with the facts about it, with its deeds and sufferings—which yield a complete description of the nature of light—is by no means the same as refusing on principle to consider the question of the nature of light. Goethe's statement simply points out that true phenomenology (structured in the way we discussed here yesterday)[86] ultimately does provide an image of the being in question.[87] To the extent that physics is or intends to be real phenomenology, it does provide—at least with respect to mechanics—an image of the essential nature of phenomena.

It can be said therefore that when we are not dealing with merely mechanical aspects of the phenomena of physics—that is, when we are dealing with fields other than mechanics—a mechanistic view hinders our ability to recognize the essential nature of things. To this extent, then, we do need to emphasize the radical difference between Goethe's intended phenomenology, which can be cultivated in Goetheanism, and any system whose principles rule out the possibility of approaching the true nature of things. This has nothing to do with the advantages of mechanistic methods for our urge to control nature.[88] It is quite understandable that the field of technology and mechanics—which has produced the greatest triumphs of the last few centuries—and its mechanistic basis for understanding nature should satisfy our urge to control nature to a certain extent.

But to what extent has this drive to understand and control nature fallen behind in other fields because they refused to press on toward the type of knowledge to which technology aspired? The difference between technology or mechanics and the fields of study beginning with physics and continuing through chemistry to biology is not that these higher fields deal only with qualitative properties or the like. The difference is simply that mechanics and mechanistic physiology are very elementary and easy-to-grasp aspects and have therefore managed to satisfy our desire for control at least to a certain extent.

At this point, however, the question arises, How do we satisfy our urge to control when we move on to higher, less mechanistic fields? In the future, we will have to count on being at least somewhat able to dominate nature in ways that go beyond mere technology. Even in the technological field, we can very easily experience failures to understand and control nature. If someone builds a bridge without adequate knowledge of the laws of mechanics that apply to railways, the bridge eventually will collapse, carrying the train with it.

We react immediately to inadequate control due to faulty information. The proof is not always so easy, however, when control is based on more complicated domains that are derived not from mechanics but from the process of developing a phenomenology. It is fairly safe to say that a bridge that collapses when the third train crosses it must have been built by someone inadequately motivated to understand the mechanics involved. In the case of a physician whose patient dies, it is not so easy to confirm a similar connection between the practitioner's desire to understand and his or her control over nature. It is easier for us to say that an engineer designed a faulty bridge than that a doctor cured the disease but killed the patient. In short, we should be somewhat less hasty to emphasize the importance of our urge to control nature simply because our mechanistic view of nature has proved capable of satisfying this urge only in the domain of mechanistic technology.

Other ways of looking at nature will be able to very differently satisfy our urge to control. Let me point again to something that I believe I mentioned yesterday from a different perspective. We can never bridge the gap between the mechanistic view of the world and the human being except by applying a true phenomenological approach.[89] Goethe's color theory not only presents the physical and physiological phenomena of color but also makes the whole subject humanly relevant by exploring the sensory and moral effects of colors.[90] In our spiritual scientific work, we can move from the effects of colors pointed out by Goethe to the broader subject of understanding the entire human being and then to the still broader subject of understanding all of nature.

In some ways it may be beneficial to draw people's attention repeatedly to the fact that a large part of the decadence we experience today in Western culture is related to satisfying our urge to control only from the mechanistic perspective. In this regard, we have done very well. We not only have developed railways, telegraphs, and telephones, and even wireless and multiple telegraphy, but we also have paved over and destroyed large parts of this continent. Thoroughly satisfying our urge to control has led to destruction.

Following the straight line of development that began with our purely technological urge to control has led to destruction. This destructive aspect will be eliminated completely when we replace our pathologically expanding mechanistic view of the phenomena of physics with a view that does not eradicate the specifics of physical phenomena simply by blanketing them in mechanistic ideas. We will move away from the mechanistic view, which admittedly has produced very good physiological explanations, to the specifics of the phenomena of physics. Our new view, which cannot be discussed down to its last consequences in one hour, also will lead to an expansion of mathematics that is based on reality.

We must realize that in the past thirty to fifty years, confused mechanistic ideas have made possible all kinds of opinions about the so-called ether. After much effort, the physicist Planck, whom I mentioned earlier in a different context, arrived at this formulation: If we want to speak about the ether in physics at all, we cannot attribute any material properties to it.[91] We must not imagine it in material terms. Planck forced physics to refrain from attributing material properties to the ether. The errors inherent in ideas and concepts about the ether are not due to having done too little mathematics or anything of that sort. They arose because proponents of the ether hypothesis were completely consumed by the trend that attempted to expand mathematics to cover the specifics of physics. Their mathematics was faulty because they behaved as if they were dealing with ponderable matter when they inserted numbers into formulas in which ether effects played a role. As soon as we realize that when we enter the domain of the ether, we can no longer insert ordinary numbers into mathematical formulas, we also will feel the need to look for a true extension of mathematics itself.

There are only two points that need to be made in this regard. The physicist Planck says that if we want to talk about the ether in physics, we must at least refrain from attributing material properties to it. And Einstein's theory of relativity—or any other theory of relativity, for that matter—forces us to eliminate the ether completely.[92] In reality, we need not eliminate it. I can give only a brief indication here, but the main point is simply that when we shift to the ether, we must insert negative numbers into the formulas of physics—that is, mathematical formulas that are applied to phenomena in physics. These numbers must be negative because when we move from positive matter through zero to the other side, as when we move from positive to negative numbers in formal physics, what we encounter in the ether is neither nothing (as Einstein believes) nor a pure negative (as Planck says) but something that we must imagine as possessing properties that are the opposite of the properties of matter just as negative numbers are the opposite of positive numbers.[93] Although we may debate what negative numbers are, the purely mathematical extension of the number line into negative numbers becomes significant for reality even before we clearly understand the character of negative numbers.

Of course, I am well aware of the significant mathematical debate in the nineteenth century between those who saw qualitative aspects in plus and minus signs and those who saw the minus sign only as a subtrahend lacking a negative minuend.[94] This debate is not especially important, but it is important to note that when physics shifts from ponderable effects to etheric effects, it is forced to take the same route that we take in formal mathematics when we move from positive to negative numbers. We should check the results of the formulas when we decide to handle the numbers in this way. Much good work has been done in formal mathematics to justify the concept of formal imaginary numbers. In physics, too, we are obliged at a certain point to substitute imaginary numbers for positive and negative numbers. At this point, we begin to interact with numbers relevant to nature.

I know that I have sketched all this very briefly and summed it up in only a few words, but I must make you aware of the possibilities. As we move from ponderable matter to the forces of life, we must insert negative numbers into our formulas to signify the inverse of the quantitative aspect of matter. And as soon as we transcend life, we must shift from negative numbers to imaginary numbers, which are not mere formal numbers but numbers with properties derived not from positive or negative matter but from the substantial aspect that is related, qualitatively and intrinsically, to both the etheric aspect or negative matter and the ponderable aspect or positive matter in the same way that the imaginary number line relates to the real number line of positive and negative numbers. Thus, there is indeed a connection between formal mathematics and certain domains of reality.

It would be highly regrettable if attempts to make our ideas approximate reality or to immerse our ideas in reality were to fail because of the trivial notion that the offerings of truly rational, rather than merely mechanistic, physics and physiology would be less effective in satisfying the human urge to control nature. In fact, they would be more effective than applying the mechanistic worldview to the technology that we have glorified to such an extent. This mechanistic technology has certainly produced great results for humanity's cultural development. But people who constantly talk about the glorious progress of the natural sciences as a result of the conventional calculations of physics should keep in mind that other areas may have suffered as a result of turning our attention totally to the technological domain. To escape from the decadence brought on by our merely technical understanding and control of nature, we would do well to turn to a physiology and physics that, unlike our mechanical and mechanistic knowledge, cannot refuse to acknowledge the essential nature of things.

You see, this mechanical domain can easily dismiss the essential nature of things precisely because this essential nature is available—spread out in space all around us. It is somewhat more difficult for the entire field of physics to progress in the way that the field of mechanics has progressed. This is the reason for all of this talk of refusing to acknowledge the essential nature of things. When physicists choose to think in purely mechanical terms, they can easily refuse to understand beings. There is no being behind the formulas that are used today to express mechanics in mathematical terms. Beings begin only when we no longer simply apply these formulas but delve into the essential nature of mathematics itself. I hope this addresses the question of how to extend the field of mathematics to cover imponderables.

*

DORNACH OCTOBER 15, 1920

A question about Copernicus's third law.

It is impossible to speak about Copernicus's third law in such a short time, so let me simply comment on its history. If you look at Copernicus's basic work, which severely shook the old Ptolemaic system and revolutionized our view of the heavenly bodies, you will find that it encompasses three laws.[96] The first of these three laws speaks about Earth's annual movement around the Sun in an eccentric circle, the second about the Earth's rotation around its axis, and the third about the Earth's movement around the Sun in relationship to the seasons and precession. As astronomy progressed, it failed to consider this third Copernican law in its entirety. In fact, Copernicus's successors effectively eliminated it. That is all I can say about this law without doing extensive drawings, which would keep us here until midnight.

On the basis of the phenomena available to him, Copernicus first calculated the daily changes caused by the Earth's circular movement around the Sun, disregarding the seasonal, yearly, and longer-term changes encompassed by his third law. He then concluded that if we consider the daily changes and those dependent on the Earth's circular movement around the Sun in the Earth's position with regard to the other heavenly bodies, the result is a view of the Earth revolving around the Sun. This view is opposed by other phenomena such as the seasons and precession, which actually nullify the assumption that the Earth revolves around the Sun.

For the sake of being able to quantify and calculate the interactions between the Earth and the other heavenly bodies, we make it easy for ourselves and disregard any changes that can be observed only over a year or over centuries, because these changes complicate the daily changes that depend on the Earth's circular movement around the Sun. Calculating the daily changes on the basis of the assumptions expressed by Copernicus in his first and second law results in the Earth's yearly revolution around the Sun. As Copernicus himself said, if we include the third law in our calculations, it counteracts the factor contained in the first law, which we calculated into the daily movement and which yields the Earth's yearly movement, and almost eliminates any such yearly movement[97]. In any case, the third Copernican law has been disregarded. People preferred the easy assumption that the Earth rotates around its axis in twenty-four hours, progressing all the while so as to move around the Sun in the course of one year.

This solution was simple as long as we clung dogmatically to the Copernican assumption that the Sun does not move at all. We were forced to abandon this assumption a long time ago, however, and the third Copernican law had to be reinstated.[98]

I can summarize this subject only briefly—as I said, a detailed mathematical and geometric explanation would take hours—but if we take the third Copernican law seriously, it does not result in movement of the Earth around the Sun. The Sun moves, it would outrun the Earth if the Earth simply revolved around the Sun. The Earth cannot revolve around the Sun because meanwhile the Sun would move away from it. In reality, the Sun moves on, and the Earth and the other planets follow it. We have a line like the thread of a screw, with the Sun at one point and the Earth at the other end. Our dual focus on the Earth and Sun and on their progressive, screwlike movement creates the illusion that the Earth is revolving around the Sun.[99] The interesting point in all this is that Copernicus was more advanced than we are today. We have simply omitted his third law from astronomy's post-Copernican development. Our astronomy has been developed without this third law, which states that other phenomena negate the yearly movements around the Sun that we calculate for the Earth. To do full justice to Copernicus, this law must be reintroduced.[100]

This subject does not attract much interest, because if we were to apply a true phenomenological approach to astronomy, we would have to realize first and foremost that, as Dr. Vreede [101] already mentioned, we are dealing with extremely complicated movements. And that the ordinary geometric constructions we use in attempting to describe these movements are suited only to descriptions of simple geometric processes. Because the heavenly bodies do not obey such simple processes, disturbances always appear, and we are forced to compensate by adding more hypotheses.[102] When we get beyond such hypotheses, astronomy will look completely different.

This will happen only when we progress to a form of natural science that truly includes the human being and observes phenomena within the human being. Taking these phenomena into account will allow us to develop a view of the events and processes of cosmic space. As Dr. Unger also mentioned,[103] the human being actually has been ousted from today's science, which disregards the human element. Ideas such as the theory of relativity,[104] which certainly do not correspond to reality, are able to take hold only because modern science is so utterly estranged from reality that it deals with everything outside human beings but nothing that happens inside them. To think in ways that correspond to reality is a skill that humanity will have to relearn.

If you have a stone lying here (reference to a drawing that has not been preserved), you can see it as leading an independent existence, at least to a certain extent. It all depends on your presuppositions. We can say that when we consider what we see within the boundaries of the stone, we develop a certain view of the stone. But now assume that instead of a stone, we are considering a rose that I have picked. It is not possible to ascribe reality to the rose in the same way that we ascribed reality to the stone within its boundaries, because a plucked rose cannot exist in isolation. It must develop in connection with something else. We are forced to say that while the stone within its described limits possesses a certain real existence, the rose does not, because it can exist only in association with its rootstock. If I separate it from its roots, the prerequisites for its existence are no longer present, and it cannot persist.

We must relearn the skill of submerging our thinking in things and taking the things themselves into account. Only when we have reacquired this skill will we have a healthy form of astronomy, for example, as a matter of course. We will be spared the terrible abstraction of such ideas as the theory of relativity. Essentially, the theory of relativity is based on ideas that are not true realities.

The ordinary formula $s = v \times t$, (distance equals speed multiplied by time) is quite illuminating. When I am describing a reality, I can write only this:

$$v = s/t.$$

When we grasp a reality by means of abstraction, I can calculate everything that is in a real object. Because it is possible to grasp many different things on an abstract level, we can perform many different calculations while remaining within the abstract. We must not believe, however, that these abstractions are realities. In the inorganic world, only speeds are realities, and both time and space are mere abstractions. Thus when we begin to perform calculations involving time and space, we enter the domain of unreality, and once we begin thinking in unreal terms, we can no longer return to reality.

These issues, therefore, are related to very significant shortcomings of our times. In recent times, humankind has disregarded the spirit completely while attempting to understand nature, and our souls have moved toward abstractions. In one sense, dealing with abstractions is extremely comfortable, because we do not need to learn to submerse ourselves in objects and events. It is easier to think in terms of space and time than to immerse ourselves in qualitative aspects or to realize that whatever we can think of as real in connection with something else, can therefore be thought about in real terms. (Editor's note: not abstractly.) You need not believe what I am about to say, but it is true nonetheless. It is torture for a person who has cultivated a capacity for thinking and a desire to understand reality to read Einstein's theory of relativity, because even though all the ideas Einstein presents are mathematically very consistent, they are literally unthinkable for someone with any sense of reality. It is impossible to pursue such thoughts to their conclusion. What does it mean and what kind of sense does it make when Einstein presents a whole complex of thoughts about someone who is sealed up in a box and journeys through space at high speed and returns to find a new generation of people and totally different circumstances?[105] When we think about such a situation, of course we are thinking only in terms of space and time and disregarding the outer bodily nature of the person or object, which would be destroyed while undergoing the experiment. Although this objection may seem naive to fanatical thinkers on the subject of relativity, it inevitably comes into consideration with regard to reality[106]. Anyone who has a sense for reality cannot see such thoughts through to the end.

Suppose that we are traveling in a car, for example, and have a flat tire. Let's assume that it makes no difference whether I think that the car, with me in it, is speeding over the ground or that the car is standing still while the ground moves out from under me. If, in fact, it makes no difference, why should the ground suddenly go on strike because of a minor breakdown that concerns only the car? If it makes no difference how we conceive of this situation, the outcome should not be affected by the outer change. As I said before, although such objections are terribly naive as far as relativity theorists are concerned, they do reflect current realities. Anyone whose thinking is grounded in reality rather than in abstraction—even an abstraction that can sustain consistent thoughts—is forced to point out such issues.

Fundamentally, therefore, we are living with a theoretical form of astronomy. A classic example is our disregard of the third Copernican law. We push it aside because it is uncomfortable. When we study it, we learn to feel uncomfortable about our customary calculations. What do we do? We apply the second Copernican law, but our calculations do not come out even, and noon falls in the wrong place. So we introduce the daily corrections known as Bessel's corrections.[107] If we realize their full implications, however, we see the need to take the third Copernican law into account—that is, we begin to deal with realities.

The point here is to acknowledge the principles behind such issues. The way we presently deal with such principles permits us to go astray in many different directions. Mr. Steffen did an excellent job of presenting three such tortuous paths in a specific field of knowledge.[108] Such misleading paths are easy to encounter today, and they influence real life. We have trained ourselves to think in ways derived from a mathematics that lacks reality, and this type of thinking gradually has become almost a touchstone of genius. In fact, a sense of reality is sometimes much more helpful than genius, because if you have a sense of reality, you must abide by the realities of the situation. You must immerse yourself in objects and events and live with them. If you have no sense of reality, you can impose all sorts of abstractions onto space and time in the most ingenious way, simply by manipulating mathematical formulas and methods. You can rise to truly terrible levels of abstraction.

These abstractions sometimes can be very seductive. I am thinking of modern set theory, which has been used as the basis for explaining infinity. Set theory dissolves number, the very principle of mathematics, because it no longer sees a number as an ordinary number but merely compares one arbitrary set with another, classifying individual entities with no regard to their qualities and sequence}.[109] Set theory makes it possible to develop certain theories of infinity, but swimming in abstractions all the while. In concrete reality, it is impossible to perform such operations. It is important to note that we gradually have become accustomed to disregarding the need to immerse ourselves in reality. In this connection, spiritual science really needs to set the record straight.

I am now going to present two opposites. This appears to have nothing to do with theory, but in truth it has a great deal to do with theory, because all of these matters deal with much more than a theory, which can be corrected if our thinking about it is sound. The real issue is the need to develop sound thinking, thinking that is not merely logical, because logic also applies to mathematics. We can incorporate logic into mathematics, and the result is a completely coherent structure that nonetheless need not apply to reality at all. By now we have reached the point of being able to show how things look to an undisciplined way of thinking that lacks any true sense of reality.

Here you have on the one hand a book that attempts to summarize everything that modern science has to offer. Thousands and thousands of copies—seventy or eighty thousand, I believe—of this famous book have already been sold. It is Oswald Spengler's book *The Decline of the West*.[110] As you know, this means that four or five times that number of people have read the book, so we know what a tremendous influence it has had on modern thought, simply because it emerged from modern thought, in a certain sense. The author of this book had the courage to formulate the ultimate consequences of modern thinking. In this book, Spengler looks at everything that astronomy, history, the natural sciences, and art have to offer, and we are forced to admit that he has amassed a huge body of evidence. Because Spengler really thinks in this way, he has the courage to draw the ultimate conclusions from the thinking of truly modern astronomers, botanists, art historians, and so on. As clearly as we can prove the second law of thermodynamics,[111] for example, Spengler's book also proves that in the beginning of the third millennium, Western civilization will have degenerated into complete barbarity.

We must admit that this book not only has shown us the decline of modern civilization but also has proved a future event as clearly as any scientific statement can be proved today. In terms of the methods of modern science, Spengler's proof of the decline of the West is certainly as good as any astronomical proof or the like and much better than any proof of the theory of relativity. His conclusions can be circumvented only by those who see factors that Spengler himself does not see, namely, by those who will provide completely new impulses for humanity from now on. Impulses that must be born out of the inmost core of the human being and that are invisible to any science based solely on contemporary thought.

But what is Spengler's thinking like? Unlike the relativity theorists, Oswald Spengler thinks in categories that correspond to reality. Not everything he thinks fits together, however. The concepts he develops about astronomy, biology, art history, architecture, sculpture, and so on do not always mesh. They form a structure that I would like to compare to crystals that have grown together. They are all confused, and they destroy each other. If we maintain a sense of reality while reading Spengler's book, we find that his concepts are very full (reference to a drawing that has not been preserved). Oswald Spengler certainly knows how to think and develop concepts, but his concepts destroy each other. They blow each other up and cut each other apart. Nothing remains whole because one concept always negates another. We see terrible destructive actions when we apply a sense of reality to the development of Spengler's ideas.

Spengler represents one pole in modern thought, the pole that constructs a unity out of concepts drawn from all different fields. The philosophers associated with this trend neatly define everything on such an abstract level that all of the concepts they derive from individual sciences can be gathered together and united into a system of sorts, in an attempt to come to a point. They fail to come to a point, however, but simply splinter and obliterate each other. Spengler is a much better philosopher of modern science than many other philosophers, whose concepts do not destroy each other because their formulators lack the courage to define them precisely enough. In their philosophies of science, these other philosophers are always confusing tiger claws with cat paws, as it were, resulting in comical constructs that are said to be the philosophical consequences of individual scientific investigations. If we consider these philosophers seriously, we see that Spengler is experienced in all the sciences and knowledgeable about anything scientific that can result from the customs of philosophy.

The other pole is represented by a philosopher who is also popular, though not revered to the extent that Spengler is, namely, Count Hermann Keyserling.[112] Keyserling differs from Oswald Spengler in that none of his concepts have any content. While Spengler's concepts are meaty, Keyserlings are empty. They never contradict each other because they are basically only empty husks of words. Keyserling's only thought, which is also an empty husk, is that the spirit must unite with the soul.[113] Count Keyserling attacks anthroposophy vehemently. In the periodical *Zukunft*, for example, he accused me of splitting the human being into various members—ether body, sentient body, sentient soul, and so on—while in fact the human being is a unity and functions as such.[114]

The thought that the spirit must unite with the soul seems fiendishly clever, but in fact it is no more clever than saying that a suit is a unity and should not be broken down into component parts, such as a vest, a pair of pants, boots, and so on. It's all a unity, so I should not have the tailor make the jacket and pants separately and then go to the cobbler for boots to match. Of course, all of these things form a unity on the human being who is wearing them. But it makes no sense to say that jacket and pants and probably the boots as well should be stitched together into a single article of clothing, even if Count Keyserling in his abstract idealism insists that they are a unity. This is the opposite pole.

We have, on the one hand, Spengler with his concepts that destroy each other and on the other hand, we have Keyserling with his totally empty concepts. For anyone who has any sense of reality, it is a torment to read Spengler and to see all his concepts colliding with and crushing each other and forcing their way into each other. You really are compelled to experience all this, especially if you have any artistic sensibility. Spengler's book is a totally inartistic construct, but when you read Keyserling's book, you stop and gasp for breath after one page, because his concepts have no air in them.[115] We want to form a thought, but there is nothing there, which makes it very easy for people to understand these concepts and feel comfortable with them. This is especially true if this impotent nonthinker also tells them that while there may be some truth to the facts that spiritual science confirms, he himself cannot corroborate them and therefore will not assume that they are true, since he is not one of those people who has intuitions, and so on and so forth.[116]

Of course, people lap up this kind of talk, especially if they themselves cannot supply the necessary proof. Especially today, such people much prefer a writer who admits to being unable to confirm the facts to one they have to struggle to keep up with. Keyserling's scribblings on art, in particular, are enough make your hair stand on end, but they are very popular. That is all I have to say on this subject.

By now, you may have developed a sense for what it means when Goethe says, "Consider the *What*, but consider *How* seriously."[117] You can consider the What when you read Spengler, because he has a lot of What to offer. But Goethe knew that a worldview depends on how we see the whole in the coordination, organization, and inherent harmony of ideas. That is why we can say, referring to Spengler, consider the What. Spengler does consider the What as it should be considered, but he fails to consider the How at all. Above all else, Goethe challenges us to consider *how* ideas are arranged. With regard to Keyserling, we might say that he appears to possess the How—in fact, his work is teaming with How, but there is no What, no content.

STUTTGART JANUARY 15, 1921

A question about the need for the anthroposophical position on the Einstein problem. Why must we suddenly reverse the sign when we leave the realm of the tangible for the ether?

Of course this also can be done without taking a specifically anthroposophical position, simply by studying the phenomena, as is done in many other scientific fields. (I illustrated an unbiased view of the phenomena of so-called heat theory in a course I gave to a small audience here a few months ago.)[119] We then must attempt to express these phenomena in mathematical formulas. The peculiar feature of such formulas is that they are correct only when they correspond to processes we can observe, that is, when the results of the formulas correspond to, and can be verified by, reality. If you want to understand what happens when a gas contained under pressure is heated, it is artificial to apply the formulas worked out by Clausius and others, although it can be done.[120] As is officially admitted today, however, that the facts do not correspond to the formulas.[121]

In connection with Einstein's theory, it is strange to note the experiments that have been conducted. These experiments were set up on the supposition that a certain theory was correct. Because the experiments did not confirm the theory, another theory, based exclusively on experiments that exist only in thought, was then developed.[122] In contrast, if you attempt to deal with heat phenomena by simply inserting the relevant positive and negative signs into the formulas, depending on whether you are dealing with conductive or radiant heat, you will find that reality confirms the formulas.[123]

Admittedly, when we move on to other imponderables, simply changing the sign to negative is not enough, and we must include other considerations. We must imagine that forces in the tangible realm work radially, while those belonging to the etheric realm come from the periphery, have negative values, and work only within a circular area. Thus, when we move on to other imponderables, we must insert the corresponding values differently. We then will find that we arrive at formulas that are verified by actual phenomena. Anyone can take this approach, with or without becoming involved in anthroposophy.

I would like to emphasize a different point here. You must not think that what I told you in these four lectures simply stems from my anthroposophical approach. I have told you these things because they are true. The so-called anthroposophical approach does not anticipate phenomena, it results from them. It is simply the consequence of an appropriate overview. If we attempt to recognize and understand objects and events without bias, an anthroposophical approach can result. The prospects for what I have told you would be poor if we had to take a biased view as our starting point, but that is not the case. We must pursue the relevant phenomena on a strictly empirical basis. Although I still maintain that the anthroposophical approach can be the best approach, it is only the end result.

After answering other questions, Rudolf Steiner says in conclusion:

I can emphasize repeatedly only that the anthroposophically oriented spiritual science that is developing here in Stuttgart is not a sectarian or amateurish movement. Although its forces are still weak, it is striving for real, authentic science. The more you test spiritual science, the more you will realize that it is a match for any scientific method of testing.

The many misunderstandings to which spiritual science is subject today are not the results of a truly scientific approach. The opponents of spiritual science battle it not because they themselves are too scientific but because they are not scientific enough, as further investigation will show.[124] In future, however, we must become more scientific rather than less so. Science must make real progress, namely, it must lead us into the spiritual realm as accurately as it leads us into the material realm.

DORNACH APRIL 7, 1921

QUESTION: *It has been said that the three dimensions of space differ in structure. Where does this difference lie?*

This statement was never formulated like that—"The three dimensions of space differ in structure." You are probably referring to the following thought.

First we have mathematical space, which we imagine—if indeed we imagine it with any precision at all—as consisting of three perpendicular dimensions or directions, which we define by means of a coordinate system on three perpendicular axes. When we consider this space from the usual mathematical perspective, we treat the three dimensions as if they were exactly the same. We make so little distinction between the dimensions of up and down, right and left, and forward and backward that we even can believe them to be interchangeable. In terms of merely mathematical space, it ultimately makes no difference whether we say that the plane of the *y*-axis, which is perpendicular to the plane formed by the *x*- and *z*-axes (which are also perpendicular to each other), is "horizontal" or "vertical." We are equally unconcerned about the boundedness of this type of space, which does not mean that we ordinarily get so far as to imagine it as limitless. We simply do not worry about its limits. We assume that from any point on the *x*-axis, for example, we can continue to move along the axis indefinitely, without ever reaching the end.

During the nineteenth century, metageometry presented many ideas contrary to this Euclidean concept of space.[126] Let me simply remind you, for example, how Riemann distinguished between the "limitlessness" of space and the "infinity" of space.[127] From the perspective of purely conceptual thinking, too, there is no need to assume that limitlessness and infinity are identical. Take the outer surface of a sphere, for instance. When you draw on such a surface, you never encounter any spatial limit that prevents you from continuing your drawing. Eventually, of course, you will intersect your previous drawing, but as long as you remain on the sphere's surface, you will never encounter a boundary that forces you to stop. Thus, you can say that a sphere's surface is limitless with regard to your ability to draw on it. This does not mean, however, that anyone claims that such a surface is infinite. In this way, on a purely conceptual level, we can distinguish between limitlessness and infinity.

Under specific mathematical conditions, this distinction also can be extended to space as a whole. If we imagine that we never will be hindered from extending an *x*- or *y*-axis by continuing to add segments to it, this property of space speaks for its limitlessness but not for its infinity. The fact that I can continue adding segments indefinitely does not mean that space is necessarily infinite. It might be simply limitless. We must distinguish between these two concepts. If space is limitless but not infinite, we can assume that it is inherently curved and returns to its starting point in some way, just as a spherical surface does. Certain ideas in modern metageometry depend on such assumptions. It is not easy to raise objections to these assumptions, because we cannot conclude that space is infinite from our experience of it. It equally well could be curved and finite.

I cannot carry this train of thought to its conclusion, of course, without explaining almost all of recent metageometry. Treatises by Riemann, Gauss, and others are readily available, however, and will provide you with plenty of food for thought if you are interested in mathematical ideas of this sort.[128] These are the purely mathematical arguments against the fixed, neutral space of Euclidean geometry. All of the arguments I have mentioned so far are based purely on the concept of *limitlessness*. Your question, however, is rooted elsewhere, in the idea that space—the space of our calculations and the space we encounter in analytical geometry, for example, when we are dealing with a coordinate system of three perpendicular axes—is an abstraction. And what is an abstraction? This question must be answered first.

It is important to know whether we are restricted to an abstract idea of space. Is abstract space the only space we can talk about? To put it better, if this abstract concept of space is the only one we are justified in speaking of, only one objection is possible, and this one objection has been raised adequately by Riemann's geometry or other forms of metageometry.[129]

Kant's definitions of space, for example, rest soundly on a very abstract concept of space. His concept is initially unconcerned with limitlessness or infinity. In the course of the nineteenth century, this concept of space was shattered—also internally, with regard to its conceptual content—by mathematics.[130] It is impossible to imagine applying Kant's definitions to a space that is limitless but not infinite. Much of what Kant presents later in his *Critique of Pure Reason—his* theory of paralogisms, for example—would begin to totter if we were forced to substitute the concept of a limitless, curved space.[131]

I know that this concept of curved space poses problems for our ordinary way of imagining things. But from the purely mathematical or geometric perspective, the only possible argument against the assumption that space is curved is that it forces us to move into a realm of pure abstraction that is initially quite remote from reality. Looking at the situation more closely, we discover that a curious circular argument exists in the derivations of modern metageometry, namely, that we arrive at them by taking as our starting point the ideas of Euclidean geometry, which is unconcerned with any limitations of space. We then move on to certain derivative ideas, such as those that apply to the surface of a sphere. On the basis of these derivatives and the forms that result, we can undertake certain transpositions and then make reinterpretations of space. Everything we say, however, presupposes Euclidean coordinate geometry. Under this presupposition, we get a specific rate of curvature. We arrive at the derivations. All this calculation presupposes Euclidean geometry. Here we come to a turning point, however. We use ideas such as the rate of curvature, which we developed only with the help of Euclidean geometry, to arrive at another idea that can lead to a new view and an interpretation of what we have gained from the curved forms.[132] Essentially, we are functioning in a realm remote from reality by deriving abstractions from abstractions. This activity is justified only when an empirical reality forces us to align ourselves with the results of such abstractions. Thus the question is, Where does abstract space correspond to our experience? Space as such, as Euclid imagined it, is an abstraction.[133] Where does its perceptible, empirical aspect lie?

We must take our human experience of space as our starting point. We actually perceive only one dimension of space—namely, the dimension of depth—as a result of our own active experience. This active perception of depth is based on a process in our consciousness that we very frequently overlook. This active perception, however, is very different from the idea of a plane, of extension in two dimensions. When we look out into the world with both eyes, these two dimensions are not the result of our own soul activity. They are there as givens, while the third dimension comes about as a result of activity that usually does not become conscious. We need to work at recognizing depths, at knowing how distant an object is from us. We do not work out the extent of a plane, direct perception provides us with that knowledge. We do, however, use both eyes to work out the dimension of depth. The way we experience depth lies very close to the boundary between the conscious and the unconscious. But when we learn to pay attention to such processes, we know that the never fully conscious activity of estimating depth—it is at most semiconscious or one-third conscious—more closely approximates a rational activity, an active soul process, than does seeing objects only in a plane.

In this way, we actively acquire one dimension of three-dimensional space on behalf of our objective consciousness. And we are forced to say that our upright position contributes a quality to the dimension of depth—that is, forward and backward—that makes it non-interchangeable with any other dimension. The fact that we stand there actively experiencing this dimension makes it non-interchangeable with any other dimension. For the individual human being, the dimension of depth is not interchangeable with the other dimensions. It is also true that our perception of two-dimensionality—that is, of up and down and right and left, even when these two dimensions are in front of us—is associated with different parts of the brain. This perception is inherent in the sensory process of seeing, while the third dimension arises for us in parts of the brain located very close to the centers associated with rational activity. Thus, we see that even in terms of our experience, the third dimension arises in a way that is very different from the other two dimensions.

When we rise to the level of imagination, however, we leave our experience of the third dimension behind and see in two dimensions. At this level, we must work to experience right and left, just as experiencing forward and backward in our ordinary consciousness requires work of which we are not fully aware. And, finally, when we rise to the level of inspiration, the same is true of the dimension of above and below.[134] As far as our ordinary nerve-related perception is concerned, we must work to experience the third dimension. When we exclude the ordinary activity of this system, however, and turn directly to the rhythmic system, we experience the second dimension. In a certain respect, this is what happens when we rise to the level of Imagination. I have not expressed this very precisely, but it will do for now. And we experience the first dimension when we rise to the level of Inspiration—that is, to the third member of our human organization.

What we encounter in abstract space proves to be exactly what it appears to be, because all of our mathematical accomplishments come from within ourselves. The mathematical consequence, threefold space, is something we derive from ourselves. When we move down through the levels of suprasensible perception, the result is not abstract space with three equivalent directions, but rather three different values for the three different dimensions of forward and backward, right and left, and above and below. These dimensions are not interchangeable.[135]

We can then conclude that we also need not imagine the three dimensions as having the same intensity, which is essentially how we imagine the x-, y-, and z-axes in Euclidean space. If we want to abide by the equations of analytical geometry, we must see the x-, y-, and z-axes as equivalent in intensity. If we make the x-axis larger, stretching it with a certain intensity as if it were elastic, the *y*- and *z*-axes must grow with the same intensity. In other words, when I apply a certain intensity to expanding one dimension, the force of expansion must be the same for all three axes, that is, all three dimensions of Euclidean space. That is why I would like to call this type of space "fixed space."

Fixed space is an abstraction of real space, which is developed from within the human being, and the principle of equivalent intensity does not apply to real space. When we consider real space, we can no longer say that the intensity of expansion is the same for all three dimensions. Instead, it depends on human proportions, which are the result of spatial expansion intensities. For example, take the *y*-axis, the up-down direction. We must imagine its expansion intensity as greater than that of the *x*-axis, which corresponds to the left-right direction. The formula that is an abstract expression of real space—we must be aware that this formula, too, is an abstraction—describes an ellipsoid with three axes.

Suprasensible perception dwells within the three very different expansion possibilities of this triaxial space. Our physical body provides direct experience of the three axes, and such experience tells us that this space also expresses the relationships among the effects of the heavenly bodies within it. Visualizing space in this way, we must also consider that everything we think of as existing in the three-dimensional universe cannot be accounted for if the expansion intensity of the *x*-, *y*-, and *z*-axes is the same, as is the case in Euclidean space. We must imagine the universe with a configuration of its own, corresponding to an ellipsoid with three axes. The configuration of certain stars suggests that this idea is correct. For example, we usually say that our Milky Way galaxy is lens-shaped, and so on. We cannot possibly imagine it as a sphere. We must find a different way of imagining it if we want to accommodate the facts of physics.

The way we treat space demonstrates how poorly modern thinking coincides with nature. In ancient times and cultures, the concept of fixed space did not occur to anyone. We cannot even say that the original Euclidean geometry incorporated a clear idea of fixed space with three equal expansion intensities and three perpendicular lines. It was only in fairly recent times, when abstraction became an essential attribute of our thinking and we began to apply calculations to Euclidean space, that the abstract concept of space emerged.[136] The knowledge available to people in ancient times was very similar to what can be redeveloped now on the basis of suprasensible insights. As you see, concepts that we depend on heavily and take for granted today assume a high degree of importance only because they work in a sphere that is foreign to reality. The space we reckon with today is one such abstraction. It is far removed from anything real experience can teach us. We are often content with abstractions today. We harp on empiricism, but we refer very frequently to abstractions without even being aware of doing so. We believe that we are dealing with real things in the real world. You can see, however, how badly our ideas need correction in this respect.

Spiritual researchers do not simply ask if every idea they encounter is logical. Riemann's concept of space is thoroughly logical, though in a certain respect it depends on Euclidean space. It cannot be thought through to its conclusion, however, because we approach it by means of highly abstract thinking, and in this process our thinking is turned upside down because of one of the conclusions we draw.[137] Spiritual researchers do not simply ask whether an idea is logical. They also ask whether it corresponds to reality. For them, that is the decisive factor in accepting or rejecting an idea. They accept an idea only if it corresponds to reality.

Correspondence to reality will apply as a criterion when we begin to deal appropriately with such ideas as the justification of the theory of relativity. In itself, this theory is as logical as it can possibly be, because it is understood purely in the domain of logical abstractions. Nothing can be more logical than the theory of relativity. The other question, however, is whether we can act on it. If you simply look at the analogies presented in support of this theory, you will discover that they are very foreign to reality. They are simply ideas being tossed around. The proponents of relativity theory tell us that these ideas are there only as symbols to help us visualize the issues. They are not merely symbols, however. Without them, the entire process would be left hanging in the air.[138] This, then, is what I wanted to say in reference to your question. As you see, there is no easy answer to questions that touch on such domains.

DORNACH AUGUST 26, 1921

QUESTION: Are we meant to understand that the Sun moves through space in a spiral and that the Earth also moves in a spiral as it follows the Sun and therefore does not revolve around the Sun?

In a longer lecture series, it would be relatively easy to discuss these issues in more detail; I have referred to them only briefly here. It is almost impossible to explain their foundations in a few words. Let me begin to respond to your question by simply summarizing the results of spiritual scientific research.[140] First of all, any conclusions we draw about (spatial) relationships in the universe on the basis of observation and from specific perspectives are always one-sided. The Ptolemaic solar system represented a one-sided view, and so do all other models of the solar system, including the Copernican model. Our conclusions about the relationships of moving objects are based on our specific vantage point, and these relationships are invariably supplemented or altered by movements that cannot be measured from that perspective.

Having stated this cautious presupposition, I ask you to consider another spiritual scientific finding that will help us develop a view of the relationship of the Earth's movement to that of the Sun. We must imagine that the Sun moves through space on a curved path. If we trace this curve far enough, it proves to be a complicated spiral form. A simplified version looks like this (Figure 65a):

Figure 65a

The Earth moves along the same path, following the Sun. When you consider the Earth's possible locations in relationship to the Sun, you discover that when the Earth is here, an observer would have to look to the right to see the Sun.

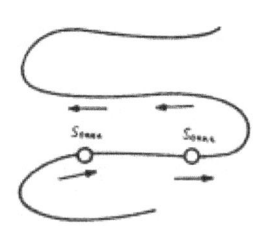

Figure 65b

Now let me sketch another possible location (Figure 65b). The arrows indicate the direction of view. In the first instance, we saw the Sun by looking in one direction, and now we see it by looking in the opposite direction. As you will easily understand if you visualize this model correctly, the consequence of the Earth following the Sun is that we see the Sun first from one side, and then from the other, and the Earth appears to move around the Sun in a circular or elliptical orbit. The primary component of this movement, the fact that the Earth follows the Sun, is differentiated still further by certain other relationships that would take hours to explain. The truth of the matter, however, is that only our direction of view rotates.

As I said, this summary represents the results of lengthy spiritual scientific investigations and is complicated even more when we take other relationships into account. We must realize that as we gain a better overview of the Sun's movements, the simple lines we use to describe the Copernican system to schoolchildren become increasingly complex, until ultimately they can no longer be drawn at all and fall out of the spatial realm altogether.[141] This is what I wanted to say from the perspective of spiritual science.

From the perspective of the history of the physical sciences, I would like to comment that what we find so striking today about the research results I outlined above is inherent in the Copernican view. Copernicus postulated three laws. The first states that the Earth rotates around its own axis; the second, that the Earth revolves around the Sun; and the third, that the Earth's movement around the Sun provides only a provisional explanation on the conceptual level. While in fact the Earth stands in a fixed relationship to the Sun.[142]

This third law proves that Copernicus was truly convinced that the second movement he describes, the Earth's revolution around the Sun, was merely a convention assumed for the convenience of certain calculations and that he did not intend to state it as fact. Today, we consistently disregard this third law and believe that the Copernican model of the solar system encompasses only the first two laws. If we were truly to study the entire Copernican view, however, we would quickly conclude that this [third law] is indeed necessary, simply on the basis of astronomical calculations.[143] You see what often happens in the history of science.

THE HAGUE APRIL 12, 1922

QUESTION about higher-dimensional space.

We can say that the ordinary axial coordinate system describes three-dimensional space. Schematically speaking, we can proceed on the basis of certain algebraic assumptions and, on an abstract level, repeat the process that led us from a plane to three-dimensional space. The result is four-, five-, or n-dimensional space. We can even construct figures such as Hinton's tessaract. The tessaract, however, is not a real figure but simply the projection of a true tessaract into three-dimensional space.[145]

On a purely theoretical and abstract level, there is nothing wrong with such deductions. On a theoretical level, we also can move from three-dimensional space to the fourth dimension in time simply by using the formulas and calculations and taking into account the leap that we are making, because moving into time is different from moving from the first to the second to the third dimension. By refining this process, however, we can indeed make the transition to time. The result is an abstract four-dimensional space. We can remain on the abstract, purely intellectual level as long as we do not need to visualize what we are doing. When we attempt to do so, however, we are confronted with a problem of elasticity, whereas our purely abstract train of thoughts led to a *regressus in infinitum*. We also can imagine initially that a pendulum simply will continue to swing indefinitely, but in dynamics we have oscillations. That is the reality of the situation.

When we rise to the level of imaginative perception, we cannot simply repeat the process indefinitely, assuming the existence of a fourth and subsequent dimensions. If we use the notation $+a$ for the first dimension, $+b$ for the second, and $+c$ for the third, we cannot, if we are describing real space, write the fourth dimension as $+d$. Instead, the reality of the situation forces us to write $-c$. The fourth dimension simply nullifies the third, and only two remain. At the end of the process, therefore, we are left with two dimensions instead of four. Similarly, if we assume the existence of a fifth dimension, we must use the notation $-b$ for it and $-a$ for the sixth. That is, we come back to a point.[146] Through the principle of elasticity, we have returned to the starting point. This phenomenon not only is present in Imagination—that is, as a subjective experiment—but also becomes a reality in the way I described the day before yesterday.[147]

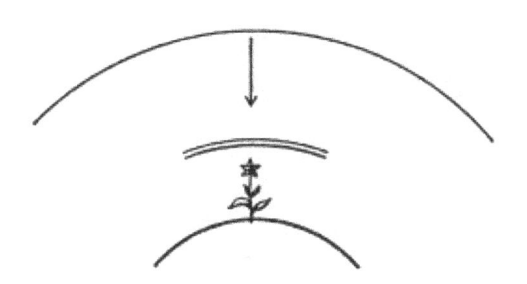

Figure 66a

As long as we are looking at the Earth's surface here and plant roots here (Figure 66a), we are dealing with a specific manifestation of gravity and remain within the ordinary dimensions of space. When we attempt to explain the shape of a flower, however, these ordinary dimensions no longer suffice. Instead of taking the intersection of the axes as our starting point, we must begin with infinite space, which is simply the counterpart of the point. Instead of moving centrifugally outward, we must move centripetally inward (Figure 66a). The result is a wavy surface. Instead of dissipating into the distance, pressure is exerted from outside, resulting in gliding and scraping movements. Such movements, which result from pressure, cannot be described correctly by taking the intersection of axes as the starting point for our coordinates. Instead, we must take an infinitely large sphere as the center of the coordinates, and the coordinates must all move toward the center.[148] That is, as soon as we move into the etheric realm, we need to apply an axial coordinate system that is the opposite—also qualitatively speaking—of the ordinary coordinate system. Ordinary theories about the ether of physics err in not taking this difference into account, making it difficult to define the ether. It is sometimes seen as a fluid and sometimes as a gas. It is wrong to apply a coordinate system that radiates from a central point to the ether. As soon as we enter the ether, we must take a sphere and construct the whole system from the outside in, instead of the other way around.

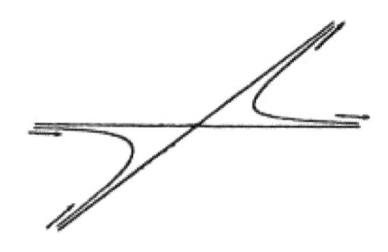

Figure 66b

Such issues become interesting when they are traced mathematically and enter the domain of physics. Developing our theories, which begin to seem very realistic, would contribute a great deal to solving problems of limits. At present, however, such theories meet with very little understanding. For example, I once attempted to introduce this subject in a lecture to the mathematical society of a university.[149] In this lecture, I said that if these are the asymptotes of a hyperbola and these its branches, we must imagine that the part on the right is dissipating, while the part on the left is becoming concentrated. That is, a complete reversal takes place (Figure 66b). Such considerations gradually lead us to a more concrete treatment of space, but this treatment finds little acceptance. Purely analytical mathematicians often are somewhat biased against synthetic geometry. Modern synthetic geometry, however, permits us to move away from purely formal mathematics and tackle empirical problems. As long as we apply only purely analytical geometry, we cannot approach the domain of reality. Analytical geometry allows us to establish only the endpoints of coordinates, their geometric locations, and so on. When we restrict our constructions to lines and circles, we need the help of images and are forced to turn to visualization for help. What makes synthetic geometry so beneficial is that it allows us to leave behind the formal aspect of mathematics. It shows us how we must conceive of the mathematical element in nature.[150]

QUESTION about the theory of relativity.

The discussion about the theory of relativity is endless.[151] This theory cannot be refuted from our vantage point as observers of cosmic events in three-dimensional space. That is, it is impossible to refute the theory of relativity on the basis of perceived space. As far as our perception is concerned, of course, it makes no difference whether a sphere flattens out or space as a whole expands inward in the direction of the sphere's flattening. Thus, as long as we are dealing with the perspective of three-dimensional space, Einstein's theory of relativity is absolutely correct. This theory appeared at the very moment in humanity's evolution and in the history of science when we first managed to think in purely spatial terms—that is, to take Euclidean space as our starting point for further thinking, whether in the sense of non-Euclidean spaces or in the sense of relativity theory. It is impossible to refute Einstein's theory in three-dimensional space.

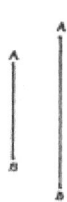

Figure 67a

We can begin to discuss the possibility of refuting this theory only when we discover how to make the transition to the etheric realm—that is, the transition from the three-dimensional spatial body to the ether body. The ether body is centripetally, rather than centrifugally, formed. In your ether body, you dwell within the totality of space. For example, your inner perception of the distance between point *A* and point *B* is sometimes this and sometimes that ([Figure 67a](#)). Having recognized this phenomenon, you can say that one or the other of the points must have moved, in absolute terms, but to do that you yourself must stand within the totality of space. At this point, discussion becomes possible. For this reason, I am convinced that all of our discussions of current concepts about the theory of relativity must end in the question, "Well, how do you know that?" In contrast, as soon as we make the transition to inner perception—a domain where absolutes can be discovered—we are forced to realize that issues such as the theory of relativity show us that we have arrived at what Nietsche calls the observer's standpoint, of which the theory of relativity represents the most extreme version. For anyone who accepts this standpoint, the theory of relativity is simply a fact, and no arguments against it are possible. It can, however, be eliminated from practical considerations. A fanatical relativity theorist in Stuttgart once explained why it makes no difference whether we make a movement in one direction or the opposite direction. If I hold a matchbox in one hand and a match in the other, the result is the same whether I move the match past the box or the box past the match. Of course, in such cases the theory of relativity is absolutely correct, but I would have liked to shout out, "Please try again with the box nailed to the wall!"

This in no way diminishes the validity of the theory of relativity. It simply shows that just as we can move from two-dimensional space into the dimension of depth, we can move into the spiritual element from any location in the world. Then and only then does the theory of relativity cease to be valid. That's why I said that discussions about the theory of relativity tend to go on ad infinitum, because it is irrefutable from the observer's standpoint. Any arguments against the theory can always be disputed.

As an observer, you stand outside what you are observing; you must make a radical distinction between subject and object. As soon as you rise to higher levels of knowledge, subjectivity and objectivity cease. There is much more that could be said on this subject than can possibly be said in the context of a question-and-answer session, but I would like to submit one more idea as a stimulus to further thinking. As long as we remain in the beholder's world, in the world of space, relativity theory as such is irrefutable. On first escaping from this world, we enter worlds where we are not mere beholders but share the experience of the object, such as pain, for example. As soon as you learn to shift from mere relationships with other beings—and it is understandable enough that a theory of relativity is possible only within relationships—to the pain of shared inner experience, to use an example, it is no longer possible to speculate about whether this experience is relative. Thus, you cannot construct contradictions and then say that because a contradiction exists, the situation is not real. In life, contradictions are reality, because the beings that constitute life belong to different but intersecting spheres. As soon as you make the transition to reality, it is no longer permissible to say that any contradiction that exists must be resolved. If it is real, it cannot be resolved. My point here is that the theory of relativity is a natural development in the world of relationships. No arguments could be raised against this theory if the beholder's standpoint were the only possible perspective. As soon as we become involved in beings, however, and in pain and pleasure, the theory of relativity is no longer tenable.

QUESTION: *Dr. Steiner, what do you mean when you say that the physical body is a spatial body while the body of formative forces is a temporal body? The physical body is also active in time when it grows and declines.*

Yes, but your statement is based on imprecise thinking, if I may say so. To give it a more exact foundation, you first would have to analyze the concept of time. Consider this: In the reality we usually encounter, space and time intermingle. We can conceive of the physical body as spatial and the body of formative forces as temporal only when we separate space and time. In our usual objective knowledge, time is not present as a given. As you know, time is measured in terms of space; that is, changes in spatial units are our means of knowing about what we call time. But now imagine a different way of measuring time. You no longer measure time in terms of space when you shift to a true experience of time, which people usually do unconsciously. Our thinking actually becomes conscious through imaginative cognition.

You have a true experience of time, for example, if you examine your soul life on April 12, 1922, at 4:04 and however many seconds. You see a temporal cross-section of your soul life. Although you cannot say that this temporal section contains any particular spatial section, it includes all of your immediate earthly past. If you want to draw it schematically, and the stream of your experience flows from *a* to *b*, you must draw the section *AB* (Figure 67b).

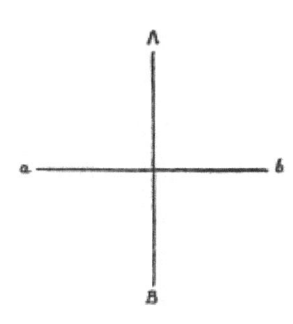

Figure 67b

You cannot avoid interposing your entire experience into this section, and yet there is a perspective in it. You can say that events lying further back in time are reproduced with less intensity than more recent events. All of these events, however, are present in the single section. As a result, the connections are different from what they are when you analyze time. We can raise time to the level of a mental image only when we refrain from analyzing it as we do in physics, according to methods of understanding space, and instead reflect on our soul life. As long as you have only abstract thoughts, however, your soul life remains stuck in the time body.

It is important to be able to see this time body as an organism. As you know, when you have a digestive disturbance, for example, you may find that other parts of your spatial organism also are affected adversely. In the spatial organism, individual areas are spatially separate from each other, while in our time organism—in spite of the fact that we differentiate between later and earlier—different times are related organically. I sometimes use the following example. When some very old people talk to younger ones, especially to children, their words seem to bounce right off; they mean nothing to the children. This is not the case with other old people. When they talk to children, their words seem to flow straight into the children's souls. To find the origin of the power of old people to bless others, you sometimes have to go back to their early childhood. (We usually do not study matters such as this, because we very seldom look at the whole person. We do not focus our attention long enough to observe such things. The scope of our present powers of observation is inadequate. That is a task for anthroposophy.) If you go back far enough, you will find that those who possess an unusual spiritual power to bless others in their old age, whose words flow as blessings into young people, learned how to pray in their own childhood. Metaphorically speaking, we can say that the folded hands of childhood become the blessing hands of old age.[152]

Here you see a connection between a person's influence on others in old age and the pious sentiments and so on that were present in that person's early childhood. Earlier qualities and later ones are connected organically. There are an infinite number of such connections in each person, but we see them only when we understand the whole human being. Today our whole life is external to this reality. We think we are steeped in reality, but we deceive ourselves. In today's culture, we are abstractionists. We pay no attention to true reality and therefore disregard qualities such as those I mentioned. We also pay no attention to the fact that when we teach children, especially in the elementary grades, we must avoid giving them sharply defined concepts. The effect of such concepts on later life is similar to that of binding limbs and not allowing them to grow larger. What we communicate to children must be an organism, and it must be flexible. I hope that you are gradually becoming able to see what I mean by an organism. Of course, Imagination alone makes it possible to grasp this meaning completely. Nonetheless, it is possible to gain an idea of the nature of an organism simply by realizing that the temporal course of events in the life of a human being is related to the time organism rather than to the space organism.

You see, time possesses an inherent reality, as you can infer from mathematics. I believe it was Ostwald—in any case, it was not an anthroposophist but simply someone who is not a materialist—who pointed out in a wonderful discussion of this subject that, unlike mechanical processes, organic processes that take place over time are not reversible.[153] In fact, ordinary calculations always remain external to temporal processes and do not allow us to approach them. For example, if you insert negative numbers into a formula for calculating eclipses of the Moon, you get instances in the more distant past, but you do not move away with the things. You move only in the sphere of space. Thus, we develop a correct idea of the actual physical human body only when we are able to separate the temporal element from the spatial. This is fundamentally important with regard to human beings, because we cannot come to any understanding of human beings if we do not know that the temporal element in humans runs its course as an independent entity and that the spatial element is governed by the temporal or dynamic element. In machines, however, the temporal element is only a function of activity in space. That is the difference. In humans, the temporal element is a real entity, while in mechanical devices the temporal element is only a function of space.

QUESTION: *Einstein says that the time-space continuum is four-dimensional. If I understood correctly, you said that the fourth dimension becomes two dimensional because the fourth dimension is a negative third dimension. Should this be interpreted to mean that there is a connection between the imaginative world and Einstein's continuum? According to conventional scientific thinking, I would have to conclude that such a space is a plane. Consequently, the imaginative world would be a very specific plane in three-dimensional space. It would not have to be straight, and it would not have to remain in the same place, but it would have to be possible to confirm its presence at any given moment. My thoughts on this subject are probably not in line with anthroposophy, but I would like to know what anthroposophy has to say about it.*

With the exception of a few comments, your thoughts are quite in line with anthroposophy. I would like to add that it is absolutely correct that when we attempt to shift from the three dimensions to the fourth on a real rather than abstract level, we must use a negative sign to describe the fourth dimension. That is, the transition to the fourth dimension simply eliminates or cancels out the third, just as debt cancels out savings. There is no other way of imagining the situation. But if we simply hurry on abstractly, we come to the *regressus in infinitum* that assumes the existence of more and more dimensions. This, however, is an abstract way of continuing and is not based on actually looking at the situation. When we enter the imaginative world, we do indeed confront a plane world, to use an expression borrowed from geometry. We confront the world of the plane of time. One peculiar feature of this world is that it can no longer be referred back to the third dimension of space. This is difficult to understand, but you will find an analogous situation in synthetic geometry, which is forced to consider the boundary of three-dimensionality—if, in fact, we impose boundaries on the three-dimensional world—as a surface and as a plane surface rather than a spherical surface. That is, synthetic geometry assumes that three-dimensional space is bounded by a plane. When you reach the boundary of three-dimensionality, you find a plane whose limit, in turn, must be imagined as a straight line rather than a circle, and this straight line has one, rather than two, endpoints.[154] At this juncture, your thinking and your perception cannot completely coincide, no matter how consistent it is to speak of a plane as the boundary of three-dimensional space, of a straight line as the boundary of a plane, and of a single infinitely distant point as the limit of a straight line. To synthetic geometry, these ideas are real. Synthetic geometry plays into the perception that develops in the imaginative world. But when we say that the imaginative world lies in a plane, we cannot refer this plane back to three-dimensional space by defining its coordinates. It is lifted out of three-dimensional space and is anywhere and everywhere. This is difficult to imagine because we are used to visualizing in three-dimensional space. The imaginative world, however, does not lie in three-dimensional space, and the definitions of three-dimensionality do not apply to it.

We find another analogue for the imaginative world in art, when we practice painting on the basis of color. When we do so, we are working on a flat surface, or, if we work on a curved surface, its curve does not originate in the painting but in other circumstances. When we paint on a plane, our possibilities are not limited to drawn perspective, which is a relatively recent discovery, as you may know. Perspective appeared very late in the history of painting, only a few centuries ago.[155] In addition to drawn perspective, however, we can utilize the perspective inherent in color.[156] We have been using such principles in our painting in Dornach. On the basis of feeling and color, rather than thoughts, yellow appears to come toward us so strongly that it is almost aggressive. In contrast, when we use blue paint, the color recedes, yet both colors lie on the same surface. Thus, it is possible to express three-dimensional phenomena even though only a two-dimensional expanse is available to us. This is simply an example to help you visualize the situation, because the imaginative world is not the same as the world of painting.

Although the ideas you expressed in your question are very true to anthroposophy, we cannot really say without qualification that the imaginative world has a connection to Einstein's continuum. Einstein's continuum is based on abstraction rather than perception. Its fourth dimension is constructed as an analogue to the other three dimensions, which is not acceptable when we move from objective cognition in space to real suprasensible cognition, which manifests first as Imagination and can be expressed in spatial terms only by allowing the third dimension to be cancelled out by its negative. What I am going to say next will seem very daring to some; nonetheless, it is my experience. In reality, the situation looks like this: When you function in the objective world with healthy common sense, your orientation is derived only from the three dimensions of space. The first dimension is inherent in your own upright posture, the second in your left-right dimension, and the third in the focusing of your eyes. You do not dwell in these three dimensions when you are in the imaginative world. There, you dwell only in two dimensions. If I had to locate these dimensions in space, I would have to take a vertical section through the human being. In Imagination, we can speak only of the dimensions of up and down and right and left. When you move in the imaginative world, these are the only dimensions you carry with you. For this reason I cannot say that they relate to a coordinate system in space. I cannot define them in terms of Euclidean geometry. To our perception, however, they are real. It makes no sense to talk about three dimensions in the context of the imaginative world. We must realize that we are dealing with an experience of two-dimensionality, an experience we cannot have in the objective world. Two dimensions are a reality in the imaginative world, and a single dimension is a reality in the inspired world. All Inspirations move vertically, if indeed we want to assign them a location in space. Intuition is pointlike, but it to cannot be referred to a coordinate system. In these higher realms, we cannot revert to Euclidean space.

DORNACH DECEMBER 29, 1922

DISCUSSION.
As you will have gathered from the lecture, we must make a distinction between tactile space and visual space. This difference can stimulate us to move beyond considering mathematics on the one hand and the physical world on the other. As you may know from my lectures,[157] it remains true that mathematics is a product of the human spirit or of the human being in general. And that as we move further into purely mathematical domains—that is, domains that are delineated in mathematical terms—we become less and less able to apprehend reality.[158] You have all seen the difficulties that have arisen repeatedly in modern times when people have attempted to use mathematics to describe reality.

For example, if you consider the transition from an infinitely large sphere to a plane, you scarcely will be able to reconcile this cornerstone of projective geometry with our ordinary ideas of reality, which are based on empirical interaction with the world around us.[159] Consequently, our task—and many people with the appropriate educational background would have to work very hard at it—is to attempt to use mathematical ideas to apprehend reality in very concrete domains.[160] At this point, I would like simply to present the problem. It can be solved successfully only if mathematicians really begin to work seriously on it.

I have provided a theoretical explanation of tactile space. Now try to handle this space in a way that necessarily incorporates all of our earthly experience of touch; in fact, that is what we are dealing with. We must incorporate all of our tactile experience, including its inherent dimensionality, into our relationship to gravity. We are subject to gravity, and the various centripetal forces coming in different directions from the periphery make it possible to set up differential equations. With regard to tactile space, we must handle these equations in the same way that we handle equations for determined movements in analytical geometry and analytical mechanics.[161] It then becomes possible to integrate these equations, which gives us specific integrals for what we experience in tactile space, whereas differentials always lead us out of reality.

Integrating these differentials results in the diagrams I told you about the day before yesterday[162]. If you want to return to their reality, you must do it as I indicated in that lecture. You must work with the integral equations in the domain of real touch. It will become evident that with regard to touch, the vertical dimension has a certain differentiation, so that the variable *x* in this equation must be preceded by a plus or minus sign. This makes it possible to set up integrals for our experiences of tactile space. Let me formulate it like this:

$$\int f(x) dy$$

The result would be integrals for our experiences of tactile space.

Now let's move on and apply the same principle to visual space. Once again, we set up differential equations that we must handle in the same way that we handle equations for determined movements in analytical geometry and analytical mechanics. We will see that when we integrate, we get very similar integrals, but ones that must be thought of as negative (taking into account that the variable *x* was positive in the last instance). When we handle the integration in this way (I'll dispense with all the trimmings), we get a result that leads to other integrals:

$$\int f(x) dy$$

But when I subtract the two from each other, they almost cancel each other out and the result approaches zero. That is, when I integrate with regard to visual space, the result is integrals that cancel out those for tactile space. And the integrals for tactile space remind me very much—though they are more extensive—of all the formulas I need for circumstances and relationships that refer to analytical geometry or mechanics in general. The only difference is that gravitation must be included in the mechanical formulas.

I get integrals for visual space that seem applicable if I simply can find the right way to express the spatial aspect of vision in mathematical terms. It is always the case that we begin with a trivial instance and set up constructions about vision and fail to note that we must count on inevitable vertical movement when we consider visual space. We must accept that vision is always forced to work in the opposite direction from gravitation.[163] Taking this fact into account, it becomes possible to relate the integrals to mechanics on the one hand and optics on the other hand. In this way, we formulate mechanics, optics, and so on in usable integrals that encompass the reality of a situation. It is not quite true, however, that the difference between the integrals is zero. In actual fact, it is a differential, and instead of writing zero, I must write:

$$dx = \int_+ - \int_-$$

If repeated searches for such integrals and the resulting differentials lead to differential equations corresponding to *dx*, I then will see that when I take *dx* to be positive here and negative there, *dx* is an imaginary number in the mathematical sense.

If I integrate the resulting differential equation, however, the result is astounding. You can experience it for yourselves if you solve the problem correctly. This step leads to acoustics, to acoustical formulas. Thus, you really have used mathematics to apprehend an intrinsic reality. You have learned that we must write mechanics down below on the vertical and vision up above on the vertical—since light is equal to negative gravitation—while hearing, in reality, takes place horizontally. When you set up these calculations, you not only will observe discrepancies—mathematics on the one hand and physics on the other—as a result of the LaGrange equations.[164] But you also will see that the work that can be done on this basis in the realm of mathematics and physics is just as productive as the work I pointed to earlier in the domain of phylogenetics.[165] Along these lines—by working things out, not through merely descriptive considerations—we discover the differences between modern natural science and anthroposophy. We will have to demonstrate that our calculations are firmly rooted in concrete realities.

Notes Part 1

[1]*János (Johann) Bólyai* (1802–1860), Hungarian mathematician. He studied the problem of parallel lines and, along with *Carl Friedrich Gauss* and *Nikolai Ivanovich Lobachevsky*, is considered one of the founders of hyperbolic non-Euclidean geometry. His paper on this subject, his only published work, appeared in 1832 as an appendix to the mathematics text written by his father, *Farkas (Wolfgang) Bólyai* (1775–1856). For more information on the two Bólyais, see Stäckel [1913].

Carl Friedrich Gauss (1777–1855), mathematician and physicist in Göttingen. One of the first to consider the problem of parallel lines, he concluded that explaining them required a non-Euclidean geometry. None of his work on this subject was published during his lifetime. See Reichardt [1976].

Bernhard Riemann (1826–1866), mathematician in Göttingen and the first to discover elliptical non-Euclidean geometry. His thesis on *The Hypotheses Underlying Geometry* developed differential geometry by generalized measurements in n-dimensional space. This supplied an incentive for research (then in its infancy) into higher-dimensional space. Riemann was the first to distinguish between *limitlessness* and *infinity* of space; the former is an expression of spatial relationships, that is, of the general geometric structure (topology) of space, while the latter is a consequence of numerical relationships. This distinction led to the clear differentiation between topology and differential geometry. See Scholz [1980].

[2]*Immanuel Kant* drew attention to this phenomenon in his *Prolegomena* [1783}, §13: "What can be more similar, in all its parts, to my hand or my ear than its image in a mirror? And yet I cannot replace the original with what I see in the mirror, because if the original is a right hand, its mirror image is a left hand, and the image of a right ear is a left ear and can never take the place of its original. There are no intrinsic, rationally conceivable differences between them, and yet our senses teach us that they are indeed intrinsically different, because in spite of all apparent similarity and sameness, a left hand is not contained within the same boundaries as a right hand (that is, they are not congruent) and a glove that fits one hand cannot

be worn on the other." See also Kant's *Lebendige Kräfte* ("Living Forces") [1746], §§9–11, and *Gegenden im Raum* ("Areas in Space") [1768]. Kant took this phenomenon as proof that human beings are capable of grasping only sensory perceptions of objects — that is, their appearances-and not their intrinsic nature. For an analysis of Kant's view of space with regard to the dimension problem, see Zöllner, *Wirkungen in die Ferne* ("Distant Effects") [1878a], pp. 220–227.

[3]Mirror-image figures that lie in the same plane and meet in an axis can be made to coincide by a continuous motion with each other by rotating one of the figures around the axis. If F is a figure in the plane and F^1 its mirror image on the other side of axis a, F can be transformed into F^1 by rotation around a. Figure 68 shows several stages in this rotation in normal projection onto the plane. The transformation, if interpreted as a plane figure, involves a projection orthogonal to a. (In the sense of projective geometry, this is a perspective with its axis a and center A on the line at infinity of the plane.)

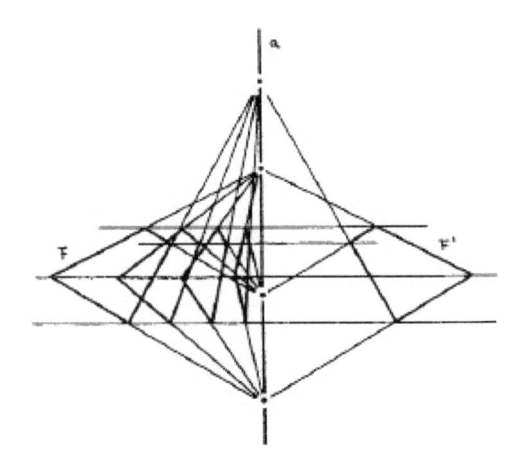

In its projection onto the plane, the figure rotated through space appears to lose a dimension as it passes through axis a and becomes parallel to the direction of projection. Note that the outlines of F and F^1 can be made to coincide through rotation within the plane (i.e., around points in the plane) only if they are broken into line segments that are then rotated around the corresponding points on axis a.

In an analogous operation, the two three-dimensional geometric figures F and F^1, which are mirror images joined by plane a, can be transformed into each other without breaking contact by means of the (three-dimensional) spatial orthogonal affinity with *a* as the plane of affinity (Figure 69). This transformation can be interpreted as an orthogonal projection (in three-dimensional space) of a four-dimensional Euclidean rotation around plane *a*. In this projection, the three-dimensional figure *F* seems to lose a dimension as it passes through the two-dimensional plane *a*.

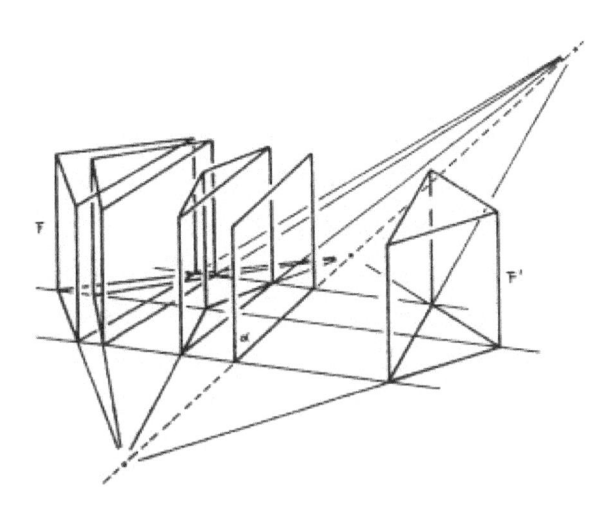

Figure 69

If the outer surface of *F* is broken into appropriate sections, these sections can be rotated around the corresponding axes in *a* to form the outer surface of figure F^1.

Basing his theories on this analogy between two-and three-dimensional mirror images, *August Ferdinand Möbius* was apparently the first mathematician to conceive of the possibility of a four-dimensional space in which three-dimensional mirror-image figures can be made to coincide without breaking contact (see *Möbius's Barycentric Calculus* [1827], §140, note). He rejected this idea as "impossible to think," however, and did not pursue it further.

> [4]The fact that we have two eyes makes depth *perception* possible for us; see also Rudolf Steiner's answers to questions by A. Strakosch, March 11, 1920, reprinted in this volume. On the significance of independent activity in perceiving the dimension of depth, see the questions and answers of April 7, 1921 (GA 76, reprinted here), and Note 17 here.
>
> [5]*(Johann Karl) Friedrich Zöllner* (1834–1882), astrophysicist in Leipzig, considered one of the founding fathers of astrophysics because of his fundamental experimental and theoretical contributions to photometry and

spectroscopy. His theory on the structure of comets set the direction for all later investigations. His book *On the Nature of Comets: Contributions to the History and Theory of Knowledge* [1886], like almost all of his treatises, contains far-reaching philosophical and historical commentary as well as polemical critiques of his contemporaries' pursuit of science.

In connection with his studies on the *Principles of an Electrodynamic Theory of Matter* [1876], *On Distant Effects* [1878a], and *On the Nature of Comets* [1886], Zöllner became familiar with contemporary studies of non-Euclidean and higher-dimensional geometry. By the early 1870s, he surmised that only curved space or a fourth dimension could explain certain phenomena of physics. Around 1875, the research of the chemist and physicist *William Crookes* (1832–1919) inspired Zöllner to study spiritualism. He developed the view that the existence of spiritualistic phenomena could be explained by assuming the existence of four-dimensional space and that these phenomena proved that four-dimensional space is a reality, not merely a conceptual possibility (Zöllner [1878a], pp. 273ff). A short time later, Zöllner began his own studies of spiritualistic phenomena (see [1878b], pp. 752ff; [1878c], pp. 330ff, and especially [1878c]).

For an overview of Zöllner's spiritualistic experiments, see Luttenberger [1977]; for a contemporary analysis of Zöllner, see Simony's *Spiritualistic Manifestations* [1884]. On spiritualism in general, see Hartmann's *Spirit Hypothesis* [1891] and *Spiritualism* [1898]. On the history of spiritualism from Rudolf Steiner's point of view, see his lectures of February 1 and May 30, 1904 (GA 52), and October 10–25, 1915 (GA 254). Zöllner conceived of Kant's "things as such" as real four-dimensional objects projected into our perceptual space as three-dimensional bodies. He found proof of this view in the existence of three-dimensional mirror-image figures, which, though mathematically congruent, cannot be made to coincide without breaking contact with each other [in three dimensions] (see Note 3): "In fact, space that can explain the world we see without contradictions *must* possess at least four dimensions, without which the actual existence of symmetrical figures can never be traced back to a [single] law."(Zöllner [1878a], p. 248). Zöllner saw Kant's ideas as a precursor to his own views (see Note 2).

In the essay quoted, Zöllner describes some of the unique characteristics of the transition from the third to the fourth dimension. Both his theoretical considerations and his spiritualistic experiments are based on these characteristics. He begins with a discussion of knots in three-dimensional space and draws attention to the fact that they can be untied only if "portions of the string temporarily disappear from three-dimensional space as far as beings of the same dimensionality are concerned [see Note 15]. The same thing would happen if, by means of a movement executed in the fourth dimension, a body were removed from within a completely enclosed three-dimensional space and relocated outside it. Thus it seems possible to nullify the law of the so-called impermeability of matter in three-dimensional space in a manner completely analogous to removing an object from within a closed curve contained in a plane by lifting the object over the boundary of the curve without touching it." (Zöllner [1878a], p. 276.) See also Note 6.

> [6]A perpendicular can be dropped to any point on a two-dimensional surface. If a point P moves away from the surface along this perpendicular, it distances itself from all points on the surface without changing its vertical projection M on the surface in any way. If this point M is the midpoint M of a circle, as point P leaves the surface, it is always equidistant from any of the points on the periphery of the circle, though this distance is constantly increasing. If we let point P move out along the perpendicular until its distance from midpoint M of the circle is greater than the radius of the circle and then rotate the perpendicular until it coincides with the plane of the circle, point P will have moved out of the circle without cutting through its circumference.

Analogously, a point P inside a sphere can move out of the interior of the sphere without piercing its surface as soon as we enlist the help of four-dimensional space. Any point in three-dimensional space can leave it and enter four-dimensional space along the straight line of a perpendicular without touching any point in the original space. If we remove the midpoint M of a sphere from three-dimensional space in this way, point M distances itself increasingly but equally from all points on the sphere's surface. As soon as the distance from the initial location M is greater than the radius of the sphere, the point has been removed from the sphere, and the operation can be made visible by rotating the straight line along which the point traveled back into three-dimensional space.

> [7]*Arthur Schopenhauer* (1788–1869): "'The world is my mental image': this is a truth that applies to any living, cognizant being." (*The World as Will and Mental Image, vol. I*, §1 [1894], p. 29).
>
> [8]Rudolf Steiner also uses this example in his book *Intuitive Thinking as a Spiritual Path: A Philosophy of Freedom* (GA 4), chapter VI, "The Human Individuality," p. 106. See also his lecture of January 14, 1921 (GA 323, p. 252).
>
> [9]Rudolf Steiner discusses these difficulties in greater detail in *Intuitive*

Thinking as a Spiritual Path: A Philosophy of Freedom (GA 4), chapter IV, "The World as Perception," and in his Introduction to Goethe's Natural Scientific Works (GA 1), chapter IX, "Goethe's Epistemologay" and chapter XVI.2, "The Archetypal Phenomenon."

[10] Rudolf Steiner also uses this comparison in his lecture of November 8, 1908 (GA 108), where he investigates more closely how sensation, perception, mental images, and concepts relate to each other.

[11] Strictly speaking, this statement about the transition from circle to straight line is valid only in Euclidean geometry. In projective geometry, the transitional circle coincides with *both* the tangent, which remains constant, and the infinitely distant straight line (see Locher [1937], chapter IV, especially pp. 69ff). only when the Euclidean plane becomes a projective plane by incorporating the infinitely distant straight line is it possible to pass through infinity (see also Ziegler [1992], chapter III).

[12] This phenomenon is directly related to the geometric fact that it is impossible to pass through infinity without leaving the domain of Euclidean geometry (see Note 11). In other words, the point we imagine as moving in one direction is *not* transformed into the point we imagine as coming back from the other side. The two portions of the straight line that we can imagine in sensory terms are connected through infinity only by a lawfulness that we can conceive; they are separated by their manifestation in points that we can visualize.

[13] Rudolf Steiner uses the metaphor of seal, sealing wax, and impression repeatedly in epistemological considerations about the relationship between the objective outer world and the consciousness of the cognizant individual. The decisive aspect of this metaphor is that in it, as in the psycho-physical domain, transmission of form is not bound to transmission of substance. See also Steiner's essays *Philosophy and Anthroposophy* (GA 35) and *Anthroposophy's Psychological Foundations and Epistemological Position* (GA 35), p. 138.

[14] *Oskar Simony* (1852–1915), mathematician and scientist in Vienna, son of the geographer and alpine researcher *Friedrich Simony* (1812–1896) and professor at the Vienna College of Agriculture from 1880 to 1913. His mathematical studies focused on number theory and the empirical and experimental topology of knots and two-dimensional surfaces in three-dimensional space (see Müller [1931] and [1951]). Some of the models Steiner mentions are illustrated in Simony's treatises.

Simony's early involvement with topology was inspired by his encounters with Zöllners spiritualistic experiments (see Note 5). He felt compelled to study the spatial problems posed by the discovery of non-Euclidean and multidimensional geometry. His investigations expanded to include physiological and epistemological considerations (see Simony [1883], [1884], and [1886]). The importance of not confusing the empirical realm and the realm of mathematical ideas was clear to him. The conceptual possibility of four-dimensional space was not a problem to him as a mathematician, but he could not accept Zöllner's thesis that all objects in three-dimensional space are projections of four-dimensional objects that are not perceptible to the senses. His intention, however, was not to reject the existence of spiritualistic phenomena out of hand. On the contrary, he, like Zöllner, advocated exact scientific investigation of such phenomena. He also considered how the spiritualistic phenomena reported by Zöllner might be proved using the traditional methods of physics and physiology, or at least reconciled with these fields (Simony, *Spiritualistic Manifestations* [1884], He felt that it was important to demonstrate that explaining such phenomena did not require leaving three-dimensional, empirical space. He pointed out that Zöllner's hypothesis of the existence of four-dimensional space contradicted our ordinary experience of space, If this hypothesis is correct, objects in the ordinary three-dimensional space of physics are shadow images that we can change at will without having direct access to their prototypes (Simony [1881b], §6, and [1884], pp. 20ff). As shown by the example of a shadow projected by a three-dimensional object onto a surface, however, no change in the shadow is possible without direct access to the object that casts it.

Simony's topological experiments were intended to investigate the nature of three-dimensional, empirical space, as opposed to curved space or any other mathematically conceivable space: "The phenomena investigated here, since they belong to the realm of our senses, [can] be incorporated only into an *empirical geometry* without being brought into connection with the theory of so-called higher manifolds. In addition, the course of development I chose also makes it clear why, in investigating various sections of the first and second type, I avoided using either analytical geometry or infinitesimal calculus in order to remain independent of any possible hypothesis about the nature of perceived space" ([1883], pp. 963ff).

As a mathematician, Simony was especially interested in how knots develop in twisted ring-shaped surfaces and in unknotted cross-shaped closed surfaces. He demonstrated that such surfaces can be cut in ways that either do not destroy their closed character or produce knots, under appropriate circumstances (Simony [1880], [1881a], [1881b]. The simplest and most famous example of this type, a closed strip incorporating a 720° twist, is mentioned by Rudolf Steiner in this lecture.

> [15]In four-dimensional space, there are no knots; that is, every knot in a closed thread or strip can be untied simply by pulling, without cutting (opening) the thread or strip.

Felix Klein (1845–1925) seems to have been the first mathematician to draw attention to this phenomenon in the early 1870s. According to an account by Zöllner [1878a], Klein spoke with him during a scientific conference on this subject shortly before publishing a treatise [1876] in which he discussed this theme in passing. Klein also reported on their meeting and expressed the opinion that it inspired Zöllner's thesis on the existence of four-dimensional space and its significance in explaining spiritualistic phenomena (Klein [1926], pp. 169ff). While Klein ([1876], p. 478) discusses the subject only in general terms, Hoppe [1879] uses an analytically formulated example to untie concretely a simple three-dimensional knot in four-dimensional space (see also Durége [1880] and Hoppe [1880]).

In *Distant Effects* ([1878a], pp. 272–274), Zöllner demonstrates the dissolution of knots in four-dimensional space with the help of an analogy. He first considers the dissolution of a two-dimensional knot in a closed curve (Figure 70): Without cutting the curve, the crossing cannot be eliminated if we remain within the plane, but by rotating a section of the curve through three-dimensional space around a straight line lying in the plane, any crossing can be undone without cutting the curve.

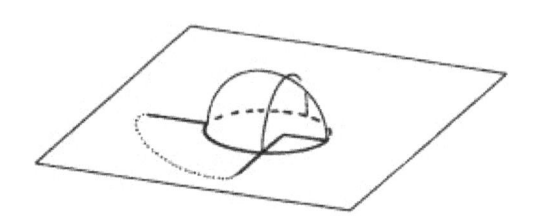

Figure 70

"If these considerations are transferred via analogy to a knot in three-dimensional space, it is easy to see that such a knot can be tied and untied only through operations in which the elements of the thread describe a doubly bent curve." Without being cut, this knot cannot be untied in three-dimensional space. "If, however, there were beings among us capable of carrying out four-dimensional movements of material objects, these beings would be able to tie and untie such knots much faster, by means of an operation fully analogous to untying the two-dimensional knot described above. [...] My observations on knot formation in a flexible thread in different dimensions of space were inspired by oral communications from Dr. Felix Klein, professor of mathematics in Munich.

"Clearly, in the operations indicated here, portions of the thread must disappear *temporarily* from three-dimensional space, as far as beings of the same dimensionality are concerned" (Zöllner [1878a], pp. 273–276).

Undoing a knot in three-dimensional space is indeed always possible if either self-crossing or passing through four-dimensional space is allowed, since the latter makes possible the results of self-crossing without the actual self-crossing (see Seifert/Threlfall [1934], p. 3 and p. 315). All we need to do is rotate a suitably shaped section of the curve in plane *a* around plane *b* through four-dimensional space ([Figure 71](#)).

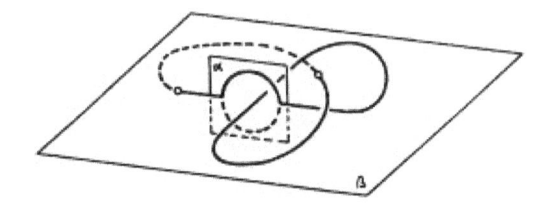

Figure 71

[16](#)Giving a strip a 360° twist before joining its ends into a ring results in a surface that is the four-dimensional equivalent of a three-dimensional cylindricalring ([Figure 72](#)).

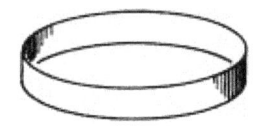

Figure 72

In other words, twists that are whole-number multiples of 360° can be undone in four-dimensional space (see later discussion). Simony was presumably aware of this phenomenon, though he does not mention it explicitly in his topological works, since he was primarily concerned with the unique qualities of empirical three-dimensional space. The equivalence of an untwisted cylindrical strip in three-dimensional space and a strip with a 360° twist in four-dimensional space results from the fact that both rings are characterized by two nonintersecting curved edges. In the second instance, these curved edges are twisted around each other, while in the first instance they are not. In four-dimensional space, the twisting can be undone without any overlapping, converting the twisted ring into an untwisted ring (see the transition from Figure 73 to 74).

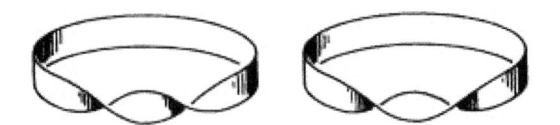

Figures 73–74

Note that this operation cannot be performed on the so-called Möbius strip, a cylindrical ring incorporating a 180° twist (Figure 75). This surface has only one edge curve, even in four-dimensional space, it cannot be transformed into an untwisted ring in any way without cutting through the surface. (This phenomenon has to do with the fact that such a surface cannot be oriented, see Seifert/Threlfall [1934], §2. The Möbius strip was first described by Möbius [1865], §11.)

Figure 75

[17]Geometrically speaking, (static) vision in a plane or in space can be interpreted as a central projection of objects in the plane or in space onto a surface. To a being in three-dimensional space with this type of vision, therefore, all objects would appear as if projected on a surface. This being has an indirect impression of the third dimension only if it is able to see *dynamically*; that is, if its visual apparatus includes two projection directions and the ability to accommodate them. If not, such a being would be able to *conclude* that the third dimension exists (as one-eyed people do on the basis of much experience and many opportunities for comparison) but would not be able to *experience* it. The very fact of three-dimensional dynamic vision in human beings is evidence of our "four-dimensional"

nature, which we cannot perceive directly (i.e. by means of our senses), though we can conclude that it exists.

On the basis of geometry and physics, *Charles Howard Hinton* (1853–1907) also concluded that human beings must be beings of four or more dimensions. "It can be argued that symmetry in any number of dimensions is the evidence of an action in a higher dimensionality. Thus considering living beings, there is evidence both in their structure, and in their different mode of activity, of a something coming in from without into the inorganic world." (Hinton, *The Fourth Dimension* [1904], p. 78).

[18]*Charles Howard Hinton* (1853–1907), mathematician and author. Hinton was strongly influenced by his father, *James Hinton* (1822–1875), a surgeon who also wrote essays, including several on the art of thinking, or "thought-artistry," in which he rejected any artificial restraints on thinking and experience due to religious, social, or legal regulation of behavior. Through his parents' contact with *Mary Everest Boole* (1832–1916), the widow of the logician and mathematician *George Boole*, (1815–1864) Hinton met the Booles' daughter, *Mary Ellen*, his future wife. Hinton studied mathematics at oxford and taught at various institutions before leaving England for Japan in 1886. He lived in Japan until 1891 and then spent the rest of his life in the United States.

Hinton's search for certainty provoked a severe crisis in 1875. He resorted to the idea that only the arrangement of objects in space could lead to absolutely certain knowledge. In his preoccupation with thought exercises and visualizations concerning the arrangement of a cube subdivided into smaller cubes, he attempted to free himself from all subjectively imposed limitations such as the concepts of "above" and "below" ("Casting out the Self" [1886], pp. 205–229). In this process, he encountered the problem of mirror-image subdivisions of two cubes and wondered whether this phenomenon might not also prove to be subjectively determined. While investigating this question, he discovered a treatise by Friedrich Zöllner on four-dimensional space [1878e] in the *Quarterly Journal of Science* (edited by William Crookes). In this paper, Zöllner briefly presented his experiments and views on the reality of the fourth dimension. Crookes (a chemist and physicist) and Zöllner both belonged to the group of university-based researchers who were attempting, though with little success, to use scientific methods to approach spiritualism.

Hinton spent the rest of his life studying the problem of the fourth dimension. His works concentrated on popularizing ideas about four-dimensional space and dealt especially with how to acquire the ability to visualize it. In this connection, Hinton studied the transition from the second to the third dimension in many different ways in order to create a solid foundation for depicting the fourth dimension in three-dimensional perceived space. In particular, he developed methodical exercises for acquiring a consistent view of three-dimensional space and for a time held the opinion that it was possible to acquire a nonsensory view of four-dimensional space in the same way (see *A New Era of Thought* [1900] and *The Fourth Dimension* [1904]). Hinton believed that the world included a material extension into the fourth dimension and attempted to prove this hypothesis through various experiments in psychology and physics. This view met with resistance both from materialists, who accepted the existence of only three spatial dimensions, and from spiritualists, who preferred to interpret the fourth dimension as purely spiritual in character (see Ballard [1980]). Hinton was a controversial writer who was avidly read and highly esteemed by the lay public, especially theosophists and avant-garde artists (see Henderson [1983] and [1988]). He was rejected or ignored in academic circles.

[19] See the corresponding explanations in the previous lecture.

[20] See Rudolf Steiner, *An Outline of Esoteric Science* (GA 13), chapter IV: "Cosmic Evolution and the Human Being."

[21] A definitive reconstruction of what Steiner meant by this analogy is not possible, and there is nothing in Hinton's works that corresponds to this train of thought. Although Hinton also uses colors to illustrate the transition from the second to the third dimension and especially the transition from the third to the fourth, he uses them very differently. In his lecture of May 24, 1905, reprinted in this volume, Steiner gives a review of Hinton's thoughts on this subject.

The geometric basis of the thoughts Steiner presents here is as follows: A line segment bisected in the middle can be developed into a square by allowing each half of the segment to form the shared side of two adjacent smaller squares. The result is a larger square divided into four smaller ones (Figure 16). A cube divided into eight smaller cubes can then be constructed by allowing each of the smaller squares to form the shared surface of two adjacent cubes (Figure 17). The corresponding four-dimensional figure, the four-dimensional cube, results when each of the eight sub-cubes of the three-dimensional cube is interpreted as the shared boundary between two four-dimensional cubes. The result is a four-dimensional cube divided into sixteen sub-cubes.

BERLIN, MAY 1905

[22]Mr. *Schouten*. In all probability, *Jan Arnoldus Schouten* (1883–1971), a Dutch mathematician from Delft.

In the archives of the Rudolf Steiner Nachlassverwaltung, there is a letter from Schouten to Steiner. The part that relates to this lecture reads:

Delft

December 1, 1905

Dear Dr. Steiner,

Before leaving for home in July of this year, I stopped in to say goodbye to you, but unfortunately you had already left. Consequently, the models you needed for your lecture are still in your possession. Since I intend to give several lectures here on the fourth dimension, could you please send the models to me? These lectures are intended for several lodges, including the one in Delft, which was founded a short time ago.

Sincerely yours, J. A. Schouten

M. T. S.

After studying electrical engineering at the technical college in Delft, Schouten practiced his profession for several years in Rotterdam and Berlin. In order to be able to understand the theory of special relativity, Schouten studied mathematics privately and wrote the book *Grundlagen der Vektor-und Affinoranalysis* ("The Bases of Vector and Affine Analysis") [1914], which he submitted as his dissertation to the University of Delft. Shortly thereafter, he was named professor at Delft, where he remained until 1943.

Schouten's book [1914], with a personal dedication by the author, was found in Rudolf Steiner's library. Schouten's mother, H. Schouten (1849–19??) was a member of the Theosophical Society and later of the Anthroposophical Society. To date, only one other indication of a connection between Schouten and Rudolf Steiner has been found, in a letter (also in the Steiner archives) to Rudolf Steiner from Schouten's mother, dated March 4, 1913. This letter reads in part:

I was very confident that my son, now that he intends to give up his membership in the Theosophical Society, would become a member of the Anthroposophical Society, but he says that for the moment he cannot do so with a clear conscience because he has not been able to keep up his theosophical studies. He told me that he makes a point of seriously studying everything he undertakes in life, and that because his own academic work is so demanding at the moment that he has almost no time to go out, he is temporarily unable to take up the study of theosophy again. The first draft of his paper has been sent to the Royal Academy. In addition to his private work, he is lecturing weekly on mathematics in Delft and on electricity in Rotterdam. In the week when you will be in the Hague, the Philosophical Society in Amsterdam has asked him to give a lecture on his concepts of nonmaterial mathematics. Praise God, both he and his wife have absorbed the truths of reincarnation and karma. They would like to attend your public lectures, and my son also thought that some of his colleagues might attend if the subject appealed to them. I hope you and my son will find the opportunity to meet.

Schouten's first paper in the *Verslagen en Mededeelingen der Koninglijke Akademie van Wetenschappen* appeared in 1917 in volume 26, a paper in the *Verhandelingen der Koninglijke Akademie van Wetenschappen te Amersterdam* appeared in 1918 in volume 12.

[23]Kronos (not to be confused with Chronos, or Time) is one of the sons of Uranus and Gaia. He married his sister Rhea, who gave birth to three daughters (Hestia, Demeter, and Hera) and two sons (Poseidon and Zeus). Kronos devoured all of them except Zeus, whom Rhea had entrusted to her mother, Gaia. (See *Kérenyi, Die Mythologie der Griechen* ["The Mythology of the Greeks"] [1966], volume I, chapter I, sections 1 and 2.)

[24]See Rudolf Steiner's *Theosophy*.

[25]*Johann von Wolfgang Goethe* (1749–1832).

Meanwhile the golden king said to the man with the lamp, "How many mysteries do you know?" "Three," answered the old man. "Which is the most important?" "The revealed one," answered the old man.

[26]*Plato* (427–347 BC). *Timaeus* 36b–37a. See also Rudolf Steiner's *Christianity as Mystical Fact* (GA 8), pp. 65 ff.

[27]In the course of his life, Hinton developed and popularized not one but many methods of representing four-dimensional space in three-dimensional perceived space. He was noted more for his popularization of the subject than for his mathematical originality. See the list of Hinton's works in the bibliography.

[28]Hinton employed several different color systems and distributions of color. He saw the two-dimensional representation of three-dimensional figures as preparation for the three-dimensional representation of four-dimensional figures (see *A New Era of Thought* [1900], part II, chapters I-IV and VII, and *The Fourth Dimension* [1904], chapters XI-XIII). Steiner

seems to be referring to a very simplified version of one of Hinton's systems.

It is not evident from the context of the lecture whether Steiner intended the colors to suggest specific attributes of the corresponding dimensions, but it seems unlikely. The various transcriptions of the lecture differ substantially at this point, presumably owing to different ways of adapting Steiner's use of color (especially white) on the dark board to white paper.

[29] These models were not found among Steiner's belongings after his death. Presumably, they were returned to J. A. Schouten (see the letter to that effect in Note 1 of Lecture 3).

[30] A cube bounded by six surfaces can be created by moving a square with its four edges in three-dimensional space. The six surfaces consist of the initial and final cubes plus the four produced by the movement of the edges. This is immediately apparent in the parallel projection of this movement onto a plane—that is, into two-dimensional space (see Figure 88). Similarly, the movement of a cube with six surfaces in four-dimensional space creates a figure with eight cubes forming its boundaries-the initial and final cubes plus the six created through the movement of the sides-as is easily apparent from a parallel projection of the cube's movement into three-dimensional space (see Figure 90).

[31] Hinton seems to have coined the term *tessaract* for the four-dimensional figure analogous to the cube. The spelling *tessarakt* also occurs in his works.

[32] Hinton's *The Fourth Dimension* [1904], chapter XII, contains almost the same reasoning and identical figures.

[33] Goethe, *Faust*, part I, scene 4, Faust's study, verses 2065ff:

Mephistopheles:

So now we simply spread the cloak

That is to carry both of us through the air.

But do not bring too large a bundle

As you take this daring step.

A little fire-air I shall create

To lift us swiftly from the earth.

Once lightened, we shall quickly rise,

Congratulations on your new career!

[34]Genesis 1:2. See Rudolf Steiner, *Genes is The Secrets of the Biblical Story of Creation* (GA 122), especially the lecture of August 20, 1910.
[35]Ibid.
[36]See note 30 from the Fourth Lecture.
[37]The situation described here corresponds to Figure 76 in the case of a cube laid out in a plane:

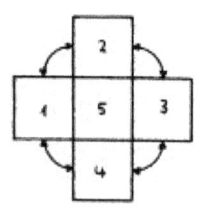

Figure 76

The location of square 6, directly "above" square 5, cannot be directly depicted in a plane. The upper edge of square 2, the lower edge of square 4, and the right and left edges of squares 3 and 1, respectively, must be seen as identical to the edges of square 6.

Correspondingly, cubes 7 and 8 "coincide" and cannot be distinguished in three-dimensional space by any direct means. The upper and lower surfaces of cubes 5 and 6, respectively, the left and right surfaces of 3 and 4, respectively, and the front and back surfaces of 1 and 2, respectively, also constitute the surfaces of cube 8. unfolding a cube makes it easier to note the coincidence between the edges of the sixth square and those of its neighboring squares (Figure 77).

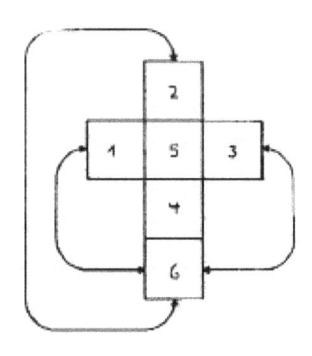

Figure 77

Figure 78 shows the corresponding situation in the case of a tessaract. The surfaces of the eighth cube must be seen as identical to the corresponding surfaces of neighboring cubes.

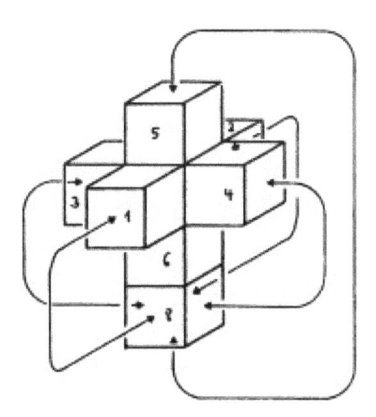

Figure 78

> [38]In each of the five regular convex polyhedrons—cube, tetrahedron, octahedron, dodecahedron, and icosahedron—all the angles of surface intersection are equal. The angle of intersection is unique to each regular polyhedron.

The surfaces of any regular polyhedron are polygons that are both similar and regular, that is, all of their edges are of equal length, and all of their angles are equal. Thus, we simply need to investigate how many polygons can meet at one vertex in order to gain a complete overview of all possible regular polyhedrons. Let's begin with equilateral triangles (Figure 79). Two equilateral triangles cannot be joined together to form one vertex of a polyhedron. Three such triangles yield a tetrahedron, four form one vertex of an octahedron, and five form one vertex of an icosahedron. Six triangles lie flat in a plane and cannot form a vertex.

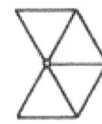

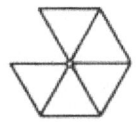

Figure 79

Three regular rectangular solids (i.e., squares) form one vertex of a cube, while four lie flat in a plane. Three pentagons form one vertex of a dodecahedron, but four pentagons would overlap (Figure 80).

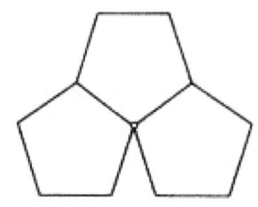

Figure 80

Three hexagons lie flat in a plane, and three heptagons overlap. Thus, there cannot possibly be more than the five types of regular polyhedrons mentioned earlier.

> [39] Rudolf Steiner refers here to a standard procedure in geometric crystallography. The seven classes of crystals are based on the symmetries of the seven possible crystallographic systems of axes. A symmetry group, which represents all of the symmetry elements of one class, is called a holohedry. The polyhedrons belonging to such symmetry groups are called holohedral shapes. They are simple polyhedrons that can be converted into each other through symmetrical operations that all belong to a single crystal system. Hemihedral forms are polyhedrons with half as many surfaces as the corresponding holohedral forms. Hemihedrons are derived from holohedrons through the extension of some of the surfaces of the holohedrons and the disappearances of others. The symmetry group of the hemihedrons is correspondingly reduced (subgroup of holohedries of index 2). In this sense, a tetrahedron is a hemihedral variation on an octahedron because it has half the number of surfaces.

Crystallographers also have introduced tetardohedrons, polyhedrons with one-fourth the number of surfaces of the corresponding holohedral figures and a correspondingly reduced symmetry group (subgroup of holohedries of index 4). For more information, see Hochstetter/Bisching [1868], pp. 20ff, Schoute [1905], pp. 190ff, and Niggli [1924], pp. 70ff and 129ff.

[40] In a cube, any two intersecting surfaces meet in a right angle. No matter which surfaces we choose, extending them always will result in a figure with 90° angles of intersection. In a cube, however, reducing the number of surfaces no longer results in a *closed* polyhedron.

[41] In this case, the axes of a cube are the three perpendicular directions that intersect in the cube's midpoint, one pair of surfaces is perpendicular to each axis. These axes are also the axes of the three zones of a cube (Figure 81). A *zone* or *zone association* is a set of at least three surfaces that are parallel to the straight line of a zone axis.

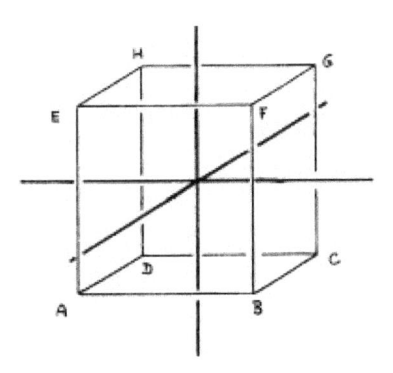

Figure 81

A rhombic dodecahedron is easy to construct with the help of a cube. First all six diagonal planes connecting opposite edges of the cube are constructed (Figure 82). Then the mirror images of the resulting six internal pyramids are constructed on the outside of the cube (Figure 83). The four "axes" mentioned in the lecture are the diagonals of the rhombic dodecahedron that coincide with the diagonals of the cube.

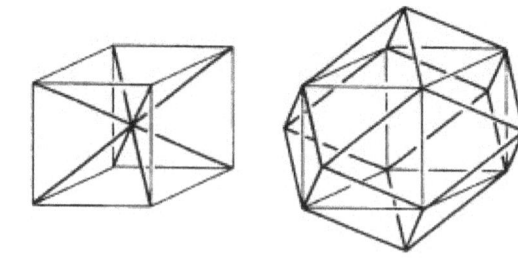

Figures 82–83

These four axes are the four *zone axes* of the rhombic dodecahedron—that is, each of them is parallel to six surfaces of this figure. These four groups of six planes are called the *zones* of the rhombic dodecahedron.

Because its vertices are not all similar, a rhombic dodecahedron is not a regular polyhedron. Three surfaces intersect in each of the vertices that emerge from the cube, while four surfaces intersect in each of the other vertices. The zone axes pass through the vertex points where three surfaces meet. Note that the "axes" described here represent a specific selection from the seven possible diagonals (straight line segments connecting opposite corner points).

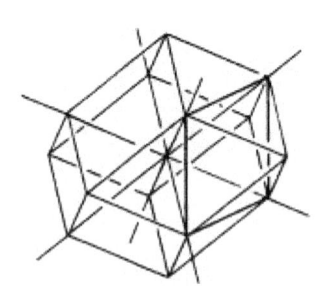

Figure 84

About the drawings: The rhombic dodecahedron, like the other geometric figures depicted here, is drawn in oblique parallel projection, which is best suited to freehand drawing on the board. This projection results in slight distortions of subsequent figures, which must be taken into account.

[42] In addition to the axes described in the previous note, a rhombic dodecahedron also has axes perpendicular to its surfaces. If a rhombic dodecahedron is held in place while its four zone axes are rotated 45° around the perpendicular axis of the underlying cube, the axes then intersect the midpoints of eight of the rhombic dodecahedron's surfaces. The figure formed by these surfaces is an octahedron consisting of the four pairs of

surfaces that are perpendicular to the zone axes (rotated 45°) of the rhombic dodecahedron (Figure 85). Adding to these four axes the two horizontal axes (also rotated 45°) of the cube (see previous note) results in a system of six "axes"; each surface of the rhombic dodecahedron is perpendicular to one of them.

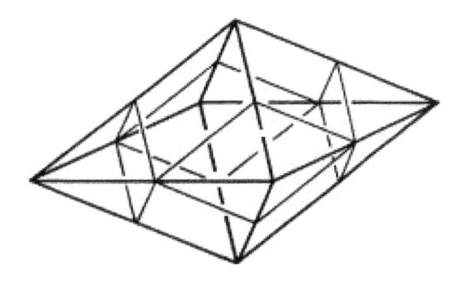

Figure 85

[43]Halving the number of surfaces of a cube does not produce any new surface angles. A rhombic dodecahedron can be "halved" in several different ways (Figures 86 and 87). When this operation produces a closed polyhedron, it is an oblique parallelepiped.

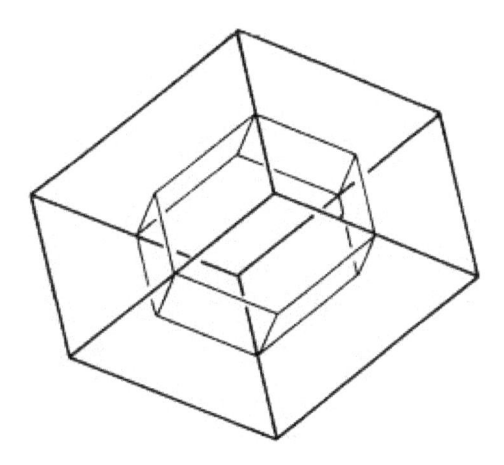

Figure 86

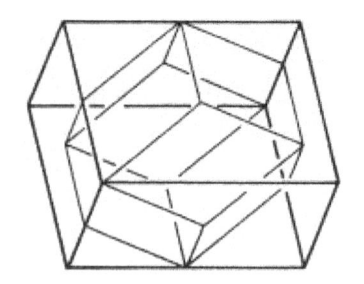

Figure 87

[44] This statement presupposes that the cuts in the tetrahedron or cube are made parallel to existing surfaces. Successively cutting off the vertices of a cube so that the cut surfaces are perpendicular to the cube's diagonals results first in a cube-octahedron and eventually in an octahedron.

[45] See also Steiner's lecture of March 31, 1905. No matter which three of the six planes defining a cube are selected, the result of extending them into space results in a "figure" that stretches to infinity. If the three surfaces we select are perpendicular to each other, the result is a geometric figure consisting of three perpendicular axes and the planes that connect them in pairs. Such a figure can be seen as representing three-dimensional Euclidean space and is also the geometric basis of every Euclidean or Cartesian coordinate system.

[46] Here and in the remainder of the lectures, Steiner's presentation seems to have been substantially abridged, and, as a result, various perspectives overlap.

To the series square-cube-tessaract, we can add another series of geometrical figures where the planes or faces of the figure are curved rather than straight or flat. We can call the figures of this second series curved squares, curved cubes, and curved tessaracts. In such a figure, the elements forming its edges or sides have the same number of dimensions as the total figure.

The circle, the spherical surface (two-dimensional sphere), and the solid (three-dimensional) sphere are topologically equivalent to the rectilinear elements defining the boundaries of a square, a cube, and a tessaract respectively. The disc, ball, and four-dimensional ball are topologically equivalent to the square, the cube, and the tessaract respectively.

On the other hand, suitable bending of a one-dimensional line segment results in a two-dimensional segment of a curve or—in a special instance—in a segment of a circle. Bending a disc produces a three-dimensional figure, a hollow hemisphere. Bending a solid sphere produces a four-dimensional figure (in a special instance, a section of a four-dimensional sphere).

In this way, a circle can be constructed from two curved line segments whose ends are joined. Similarly, in three-dimensional space, a spherical surface can be constructed from two discs that are first curved and then joined at their edges. In four-dimensional space, a three-dimensional sphere results when two curved solid spheres are joined at their surfaces (two-dimensional spheres). This three-dimensional sphere relates to three-dimensional space as a ball (the surface of an ordinary sphere) relates to a plane. [Mathematician David Cooper comments: You are comparing filled-in figures rather than boundaries in both cases. A sphere (the boundary of a ball) is two-dimensional, so the two-dimensional sphere's volume means the (three-dimensional) ball.]

[47]Presumably, this reference is to Hinton's books *Scientific Romances* [1886], *A New Era of Thought* [1900], and *The Fourth Dimension* [1904].

[48]Strictly speaking, the depiction of a tessaract in the previous lecture (May 31, 1905) is not a projection but simply an unfolded view. In the present lecture, Steiner proceeds to construct an orthogonal parallel projection of a tessaract in three-dimensional space, taking one of its diagonals as the direction of projection.

[49]Considering the framework formed by the edges of a cube, an oblique parallel projection of the cube onto a plane generally consists of two parallel, non-coinciding cubes and the line segments connecting their corresponding corners (Figure 88: oblique parallel projections of a cube).

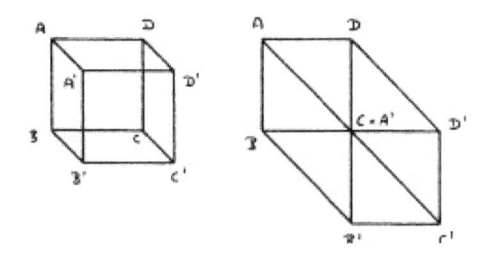

Figure 88

If the diagonal A'C is selected as the direction of projection, vertices A' and C coincide, producing an oblique hexagon and its diagonals. The images of the six individual faces of the cube can be reconstructed from this hexagon by tracing all the possible parallelograms defined by the existing structure of lines. Each of these parallelograms overlaps with two others, and the hexagon's surface is covered twice by the faces of the cube. When the direction of projection is perpendicular to the plane of projection, the resulting image of a cube is a regular hexagon (Figure 89: orthogonal parallel projections of a cube).

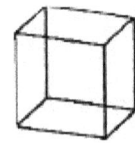

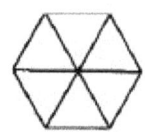

Figure 89

Note that the three diagonals of the hexagon also represent the three (zone) axes of the cube. The zone associations belonging to each of these axes—that is, the four faces of the cube that parallel it—appear as four parallelograms or rhombuses with one edge coinciding with the corresponding axis.

> [50] Earlier in this lecture, Steiner called a distorted or oblique square a "rhombus," which is a parallelogram with four equal sides. The corresponding solid figure, Steiner's "rhombic parallelepiped," is an oblique cube—i.e., a parallelepiped whose edges are all the same length.
>
> [51] If we see the tessaract as the framework formed by its edges, the result of projecting the tessaract into three-dimensional space generally consists of two parallel, displaced oblique cubes and the line segments connecting their corresponding vertices (Figure 90: oblique parallel projections of a tessaract).

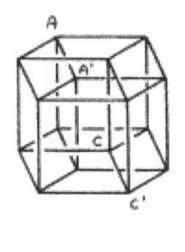

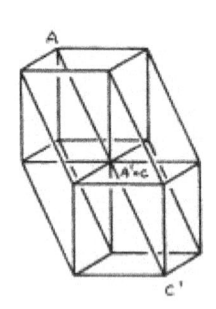

Figure 90

When the direction of projection passes through the diagonal A'C, the endpoints A' and C coincide, resulting in a rhombic dodecahedron with four diagonals. In the first figure, it is easy to trace the images of the eight cubes defining the boundaries of a tessaract: they are all the possible parallelepipeds formed by the edges of the existing framework. These parallelepipeds include the original cube, the displaced cube, and the six parallelepipeds that share one face each with the original and displaced cubes. This situation does not change fundamentally when we make the transition to the rhombic dodecahedron, except that in this instance all of the "rhombic cubes" (parallelepipeds) interpenetrate in such a way that they fill the internal space of the rhombic dodecahedron exactly twice, with each parallelepiped including portions of three others.

The four diagonals of the rhombic dodecahedron that appear in the projection of the tessaract are the *zone axes* of the rhombic dodecahedron's four associations of six faces each. Each such face association consists of all six surfaces that are parallel to a single zone axis. (Note that in a rhombic dodecahedron the axes pass through vertices rather than through the centers of faces, as in a cube.)

These four axes, however, are also the projections of the tessaract's four perpendicular axes in four-dimensional space. A cube's three axes pass through the centers of its square sides. Analogously, a tessaract's axes pass through the middle of the cubes that form its sides. In parallel projection, the middle of a cube is transformed into the middle of the corresponding parallelepiped. As we can ascertain by studying all eight parallelepipeds in a rhombic dodecahedron, the four axes pass exactly through the middles of these parallelepipeds.

A cube's four perpendicular axes are simultaneously the zone axes of its three face associations of four faces each. Similarly, a tessaract's four axes are also the zone axes of four cell associations of six cells each *(cell* equals the cube forming a side of the tessaract). In the rhombic dodecahedron, the cells belonging to each axis are easy to find: they are the six parallelepipeds with one edge coinciding with that axis.

[52]*Plato, The Republic,* book 7, 514a-518c. It has not yet been possible to ascertain where Schopenhauer used this metaphor.

[53]Zöllner drew attention to this interpretation of Plato's cave metaphor in his essay *Über Wirkungen in die Ferne* [1878a], pp. 260ff.

[54]See the lecture of March 24, 1905.

[55]What Steiner seems to mean here by spherical tessaract is not a four-dimensional cube in the narrower sense but rather its topological equivalent, the three-dimensional sphere in four-dimensional space, which is produced by curving and attaching two solid three-dimensional spheres. See Note 11, Lecture 5.

[56]See Note 9 above and Note 11, Lecture 5.

[57] The remaining text of this lecture incorporates fragments of transcripts quoted in Haase's essay [1916], which helped clarify the meaning.

[58] Exodus 19, also Exodus 33 and 34.

[59] In theosophical literature, the three upper regions of the land of spirit were called Arupa regions, in contrast to the four lower, or Rupa, regions. See the editor's note to Rudolf Steiner's *Die Grundelemente der Esoterik* "The Basic Elements of Esotericism" (GA 93a), p. 281 ff. On the seven regions of the land of spirit, see Rudolf Steiner, *Theosophy* (GA 9), "The Country of Spirit Beings." On the problem of dimensionality in connection with the planes or regions of the spirit world, see also Rudolf Steiner's lecture of May 17, 1905, his response to questions asked by A. Strakosch on March 11, 1920, the questions and answers of April 7, 1921 (GA 76), and April 12, 1922 (GA 82), and the lectures of August 19, 29, 22, and 26, 1923 (GA 227).

[60] See Steiner's lectures of March 24 and 31, 1905, and the relevant notes.

[61] See Note 6, (March 24, 1905).

[62] See Rudolf Steiner's autobiography, *Autobiography; Chapters in the Course of my Life* (GA 28), chapter III, p. 63, and his lecture of April 3, 1922, "Die Stellung der Anthroposophie in den Wissenschaften" in *Damit der Mensch ganz Mensch werde: Die Bedeutung der Anthroposophie im Geistesleben der Gegenwart* (GA 82).

[63] In this passage, Rudolf Steiner refers to the distant (or absolute) plane of Euclidean space, resulting in a projective space. A projective space is self-contained and has no limits or boundaries, meaning that we can travel to "infinity" in any direction and return from the other side.

[64] See also the explanation in his lecture of March 24, 1905 and the accompanying notes.

[65] See the explanations at the beginning of the preceding lecture (June 7, 1905) and the accompanying notes.

[66] The upper and lower devachen are heavenly realms through which the soul apsses through after death. See Rudolf Steiner's *Theosophy*.

[67] The first mathematical studies of the problem of higher-dimensional space date from the middle of the nineteenth century. See the introduction to Manning's *Geometry of Four Dimensions* [1914].

[68] In the passages that follow, Rudolf Steiner bases himself on Riemann's studies on the geometry of n-dimensional manifolds. See Note 1, Lecture 1 (March 24, 1905).

[69] See also the following books, which were well-known and popular in their time: Abbott, *Flatland* [1884], Hinton, the chapter "A Plane World" in *Scientific Romances* [1886] (pp. 129-159), and Hinton, *An Episode of Flatland* [1907].

[70] See also Rudolf Steiner's lecture of April 10, 1912 (GA 136). We have not been able to confirm the assumption that this statement of Steiner's refers to Zöllner's views on the subject. Zöllner's comet theory (see Zöllner [1886]) became the basis and point of departure for modern conventional comet theories, and there is no indication that Zöllner saw any connection between his comet theory and his spiritualistic ideas about four-dimensional space.

Notes Part 2

[1] These comments were made after a lecture on Christianity (not yet published in the complete edition of Rudolf Steiner's works) to the Berlin branch.

[2] Jan *Arnoldus Schouten* (1883–1971) See Note 1, Lecture 3 (May 17, 1905). This question suggests that the problem of the fourth dimension was topical even in Rudolf Steiner's immediate circle and that his lectures on the subject were meant above all to address related spiritual scientific questions.

[3] This question-and-answer session took place during the lecture cycle *Vor dem Tore der Theosophie* (GA 95).

[4] By space, Rudolf Steiner apparently means ordinary, perceived space that is defined by the laws of Euclidean geometry. In this type of space, infinity (or, when this space is embedded in projective space, the distant plane) is an impenetrable boundary. According to Steiner, the same does not apply to astral space, whose structure is related to that of projective space. In this type of space there is no boundary, no unattainable infinity. Projective space is self-contained; we can set out in any direction from a fixed starting point and ultimately return to the same point.

[5] It has not been possible to reconstruct exactly what this sentence means. On the basis of the drawing that has been preserved (Figure 62), the sentence may be a fragment of an explanation with approximately the following contents: In the second dimension, a two-dimensional object within a circle cannot leave the circle without crossing the circumference. The object can easily be moved outside the circle, however, by enlisting the help of the third dimension. Similarly, an object located within a sphere in three-dimensional space cannot be removed without puncturing the sphere, except by passing through the fourth dimension. (See the explanations in the lecture of March 24, 1905, and the accompanying notes.)

[6] This question-and-answer session took place during the lecture cycle *The Apocalypse of St. John* (GA 104).

[7] Kant, *Prolegomena to Any Future Metaphysics* [1783], "Cosmological Ideas", §50–53, and *Critique of Pure Reason* [1787], "The Antinomies of Pure Reason, the First Conflict of Transcendental Ideas," §454ff. Kant shows that arguments can be presented both for and against the infinity of space. For him, the origin of this contradiction lies in the implicit assumption that space and its objects must be taken as absolute givens and as objective laws of things as they are (*"von Dingen an sich"*). If they were understood as what Kant says they are—namely, mere mental images (ways of looking at things, or phenomena) of things as they are—then the "conflict of ideas" dissolves.

[8] Rudolf Steiner's statements here are based on the discovery that Euclidean geometry is embedded in projective geometry. A Euclidean straight line disappears into infinity in both directions, and the right and left directions are separated by infinity (the distant point). A projective straight line has no such limits—with regard to the sequence of its points, it is closed like a circle.

[9] The text that has been preserved is insufficient to reconstruct whether Steiner attributes an actual geometric curve to astral space. In any case, a self-contained projective straight line is not curved. It is possible that Steiner simply wanted to point out the structural relationships on a projective straight line and how they behave on the circumference of a circle.

[10] Here, too, Steiner presumably uses the term sphere only to draw attention to the self-contained character of astral space in the sense of a projective space. In the topological sense, neither the projective plane of a two-dimensional sphere nor the projective space of a three-dimensional sphere is equivalent.

[11] This question-and-answer session and the following one took place during the lecture cycle *The Spiritual Hierarchies and the Physical World* (GA 110).

[12] This statement cannot be found in Plato's works. It comes from the table conversations recounted by Plutarch that form one section of his *Moralia*. There, one participant in the conversations says, "God is constantly doing geometry—if this statement actually can be ascribed to Plato." Plutarch adds, "This statement is nowhere to be found in Plato's writings, but there is sufficient evidence that it is his, and it is in harmony with his character" (Plutarch, *Moralia*, "Quaestiones convivales," book VIII, question 2, Stephanus 718c).

[13] See also Rudolf Steiner's essay "Mathematik und Okkultismus" (1904) in *Philosophie und Anthroposophie* (GA 35).

[14] See the notes to the questions and answers of September 2, 1906, and June 28, 1908. The term *positional geometry* is an outdated name for synthetic projective geometry.

[15] From the perspective of projective geometry, all theorems in Euclidean geometry having only to do with the position and arrangements of points, lines, and planes (and not with any measurements) are seen as special or "borderline" instances of general projective theorems.

[16] Two points A and B of a projective straight line s separate the line into two segments (Figure 91), one of which includes the distant point of line s. In projective geometry, both segments are considered to connect points A and B. In Euclidean geometry, however, only the segment that does not include the distant point of the straight line g is considered a connection between A and B.

Figure 91

[17] Gall wasp: Similar discussions about the possibility of individual parts of a whole affecting each other without being spatially connected also are found in Rudolf Steiner's lectures of October 22, 1906, in Berlin (in GA 96) and March 22, 1922, in Dornach (in GA 222). None of the many subspecies of gall wasps described in the scientific literature match Rudolf Steiner's description, but a long, stemlike connection between the head and the abdomen occurs in several species of grave wasps, especially in the sand wasp subspecies. The note taker may have misheard the name of this insect.

[18] Notes of a question-and answer-session during the lecture cycle "Psychosophie," in *Anthroposophie-Psychosophie-Pneumatosophie* (GA 115).

[19] Additions to the original German text were added by the original editors to clarify the meaning and are based on Rudolf Steiner's lecture of June 7, 1905, and questions and answers after his lecture of May 17, 1905.

[20] Notes of a question-and-answer session after the lecture to members entitled "Die Ätherisation des Blutes. Das Eingreifen des ätherischen

Christus in die Erdenentwickelung" in *Das esoterische Christentum und die geistige Führung der Menschheit* (GA 130).

[21] This question and answer session took place after a public lecture on "Wahrheiten der Geistesforschung," which was published in the periodical *Mensch und Welt: Blätter für Anthroposophie*, vol. 20, 1968, no. 5, pp.167–177. It has not yet been published in the complete edition (GA) of Rudolf Steiner's works.

[22] Here Rudolf Steiner refers again to Bernhard Riemann's studies, mentioned several times in the lectures. See Note 1, Lecture I.

[23] *Oskar Simony* (1852–1915). See Rudolf Steiner's lecture of March 24, 1905 (Lecture I), and Note 14, Lecture I.

[24] See Rudolf Steiner, *Autobiography* (GA 28).

[25] See the answers to the preceding questions and the accompanying notes.

[26] Notes of a question-and-answer session after a public lecture in Berlin in the House of Architects on "Lionardos geistige Grösse am Wendepunkt zur neueren Zeit" (GA 62).

[27] Goethe's *Das Märchen*. See Note 3, Lecture 3.

[28] For further discussion of the general occult law of repetition and varied repetition, see Rudolf Steiner's *Outline of Esoteric Science* (GA 13), chapter 4, "Cosmic Evolution and the Human Being." On the law of repetition as an elementary principle of the etheric realm, see, for example, Rudolf Steiner's lecture of October 21, 1908 (GA 107), where he illustrates this principle using the example of plant growth and points out the varied repetition in the ongoing process of leaf formation.

[29] The significance of repetitions in the Buddha's talks is also mentioned in lectures Rudolf Steiner gave on September 18, 1912 (GA 139), and on the afternoon of September 27, 1921 (included in GA 343).

[30] *Fra Luca Pacioli* (ca. 1445–1517), who was influenced by *Piero della Francesca* (1410–1492) and *Leonardo da Vinci* (1452–1519), wrote the paper *Divina propor-tione* (Venice, 1509) using drawings copied from his friend Leonardo. This paper was the first thorough study to focus on the mathematical and aesthetic characteristics of the Golden Section.

The golden section *(sectio aurea)*, also called "constant division," results from dividing a line segment into two parts in such a way that the ratio of the smaller portion to the larger is the same as that of the larger to the whole. When we continue to divide a line segment according to the golden section, the result is a sequence of line segments such that the proportion between any two adjacent sections is the golden section. This explains the term *constant division*.

A further indication of the principle of repetition and varied repetition in the context of the golden section is the appearance of the proportion of the golden section in continued fractions. Furthermore, the approximation fractions of these fraction sequences are the quotients of successive members of the Fibonacci series 1, 1, 2, 3, 5, 8…., which play a major role in the arrangement of leaves in plants (phyllotaxis) (see Coxeter [1981], chapter 11).

[31] Questions and answers after the public lecture "Vom Tode," held in Berlin in the House of Architects (published in GA 63).

[32] Rudolf Steiner's lecture of March 19, 1914, "Zwischen Tod und Wiedergeburt des Menschen" (published in GA 63).

[33] With regard to the remainder of this question-and-answer session, see also the questions and answers of March 7, 1920, and the accompanying notes.

[34] A handwritten note by Rudolf Steiner in response to a question asked by Georg Herberg. A facsimile of this note is included in the volume *Geisteswissenschaftliche Impulse zur Entwicklung der Physik, Erster Naturwissenschaftlicher Kurs* (GA 320), Dornach, 1987, p. 192. *Georg Herberg* (1876–1963), one of Germany's first Ph.D.s in engineering, was an independent engineering consultant in the field of heat and energy economy in Stuttgart from 1913 onward.

[35] Questions and answers during the lecture cycle *Geisteswissenschaftliche Impulse zur Entwicklung der Physik: Zweiter Naturwissenschaftlicher Kurs* (GA 321). These questions were asked by *Hermann von Baravalle* (1898–1973), mathematics and physics teacher at the first Waldorf School in Stuttgart), after a lecture he gave on the theory of relativity (Stuttgart, March 7, 1920). To date, no transcript of Baravalle's lecture has been discovered.

[36] The theory of elasticity was one of the theoretical aids used by nineteenth-century physicists in formulating their various theories of optics, which all assumed the existence of a physical ether. Later, the electromagnetic theory of light, *James Clark Maxwell* (1831–1879), in conjunction with the negative outcome of the ether drift experiment (1881ff) conducted by *Albert Michelson* (1852–1931) and *Edward Morley* (1838–1923), superseded the idea of a quasimaterial ether but failed to eliminate it totally from the field of physics. (On the evolution of ether theories and their status in the late nineteenth and early twentieth centuries, see Whittaker [1951–1953]).

In volume II of his lectures on theoretical physics [1944], §15, *Arnold*

Sommerfeld (1868–1951) discusses an ether model based on a quasi–elastic body. This model originated in the investigations of *James MacCullagh* (1809–1847); for more information, see Klein [1926]. Sommerfeld shows that the equations for the movement of this body take the form of Maxwell's electrodynamic equations for empty space.

Friedrich Dustmann [1991] shows that this ether model meets many of the requirements for a theory of light that Steiner presents here and elsewhere. In addition, the basis of this quasi-elastic ether model is a specific antisymmetrical tensor, which from the geometric perspective represents a linear complex, thus forming a bridge to the theory of hypercomplex numbers, which Steiner mentions in his response to a question by Strakosch on March 11, 1920. (For more on this subject, see Gschwind [1991], especially section 8.5, and [1986], pp. 158–161).

It is no longer possible to reconstruct whether Steiner was referring indirectly here to papers on the mechanical and elastic theory of light and was thinking of a suitable extension of or supplement to such theories from his own time. In any case, we must keep in mind that Steiner's suggestions for transforming or reformulating an ether theory for mathematics and physics must not be imagined solely in the context of a purely material and energetic phenomenology of light, see Steiner's responses to questions on March 31, 1920 (Blümel), and January 15, 1921, and the accompanying notes. From this perspective, Steiner's remarks here and in the passages that follow are not to be construed as criticizing the scientific foundations of Einstein's special theory of relativity but rather as calling for an appropriate expansion of the perspectives of physics through the methods and concepts of anthroposophical spiritual science (see also his lecture of January 6, 1923, in GA 326).

Similar-sounding remarks of Steiner's on the elastic oscillation/return of light are to be found in his lecture of December 6, 1919 (GA 194), in the teacher's" conference of September 25, 1919 (GA 300a), and in the lecture of February 16, 1924 (GA 235). Similar statements on the behavior of energy are found in the questions and answers of November 12, 1917 (GA 73).

[37]*Albert Einstein* (1879–1955), physicist in Zürich, Berlin, and Princeton, the founder of the special theory of relativity and the general theory of gravitation.

The only passage in Steiner's written works that addresses the special theory of relativity is in *The Riddles of Philosophy* (GA 18), pp. 590–593. This passage is fundamentally important for assessing all of Steiner's comments on the theory of relativity in lectures and question-and-answer sessions. To clarify Steiner's primary view on the theory of relativity, this passage will be quoted here in its entirety:

> A new direction in thinking has been stimulated by Einstein's attempt to transform fundamental concepts of physics. Until now, physics accounted for the phenomena accessible to it by imagining them arranged in empty three-dimensional space and taking place in one-dimensional time. Thus space and time were assumed to exist outside and independent of objects and events, in fixed quantities. With regard to objects, we measured distances in space, with regard to events, we measured durations in time. Distance and duration, according to this view of space and time, do not belong to the objects and events. This view now has been countered by the theory of relativity introduced by Einstein. From this perspective, the distance between two objects belongs to the objects themselves. A specific distance from another object is an attribute, a property just like any other property an object may possess. Interrelationships are inherent in objects, and outside these interrelationships there is no such thing as space. Assuming the independent existence of space makes it possible to conceive of a geometry for that space, a geometry that can be applied to the world of objects. This geometry arises in the world of pure thoughts, and objects must submit to it. We can say that relationships in the world must obey laws that were laid down in thought *before* actual objects were observed. The theory of relativity dethrones this geometry. Only objects exist, objects whose relationships can be described by means of geometry. Geometry becomes a part of physics. In that case, however, we can no longer say that the laws of geometry can be laid down *before* the objects are observed. No object has a location in space but only distances relative to other objects.

A similar assumption is made about time. No event exists at a specific point in time, it happens at a temporal distance from another event. Thus, spatial and temporal distances between interrelated objects are similar and flow together. Time becomes a fourth dimension that is similar to the three dimensions of space. An event happening to an object can be described only as taking place at a temporal and spatial distance from other events. An object's movement can be conceived of only as happening in relationship to other objects. This view alone is expected to supply faultless explanations of certain processes in physics, but assuming the existence of independent space and independent time leads to contradictory thoughts about these processes.

When we consider that many thinkers have accepted only those aspects of the natural sciences that can be presented in mathematical terms, the theory of relativity contains nothing less than the nullification of any real science of nature, because the scientific aspect of mathematics was seen as lying in its ability to ascertain the laws of space and time independent of observations of nature. Now, in contrast, natural objects and natural processes are said to determine spatial and temporal relationships, these objects and events are to provide the mathematics. The only certain factor is surrendered to uncertainty. According to this view, every thought of an essential reality that manifests its nature in existence is precluded. Everything is only in relation to something else.

To the extent that we human beings look at ourselves in the context of natural objects and processes, we will not be able to escape the conclusions of this theory of relativity. If, however, our experience of ourselves as beings prevents us from losing ourselves in mere relativities as if in a state of soul paralysis, we will no longer be permitted to seek intrinsic beingness in the domain of nature but only above and beyond nature, in the kingdom of spirit. We will not escape the theory of relativity with regard to the physical world, but it will drive us into knowledge of the spirit. The significance of the theory of relativity lies in pointing out the need for spirit knowledge that is sought by spiritual means and independently of our observations of nature. That the theory of relativity forces us to think in this way establishes its value in the evolution of our worldview.

For further discussion of the specific problems with regard to the theory of relativity addressed by this question-and-answer session, see unger [1967], chapter VIII, and Gschwind [1986] and the literature they list. See also the additions to this note in *Beiträge zur Rudolf Steiner Gesamtausgabe*, no. 114/115, Dornach, 1995.

Rudolf Steiner spoke repeatedly about the theory of relativity and apparently did not distinguish clearly between the special theory of relativity and the general theory of gravitation, which Einstein also called the general theory of relativity. The following lectures and question-and-answer sessions (Q&A) discuss or mention the theory of relativity (RT). The list does not claim to be exhaustive.

Lecture	Year	GA	Page	Keywords
November 27	1913	324a	Q&A	RT, speed
	1914	18	590–593	Einstein, RT, space, time
August 20	1915	164	251–267	speed, lumen, Einstein, Minkowski, Planck, Poincaré
April 15	1916	65	657–658	Planck's ether concept, gravity
August 21	1916	170	178–181	RT, Einstein, Lorentz
August 7	1917	176	239	RT, Einstein
August 29	1919	294	121–123	Gravity, RT, Einstein
September 25	1919	300a	92–93	RT, Einstein, Lorentz
March 1	1920	321	20–22	Einstein, RT, refraction of defraction of light
March 3	1920	321	57	Einstein, RT, fourth dimension
March 7	1920	324a	Q&A (Baravalle)	Speed of light, RT, Einstein, diffraction of light
March 7	1920	324a	Q&A (Herberg)	Mass-energy equation, Einstein
March 24	1920	73a special edition, 1950	12–13	Einstein, Lorenz, Mass/energy
March 27	1920	73a special edition, 1950	45–51	RT, ether, speed of light, Einstein, Mie, Nordström
March 31	1920	324a	Q&A	Planck's ether concept, RT, imponderable matter
April 18	1920	201	90–91	Einstein, RT
April 24	1920	201	129–131	RT, gravity, Einstein
May 1	1920	201	163	RT, mercury theory

Lecture	Year	GA	Page	Keywords
May 15	1920	201	233	Einstein, RT, gravitation
September 22	1920	300a	233	Einstein (mentioned)
October 15	1920	324a	Q&A	RT, speed, Einstein
January 15	1921	324a	Q&A	RT, Einstein (mentioned)
April 7	1921	76/324a	Q&A	RT, logic (mentioned)
April 12	1921	313	30	Ether, Einstein (mentioned)
June 27	1921	250f.		
June 28	1921	205	42–43, 51	Einstein, RT
July 8	1921	205	150–151	Einstein, RT, logic
August 7	1921	206	110	Einstein, RT (mentioned)
October 14	1921	339	74	Einstein, RT (mentioned)
October 15	1921	207	168–169	RT (mentioned)
November 4	1921	208	137	Einstein, RT (mentioned)
December 31	1921	209	186	Einstein (mentioned)
March 15	1922	300b	77	Einstein (mentioned)
April 12	1922	82/324a	Q&A	RT, Einstein, absolutes
December 27	1922	326	68	RT, Newton (mentioned)
January 2	1923	326	113	RT (mentioned)
July 28	1923	228	25–30	RT, Einstein, light
July 29	1923	228	52–53	RT, Einstein, gravity
July 29	1923	291	209–210	RT, Einstein, gravity
September 15	1923	291	126–127	RT, Einstein
November 16	1923	319	Q&A, 141	RT, properties
January 2	1924	316	25	RT (mentioned)
February 20	1924	352	Q&A, 152	Einstein, RT
February 27	1924	352	175–191	Einstein, RT, Copernicus, astronomy
March 1	1924	235	84–85	RT (mentioned)
April 16	1924	309	64	RT, Einstein (mentioned)
April 30	1924	300c	159–160	RT
May 17	1924	353	248	RT (mentioned), astronomy
July 20	1924	310	75v76	RT, Einstein, sound
July 22	1924	310	116	RT (mentioned)
August 19	1924	311	120–121	RT, Einstein

[38] This passage makes it clear that Rudolf Steiner's criticism of Einstein's thoughts does not have to do with their scientific foundation but rather with the fact that they have been applied to contexts and domains of life that are no longer solely attributable to physics as an inorganic science.

[39] The British astronomer and astrophysicist *Arthur Eddington* (1882–1944) undertook an experimental test of Einstein's prediction that light rays are influenced by gravitational fields (gravitational aberration). The test was to

measure the change in apparent location of fixed stars close to the Sun during a solar eclipse. Two British expeditions (one to the western coast of Africa, the other to northern Brazil) were assigned to photograph the environs of the Sun during the solar eclipse of May 29, 1919, and compare them to the known locations of the stars. The result was published on November 6, 1919, and proclaimed as a triumph for Einstein's theory. The deviation at the edge of the Sun, as Einstein's theory predicted, was approximately 1.75 seconds of an arc. Questions immediately arose as to whether the accuracy of the results was sufficient to confirm Einstein's theory. Steiner's objection, however, may have less to do with the inaccuracy of his contemporaries' measuring techniques, which were later superseded as this experiment and others were repeated, than with a question of principle, namely, whether even very precise quantitative experimental confirmations of a theoretical mathematical model constitute an adequate guarantee that the model is true or corresponds to reality.

In his commentary on Goethe's natural scientific works *Geschichte der Farbenlehre, Erster Teil, Sechste Abteilung. Newtons Persönlichkeit*, Steiner writes about this problem: "Mathematical judgments, like any others, are the results of certain presuppositions that must be assumed to be true. But in order to apply these presuppositions correctly to experience, the experience must correspond to the conclusions that result. We cannot draw the opposite conclusion, however. An empirical fact may correspond very well to mathematical conclusions that we have arrived at, and yet in reality the presuppositions that apply may not be those of mathematical scientific research. For example, the fact that the phenomena of interference and light refraction coincide with the conclusions of the wave theory of light does not mean that the latter must be true. It is completely wrong to assume that a hypothesis must be correct if empirical facts can be explained by it. The same effects may be due to different causes, and the justification for the presuppositions we accept must be proved *directly*, not in a roundabout way by using consequences to confirm them." *(Goethean Science,* edited by Rudolf Steiner, volume 4, GA1d.)

[40]See Einstein, *The Principle of Relativity* [1911]:

The situation is most comical when we imagine causing this clock to fly off at a constant high speed (almost equal to c) and in a constant direction. After it has covered a great distance, we then give it an impulse in the opposite direction, so that it returns to the point where it was originally thrown out into space. We then discover that the hands have scarcely moved at all during its entire trip, whereas the hands of an identical clock, which remained motionless at the starting point for the entire time, have moved considerably. We must add that what is true of this clock, which we have introduced as a simple representative of all events in physics, also applies to any other self-contained physical system. For example, a living organism that we place in a box and subject to the same motion as the clock would be relatively unchanged on returning to its starting point after the flight, while a similar organism that remained in the same place would have made way for new generations a long time ago. For an organism moving at approximately the speed of light, the long traveling time would amount to only a moment. This is an irrefutable consequence of the underlying principles that experience imposes on us....

The theory of relativity has several important conclusions for physics that must be mentioned here. We saw that according to the theory of relativity, a moving clock runs slower than an identical clock that is not moving. We will probably never be able to use a pocket watch to verify this statement, because the speeds that can be imparted to a watch are minuscule in comparison to the speed of light. Nature, however, does provide objects that are clocklike in character and that can be made to move extremely rapidly, namely, atoms that give off spectral lines. Through the use of an electrical field, these atoms can achieve speeds of several thousand kilometers (channel rays). According to the theory, it is to be expected that the influence of these atoms' movement on their frequency of oscillation is similar to what we deduced with regard to the moving clock.

Clearly, Einstein does not hesitate to extend his theories, which are based purely on considerations belonging to the field of physics, to objects not belonging to that field alone. Thus he claims implicitly that the theory of relativity does not encompass simply systems belonging to the field of physics in the narrower sense but that the entire cosmos underlies his theory. This relatively indiscriminate view is the primary reason for Steiner's harsh objections to what he calls the abstractness and lack of reality of Einstein's thinking.

That Einstein really chose not to recognize any significant difference between the different domains of reality is evident from a contemporary report by *Rudolf Lämmel* (1879–1971), a physicist and ardent popularizer of Einstein's theory of relativity. In his book *Die Grundlagen der Relativitätstheorie* [1921], Lämmel says:

The strangest consequence of these new ideas of the theory of relativity is this: distances are shorter for observers at rest than for those who travel them. Similarly, elapsed time seems longer for an observer "at rest" than for one who is traveling with the clock ... Thus, if we send an expedition out into space today, traveling at half the speed of light, when the travelers return at the same speed after an 11 1/2 year absence, they will ascertain that they spent *exactly ten* years en route.... Thus the questions "How long is this distance?" and "How long is this duration" no longer can be answered in absolute terms but only with regard to specific observers, that is, relatively. This insight is no mere philosophical remark, but a mathematically confirmed relationship.

In his Zurich lectures to the Physicalischen Gesellschaft (Society for Physics) and the Naturforschenden Gesellschaft (Society for Scientific Research), Einstein took up the above example of the duration of a space trip and concluded that under certain circumstances, the explorers might find on their return that their former contemporaries had aged considerably, while they themselves had been traveling for only a few years. This author objected to Einstein's claim and stated that the conclusion applied to units of measurement and to clocks, but not to living beings. Einstein, however, replied that ultimately all processes taking place in our blood, nerves, and so on, are periodic oscillations and therefore movements. Since the principle of relativity applies to all movements, the conclusion about unequal aging is admissible! ... (p. 84 f).

For more on the debate about the theory of relativity during the first few decades of the twentieth century, see Hentschel's thorough study [1990].

[41]The issue here later became known as the "paradox of the clocks" or "paradox of the twins." See the comparable passage in the questions and answers of october 15, 1920.

[42]See Note 36 on ether theory.

[43]See Steiner's thorough explanation in his lecture of August 20, 1915 (GA 164). If the formula $s = c \times t$ is interpreted as an equation of quantities: it is unavoidable to conclude that t is of a different dimension from s and c. In any case, t is certainly not without dimension and that is not what Steiner meant, because the result would be meaningless in the dimensional calculus of physics. Steiner's intent is not to correct the dimensional calculus but rather to point out the problem of the reality of the quantities and

calculations that appear in physics. In this sense, no *reality* can be attributed to the quantity *t*, though in formulas it must appear to have a specific dimensionality. "Time" *t* is not a dimensionless factor but a factor with no reality—that is, a pure number with no reality.

[44] See the following comparable passages on speed as a reality: questions and answers of November 27, 1913, lectures of August 20, 1915 (GA 164), December 6, 1919, December 27, 1919, and January 2, 1920 (GA 320), questions and answers of october 15, 1920, and the lecture of January 6, 1923 (GA 326).

[45] On this point, see Rudolf Steiner's *Einleitungen zu Goethes Naturwissenschaftlichen Schriften* ("Introductions to Goethe's Natural Scientific Writings") (GA 1), chapter XVI.2, "Das Urphänomen" ("The Archetypal Phenomenon").

[46] Steiner is referring here to unprotected movement through the air, not to travel in airplanes or similar vehicles. See the comparable passages in his lectures of August 7, 1917 (GA 176), September 25, 1919 (GA 300a), June 27, 1921 (GA 250f), June 28, 1921 (GA 205), April 30, 1924 (GA 300c), and July 20, 1924 (GA 310).

[47] Answers to questions raised by Georg Herberg during the lecture cycle *Geisteswissenschaftliche Impulse zur Entwickelung der Physik: Zweiter Naturwissenschaftlicher Kurs* ('Spiritual Scientific Impulses for the Evolution of Physics: Second Scientific Course") (GA 321).

[48] The date of this question-and-answer session cannot be ascertained with certainty on the basis of documents in the Rudolf Steiner archives. It is unlikely that the questions date from March 13, 1920—the time ascribed to them by Hans Schmidt in his book *Das Vortragswerk Rudolf Steiners* ("The Lectures of Rudolf Steiner"), Dornach, 1978, expanded second edition, p. 319—because the theory of relativity was not mentioned in either Steiner's lecture on that date or Eugen Kolisko's lecture on "hypothesis-free chemistry" on the same day. Steiner's approach to the question suggests that it may belong to the previous question-and-answer session (March 7, 1920), which took place after Hermann von Baravalle's lecture on the theory of relativity.

[49] The word *rotation* in the transcript of the document seems meaningless in this context and has been replaced by *radiation*.

[50] Steiner is referring here to the phenomenon of electrical conductance in rarefied gases and, in particular, to cathode rays—that is, to streams of high-speed electrons emitted from the cathode of a vacuum tube. Steiner's

remarks coincide with the standard thinking of physicists on the subject.

The kinetic energy $\frac{1}{2}mv^2 = eU$ that is imparted to the individual electrons (with the charge e) by an electrical field of voltage U plays a determining role in all calculations related to cathode rays. Furthermore, the force K (Lorentz force) with which a charge e is deflected in a magnetic field B is a function of the speed v:

$$K = evB.$$

On the subject of cathode rays, see also Steiner's lecture of January 2, 1920 (GA 320).

[51] Einstein's formula $E = mc^2$ establishes the proportionality of energy and inert matter. It is often called the most important result of the special theory of relativity. As is the case with other basic formulas in physics, there are no real proofs, but at best certain justifications (see below) of the formula $E = mc^2$. Thus, this formula is seen as a postulate underlying relativistic physics.

According to Einstein [1917], §15, where c is the speed of light, the kinetic energy of a body with a resting mass m moving at a speed v is

$$E_{kin} = \frac{mc^2}{\sqrt{1 - v^2/c^2}}$$

If we develop the relativistic term Ekin for kinetic energy in a series, the result is

$$E_{kin} = mc^2 + \tfrac{1}{2}mv^2 - \tfrac{3}{8}\frac{mv^4}{c^2} + \cdots$$

If $v \ll c$, the term remaining in the non-relativistic borderline case $v/c \to 0$ is $mc^2 + \tfrac{1}{2}mv^2$. Thus, the resting energy mc^2 must be added to the ordinary kinetic energy $\tfrac{1}{2}mv^2$ if non-relativistic mechanics is to result (as the borderline case $v/c \to 0$) from relativistic mechanics. This changes nothing in non-relativistic mechanics, because mc^2 is an unchangeable constant that influences only the conventionally determined null point on the energy scale.

[52] This passage in the transcript reads "... mass and energy are only a new disguise for the old formula, p.g. energy." It has not been possible to reconstruct the meaning of this formula, if indeed it was correctly recorded. What is intended here is probably the formula for the potential energy U of a body of mass m in the gravitational field: where g is the gravitational constant and z the z-coordinate. In fact, the thoughts presented in Note 40

show that $E = mc^2$ plays the role of a potential energy of sorts (resting energy), though it is not directly significant for calculations in non-relativistic mechanics.

$$U = mgz.$$

[53] If p is interpreted as force in the sense of *potentia*, the formula $W = p \times s$ represents the work W of an unchanging force p over a distance of s.

[54] Questions posed by *Ernst Blümel* (1884–1952) after his lecture "Über das Imaginäre und den Begriff des Unendlichen und Unmöglichen" ("On the Domain of the Imaginary and the Concepts of Infinity and Impossibility") on March 11, 1920. Blümel taught mathematics in the school of continuing education at the Goetheanum in Dornach and in the first Waldorf School in Stuttgart. To date, no transcript of his lecture has been found.

[55] *Ernst Müller* (1884–1954), mathematician, author, and Hebraic and cabalistic scholar, gave a lecture on "Methoden der Mathematik" ("The Methods of Mathematics") in Stuttgart on March 8, 1920. To date, neither a transcript of Müller's lecture nor a record of Steiner's answer to his question has been found.

[56] For further discussion of the metamorphosis of long bones into head bones, see also Steiner's lectures of September 1, 1919 (GA 293), April 10, 1920 (GA 201), and January 1, 10, 11, 15, and 17, 1921 (GA 323).

[57] On the reality of imaginary numbers, see also Steiner's lectures of March 12, 1920 (GA 321), and January 18, 1921 (GA 323).

[58] Lectures on physics: Rudolf Steiner, *Geisteswissenschaftliche Impulse zur Entwickelung der Physik: Zweiter Naturwissenschaftlicher Kurs, Die Wärme auf der Grenze Positiver und Negativer Materialität* ("Spiritual Scientific Impulses for the Evolution of Physics: Second Natural Scientific Course. Warmth on the Boundary Between Positive and Negative Matter") (GA 321). See especially the lectures of March 10 and 11, 1920.

[59] Compare the passage that follows with Steiner's lectures of March 12 and 14, 1920 (GA 321). A collection of materials on an experiment in bending the spectrum using a strong magnet can be found in *Beiträge zur Rudolf Steiner Gesamtausgabe* ("Articles on Rudolf Steiner's *Complete Works*"), vol. 95/96, 1987.

[60]A variant of the text reads "The red moves outward toward the position/situation/layer," which makes no sense in either English or German.

[61]See Steiner's explanations of the ether and negative space in his lectures of January 8, 15, and 18, 1921 (GA 323), the question-and-answer session of April 7, 1921 (GA 76), the lectures of April 8 and 9, 1922 (GA 82), and the questions and answers of April 12, 1922 (GA 82).

[62]In a lecture given on May 11, 1917 (GA 174b), Rudolf Steiner tells of a related personal experience during a class at the university of Vienna. According to Steiner's account, *Leo Königsberger* (1837–1921), a well-known mathematician of the day, rejected the concept of hypercomplex numbers because they would lead to zero factors (see Note 18). Just as complex numbers were slow to gain recognition, hyperimaginary or hypercomplex numbers were only reluctantly accepted by mathematicians. The difference of opinion between adherents of the calculus of quaternions dating back to *William Rowan Hamilton* (1805–1865) and advocates of the vector analysis developed by *Oliver Heaviside* (1850–1925) and *Josiah Gibbs* (1839–1903) formed the background of the debate Rudolf Steiner alludes to here. Vector analysis initially gained the upper hand in practical applications because of the progress in theoretical physics that accompanied its development. At approximately the same time, however, the development of abstract algebra led to the discovery and classification of different systems of hypercomplex numbers.

For more information on the above-mentioned debate, see Schouten [1914] (introduction) and Crowe [1967]. on the history of the discovery and refinement of hypercomplex number systems, see Van der Waerden [1985], on the mathematics of hypercomplex numbers, see Ebbinghaus etal. [1988], Part B. These and other generalized number systems have many applications in modern theoretical physics, see Gschwind [1991] and the bibliography to his book.

[63]In his lecture of May 11, 1917 (GA 174b), Rudolf Steiner reports becoming aware of the mathematical problem of zero factors during a lecture by Leo Königsberger. Zero factors are generalized numbers whose product is zero, though the factors themselves are not equal to zero. Königsberger mentions this problem in the first lecture in his book *Vorlesungen über die Theorie der elliptischen Funktionen* ("Lectures on the Theory of Elliptical Functions") [1874], pp. 10–12, where he says of the existence of hypercomplex numbers, "Assuming that the validity of common rules of calculation for all arithmetic quantities remains a

condition that must be met, if quantities of this sort can be incorporated into pure arithmetic, calculations that involve them and that are carried out according to the rules established for the numbers discussed earlier must lead to results that do not contradict the main propositions/ theorems of arithmetic that have been discovered for real and complex imaginary numbers. Thus, according to the rules for multipart expressions, multiplying two numbers of the same type must yield a number of the same type, and the product cannot disappear unless one of the factors becomes zero."

The passage that follows demonstrates concretely that the product of two such hypercomplex numbers can indeed disappear without one of the factors being zero, "which contradicts the basic rule for real numbers that a product of zero results only when one of the factors disappears." Later, Steiner received a copy of oskar Simony's paper *Über zwei universelle Verallgemeinerungen der algebraischen Grundoperationen* ("On Two Universal Generalizations of Basic Algebraic Operations") [1885] with a personal dedication by the author. Simony discusses the problem of the existence of zero factors at the very beginning of this article, which is devoted to the concrete construction of two systems of hypercomplex numbers, one of which includes zero factors ([1885], §8). Additional material on this subject can be found in *Beiträge zur Rudolf Steiner Gesamtausgabe* ("Articles on Rudolf Steiner's Complete Works"), vol. 114/115, Dornach, 1995, p. 5. Schouten's work [1914], also with a personal dedication to Rudolf Steiner, includes an introduction to hypercomplex number systems (which Schouten calls associative systems), zero factors are mentioned on p. 15.

[64] See Gschwind's investigations [1991] and list of references for further reading.

[65] The typed transcript reads "rotational parallelepopods," a term that does not exist in mathematics and that is probably due to an error in transcription. It seems unlikely from the context that the term "parallelopipeds" was intended. In all the transcripts the archives have received, the term "parallelepopods" is crossed out and replaced by "paraboloids" (in handwriting). Rotational paraboloids are surfaces that result from the rotation of a parabola around its axis of symmetry. This interpretation of the transcript presents the problem of how to relate such a surface to rotating cones. Without going into the problem in greater detail, Gschwind [1991] had good reasons for deciding on this wording and based important and fruitful conclusions on it. Specifically, he demonstrated a relationship between such surfaces and hypercomplex numbers. Exhaustive supplementary material can be found in *Beiträge zur Rudolf Steiner*

Gesamtausgabe ("Articles on Rudolf Steiner's Complete Works"), vol. 114/115, Dornach, 1995, pp. 5-7.

[66]Presumably Rudolf Steiner is referring here to the problem in number theory of finding whole numbers that can replace *a*, *b*, and *c* in the equation $a^2 + b^2 = c^2$. Such numbers are known as *Pythagorean triplets*. Algorithms for finding all possible solutions to this equation—that is, all possible Pythagorean triplets—have been known since antiquity.

[67]Rudolf Steiner's call for establishing the foundations of arithmetic and algebra independent of geometry had already been taken up at the end of the nineteenth century, when the tendency to arithmeticize mathematics sometimes went so far that it threatened to displace geometry. It was one of the most important mathematical accomplishments of the early twentieth century, though initially it remained an internal issue in the field of mathematics. Some time elapsed before this development found its way into textbooks and the teaching of mathematics.

[68]*Carl Friedrich Gauss* (1777–1855), mathematician in Göttingen who explained negative numbers as simply the opposites of positive numbers. He presented his general views on the subject in his *Theoria Residuorum Biquadraticorum* [1831], pp. 175ff: "Positive and negative numbers can be applied only where the union of a quantity and its opposite eradicates that quantity. Precisely speaking, this prerequisite does not apply when substances (that is, objects that can be imagined as standing on their own) are involved but only in relationships between objects that are enumerated. It is postulated that these objects are arranged in a series, such as *A*, *B*, *C*, *D*, …, and that the relationship of *A* to *B* can be considered the same as that of *B* to *C*, and so on. In this case, the concept of opposites means nothing more than reversing the members in a relationship, so that if the relationship between (or transition from) *A* to *B* is + 1, the relationship of *B* to *A* can be described as -1. Inasmuch as such a series has no limits in either direction, each real whole number represents the relationship between a member that has been selected arbitrarily as the beginning and another specified member of the series." See also the discussion in Kowol [1990], pp. 88ff.

[69]Eugen Dühring (1833–1921), philosopher and author of books on political economy. See especially the book he coauthored with his son ulrich [1884], which contains harsh criticism of Gauss' definition of negative numbers. According to the Dührings, the contrast or opposition that characterizes negative numbers results from unimplemented

subtraction, which they view as the only essential aspect of negative numbers. See [1884], p. 16: "The incisive characteristic of an isolated negative number, however, is that it not only results from a numerical operation in which subtraction cannot be carried out but also points to an operation in which subtraction can be implemented. We must carefully distinguish between these two operations—or, if you will, these two parts of a general operation." For a comparison between Gauss' and Dühring's views on negative numbers, see Kowol [1990], p. 88 ff.

[70] On Dühring's view of imaginary numbers, see E. and U. Dühring [1884], Chapters 2–4, and 13. A discussion of Dühring's thoughts compared with other attempts to deal with this issue can be found in Kowol [1990], pp. 118ff. and 122ff.

[71] See E. and U. Dühring [1884], Chapters 4, 12, 14, and 15.

[72] Question-and-answer session during the lecture cycle *Geisteswissenschaftliche Impulse zur Entwickelung der Physik: Zweiter Naturwissenschaflicher Kurs* ("Spiritual Scientific Impulses for the Development of Physics: Second Scientific Course") (GA 321). *Alexander Strakosch* (1879–1958), railway engineer and teacher at the first Waldorf School in Stuttgart, asked these questions after giving a lecture on "Mathematical Figures as an Intermediate Link Between Archetype and Copy" in Stuttgart, March 11, 1920. To date no transcript of his lecture has been found.

[73] on the relationship between archetype and image in the context of mathematics, see also Rudolf Steiner's essay on "Mathematics and Occultism" in *Philosophy and Anthroposophy* (GA 35).

[74] In the lecture of March 5, 1920 (GA 321). For further discussion of the evolution of geometric and mathematical views arising out of the will nature of the human being, see also Rudolf Steiner's lectures of January 3, 1920 (GA 320), September 29, 1920 (GA 322), March 16, 1921 (GA 324), and December 26, 1922 (GA 326).

[75] For a further discussion of fluid or mobile geometry, see also Rudolf Steiner's lecture of January 20, 1914 (GA 151).

[76] For more on the relationships between the planes or regions of the spiritual world and the higher dimensions, see also Rudolf Steiner's lectures of May 17 and June 7, 1905, the question-and-answer sessions of April 7, 1921 (GA 76) and April 12, 1922 (GA 82), and the lectures of August 19, 20, 22, and 26, 1923 (GA 227).

Ernst Blümel (1884–1952), mathematician and teacher. See Renatus Ziegler's

Notizen zur Biographie des Mathematikers und Lehrers Ernst Blümel ("Notes on the Biography of Ernst Blümel, Mathematician and Teacher"), Dornach, 1995, in *Arbeitshefte der Mathematisch-Astronomischen Sektion am Goetheanum, Kleine Reihe, Heft 1* ("Working Papers of the Section for Mathematics and Astronomy at the Goetheanum, Short Series, No. 1").

[77] Question-and-answer session after *Eugen Kolisko's* lecture on "Anthroposophy and Chemistry" during the conference on "Anthroposophy and the Specialized Sciences" held at the Goetheanum in Dornach from March 21 to April 7, 1920. *Eugen Kolisko* (1893–1939) was a physician and taught at the first Waldorf School in Stuttgart. To date, no transcript of his lecture has been discovered. See the brief report on the conference in the journal *Dreigliederung des sozialen Organismus* ("The Threefolding of the Social Organism"), vol. 1, 1919/1920, no. 45.

[78] Goethe, *Zur Farbenlehre* ("On Color Theory") [1810] and *Der Versuch als Vermittler von Objekt und Subjekt* ("The Experiment as Mediator Between Object and Subject") [1823]. See Rudolf Steiner's *Einleitungen zu Goethe's Naturwissenschaftlichen Schriften* ("Introduction to Goethe's Natural Scientific Works," GA 1), chapters X and XVI, *Grundlinien einer Erkenntnistheorie der Goetheschen Weltanschauung* ("outline of an Epistemology of the Goethean Worldview," GA 2), chapter 15, and the chapter in Goethe's *Weltanschauung* ("Goethe's Worldview," GA 6) entitled *Die Erscheinungen der Farbenwelt* ("The Phenomena of the World of Color").

[79] The discovery of non-Euclidean geometries showed that Euclidean geometry was not the only imaginable geometry. As a result, the question of which type of geometry applies to the space we experience became an epistemological problem for the sciences. For more on the impact of the discovery of non-Euclidean geometries, see also Rudolf Steiner's lectures of August 26, 1910 (GA 125), October 20, 1910 (GA 60), January 3, 1920 (GA 320), March 27, 1920 (GA 73a), January 1 and 7, 1921 (GA 323), and April 5, 1921 (GA 76). On the importance of the discovery of non-Euclidean geometry in the history of consciousness, see Ziegler [1987]. On the history of this discovery, see Bonola/Liebmann [1919], Klein [1926], chapter 4, and Reichardt [1976]. on the relationships of axioms, archetypal phenomena, and experience, see Ziegler [1992], chapters VII and VIII.

[80] In an *elliptical geometry* such as Riemann's (Riemann [1867]), the rate of curvature of measurement is greater than 1, and the sum of the angles of a triangle is always greater than 180°. In *hyperbolic geometry*, the rate of

curvature of measurement is less than 1, and the sum of the angles of a triangle is always less than 180°. The relationship of spaces or manifolds with a constant curvature to non-Euclidean geometries was discovered by *Eugenio Beltrami* (1835–1900) and *Bernhard Riemann* (1826–1866). In contrast to Euclidean geometry (Pythagorean theorem), the measurement of such a space is determined by a function of the coordinates. In general, this function is no longer a sum of squares. On this subject, see Klein [1927], chapter 3C, and Scholz [1980], chapter III.

[81] See Simony [1888b], §5, [1883], and [1886].

[82] Questions and answers after Karl Stockmeyer's lecture on "Anthroposophy and Physics" during the conference on "Anthroposophy and the Specialized Sciences" held at the Goetheanum in Dornach from March 21 to April 7, 1920. *Ernst August Karl Stockmeyer* (1886–1963) was a teacher at the first Waldorf School in Stuttgart. To date, no transcript of his lecture has been discovered. See the brief report on the conference in the journal *Dreigliederung des sozialen Organismus* ("The Threefolding of the Social Organism"), vol. 1, 1919/1920, no. 45.

[83] See the questions and answers of March 30, 1920, and Steiner's lectures of March 27, 1920 (GA 73a), and January 3, 1920 (GA 320).

[84] *Bernhard Riemann* (1826–1866), whom Steiner mentions repeatedly, typifies this trend. See also Note 1, Lecture 1 (March 24, 1905) on Bolyai, Gauss, and Riemann.

[85] See the beginning of the question-and-answer session on March 11, 1920 (E. Blümel's questions) and related notes.

[86] See the question-and-answer session of March 1, 1920.

[87] Goethe says at the very beginning of the Preface to his *Zur Farbenlehre* ("On Color Theory") [1810]:

When the subject of color is addressed, the very natural question arises of whether light should be discussed first and foremost. The brief and honest response to this question is that so much has been said about light, and so often, that it seems questionable to repeat or add to what has been said.

For, in fact, our attempts to express the essential nature of light are in vain. We become aware of the effects of a being, and a complete account of them probably does encompass its essential nature. Our efforts to describe a person's character are all in vain, but if we present all of his actions and deeds, a picture of his character will emerge.

Colors are the deeds of light, its deeds and sufferings. In this sense, we can expect them to yield conclusions about light. Colors and light are related very precisely, but we must think of both of them as belonging to all of Nature, because through them Nature and Nature alone attempts to reveal itself to the sense of sight.

[88] The editors of the German version, noting that the context requires a meaning of "control" or "understanding," substituted the word *Beherrschung* (control), here and elsewhere in the lecture for *Beharrung* (perseverance), which appeared consistently in the typescript of the stenographic notes.

[89] See also Rudolf Steiner's lecture of March 30, 1920 (GA 312), and the question-and-answer session that took place on the same date.

[90] Goethe, *Zur Farbenlehre* ("On Color Theory") [1810], section 6, *Sinnlich-sittliche Wirkung der Farbe* ("The Sensory-Moral Effect of Color"), §758–920.

[91] *Max Planck* (1858–1947), theoretical physicist in Munich, Kiel, and Berlin. The hypothesis of a quasimaterial ether that served as the medium for light processes and electrical phenomena had its roots in the thinking of *Isaac Newton* (1642–1727) and René Descartes (1596–1650). This qualitative type of ether made it possible to interpret processes whose more precise mechanisms were not yet understood. The chief characteristic of nineteenth-century ether hypotheses was quantifiability, which made it possible to incorporate such processes concretely into mathematical theories on the phenomena of physics. See also the beginning of the question-and-answer session of March 7, 1920, and the corresponding notes.

The exact wording of Planck's formulation has not been found. Planck [1910] emphasizes, however, "I believe that I will not encounter any serious opposition among physicists when I summarize this position as follows: Presupposing that the simple Maxwell-Hertz differential equations are fully valid for electrodynamic processes in pure ether excludes the possibility of explaining them mechanically" (p. 37). Later he says, "similarly, it is certainly correct to state that the first step in discovering [Einstein's] *principle of relativity* coincides with the question of what relationships must exist between natural forces if it is impossible to ascribe any material properties to the light ether—that is, if light waves replicate through space without any connection to a material vehicle. In that case, of course, it would be impossible to define—let alone measure—the speed of a moving body with regard to the light ether. I need not emphasize that the mechanical view of nature is virtually incompatible with this view. Thus, anyone who sees this view as a postulate of the thinking of physics will never be comfortable with the theory of relativity. Those who are more flexible in their judgments, however, will first ask where this principle leads us" (p. 39).

[92] See the question-and-answer session of March 7, 1920, and the corresponding notes.

[93] Compare this and the following passages to the question-and-answer sessions of March 11, 1920 (Blümel), and January 15, 1921, and to the corresponding notes.

[94] Comments about the debate surrounding the concept of negative numbers can be found at the end of the question-and-answer session of March 11, 1920 (Blümel). See Kowol [1990], chapter IV. B.

[95] Question-and-answer session during a "conversation on spiritual science" in the context of the anthroposophical conference of September 26 to october 16, 1920, at the Goetheanum in Dornach. Rudolf Steiner's introductory lectures on *Grenzen der Naturerkenntnis* ("The Limits of Our Understanding of Nature") were held from September 27 to october 3, 1920, and appeared in GA 322. Many lectures by other participants were printed in *Aenigmatisches aus Kunst und Wissenschaft* ("Enigmatic Aspects of Art and Science"), vols. I and II, Stuttgart, Der Kommende Tag Verlag 1922 (available from the Goetheanum bookstore), or in *Kultur und Erziehung* ("Culture and Education"), Stuttgart, Der Kommende Tag Verlag, 1921 (available from the Goetheanum bookstore). See also the announcement of the conference, which includes a detailed program, in the periodical *Dreigliederung des sozialen Organismus* ("The Threefolding of the Social Organism"), vol.2, 1920/1921, no. 9. Reports on this conference by Alexander Strakosch and Günther Wachsmuth appeared in the same periodical (nos. 15, 16, and 18).

[96] According to Ptolemy (*Claudius Ptolemeus, ca.* 100–170 A.D.), the basic structure of the solar system was classically geocentric, with the resting Earth in its center. In his chief work, *Almagest,* Ptolemy uses a complicated construction of concentric circles to explain the details of planetary movements. (See Ptolemy [1962], Ziegler [1976], Teichmann [1983], chapter 3.2, Van der Waerden [1988, chapter XIX.]) With regard to planetary orbits that result from combinations of circular movements,

nothing essential is changed by shifting from the geocentric Ptolemaic system to the heliocentric Copernican system, except that the Sun and the Earth exchange places, which corresponds to a simple geometric transformation. Furthermore, both Ptolemy's and Copernicus's arguments are essentially kinematic (Steiner would have said "phoronomic")—that is, they do not take force relationships into account. See Vreede [1980], *"Über das kopernikansiche System"* ("On the Copernican System"), pp. 349–359, Teichmann [1983], chapter 3, and Neugebauer [1983], section 40.

In his chief work *De Revolutionibus Orbium Coelestium*, 1543, volume 1, chapter 11, *Nicolas Copernicus* (1473–1543) separates the movement of the Earth into three components (see Copernicus [1879], pp. 28ff or [1990], pp. 139ff.). The first movement is the Earth's daily rotation around its axis, the second is its movement in an eccentric orbit around the Sun, and the third is its "movement in declination." Copernicus formulates it like this:

> Since so many important planetary phenomena testify that the Earth moves, we will describe this movement in general terms, inasmuch as it confirms the phenomena, like a hypothesis. We must assume that this movement is threefold: the first movement, which the Greeks called *nychthemerinon, daily-nightly*, is the actual circulation of day and night, which moves around the Earth's axis from west to east in the same way that we formerly believed the Earth to move in the opposite sense. This circulation defines the equinoctial circle or equator, which some call the *circle of equal days* in imitation of the Greeks, who called it *isemerinos, of equal days*. The second is the yearly movement of the center, the Earth and its satellite through the zodiac around the Sun from west to east—that is, in direct motion—between Venus and Mars. The result of this movement, as we said, is that the Sun itself seems to make a similar movement through the zodiac, so that when the Earth (the central point) is moving through Capricorn, Aquarius, and so forth, the Sun appears to be moving through Cancer, Leo, and so on. We must imagine that the slant of the equator and of the Earth's axis varies in relationship to the plane of the circle that passes through the center of the zodiac signs. If the slant were constant and only the midpoint (the Earth) moved no change in the length of days and nights would occur and we would have always either the summer solstice or the winter solstice or an equinox—in any case, an unchanging season. Thus, the third movement, or movement of declination, occurs in a yearly cycle but in the opposite direction from the movement of the midpoint (the Earth). As a result of these two almost equal but opposite movements, the Earth's axis, and thus

also the equator—the greatest parallel circle—remain pointing to almost the same area of the heavens, as if they were immobile, while the Sun, because of the progressive movement of the Earth's center, seems to move through the oblique plane of the zodiac in a way that is no different from what it would do if the Earth were the center of the solar system, if we only remember that the Sun's distance from the Earth in the sphere of fixed stars has already exceeded our perceptive capacity (Copernicus [1879], p. 28ff).

Rudolf Steiner seems to have reversed the order of the first two laws of Copernicus's *De Revolutionibus*. The above sequence, however, is the one Copernicus also uses in discussing the three movements of the Earth in *De Hypothesibus Motuum Coelestium a se Constitutus Commentariolus*, also called simply *Commentariolus*, published in 1514. (See Copernicus [1948], pp. 12ff, or [1990], pp 9ff.) In the passages that follow, we have preserved Steiner's sequence:

1. The Earth's annual movement around the Sun in an eccentric orbit
2. The Earth's daily rotation around its axis
3. Movement in declination: the Earth's axis describes a cone, moving in the opposite direction from its revolution around the Sun.

> [97]In a geometric or kinematic sense, the first movement (if considered in isolation, disregarding the second and third movements) is the Earth's revolution around the Sun. Note that the Earth's axis does not remain parallel to itself—except in a special instance when the axis is parallel to the axis of rotation, which is not the case here. Instead, it describes a cone in relationship to the Earth's midpoint. In other words, the intersection of the extension of the Earth's axis with a line perpendicular to the plane of the Earth's eccentric orbit around the Sun is a fixed point of this movement. If this movement existed in isolation, there would be no change of seasons, because the Earth's position in relationship to the Sun would always be the same.

Consequently, Copernicus had to introduce another movement to account for the phenomenon of changing seasons, on the one hand, and precession (shifting of the vernal equinox), on the other. His "movement in declination," the third movement in Steiner's sequence, served this purpose. This movement consists of the yearly rotation of the Earth's axis in the opposite direction from its movement around the Sun. It negates the rotation of the Earth's access created by the second movement, and a slight excess accounts for precession.

[98] In 1783 at the latest, the fact that the Sun itself also moves was acknowledged when *William Herschel* (1738–1822) discovered its movement (called the *apex movement*) in the direction of the constellation Hercules. (See Wolf [1891–1893], §292.)

[99] Rudolf Steiner often spoke of the spiral or screwlike movement of the Earth as it follows the movement of the Sun, see the lectures of March 24 and 31, 1905, for example. Beginning with his lecture of September 1, 1906 (GA 95), he often links the third Copernican movement to his own description of the problem of the Sun and Earth's motion. From 1916 on, he adds the aspect of a progressive lemniscatic quality of movement. (For a general overview of this problem, see Vreede [1980], *"Über das Kopernikanische System"* ["On the Copernican System"], p. 349ff.)

The following list includes most of the lectures and question-and-answer sessions (Q&A) in which Steiner discusses the problem of the Sun and Earth's motion, especially the third Copernican movement (Copernicus 3), Bessel's corrections (Bessel), and / or the problem of spiral or lemniscatic (∞) movements of the Sun and Earth. Especially important and thorough presentations include those of october 1, 1916 (GA 171), April 10, 1920 (GA 201), and January 2 and 17, 1921 (GA 323).

Lecture	Year	GA	Contents
March 24	1905	324a	Screwlike line
March 31	1905	324a	Screwlike line
September 1	1906	95	Copernicus 3
September 16	1907	101, GA284/285	Copernicus 3
April 29	1908	98	Copernicus 3, screwlike line
November 7	1910	124	
March 21	1913	145	Screw-like line
May 5	1914	286	Blood circulation and heart
July 13	1915	159	Blood circulation and heart
August 20	1916	272	Copernicus 3
October 1	1916	171	∞
May 28	1918	181	Copernicus 3, Bessel
September 4	1919	295	Copernicus 3, Bessel
September 25	1919	300a	Copernicus 3, Bessel
September 26	1919	300a	Spiral
September 28	1919	192	Copernicus 3, Bessel
October 3	1919	261	Copernicus 3, Bessel
October 3	1919	191	Copernicus 3, Bessel
April 10	1920	201	Progressive spiral
April 11	1920	201	Blood circulation and heart
April 18	1920	201	∞, Copernicus 3
May 1	1920	201	Bessel, progressive lemniscate
May 2	1920	201	Progressive lemniscate
October 15	1920	324a	Q&A, Copernicus 3, Bessel
January 2	1921	323	Copernicus 3
January 11	1921	323	∞, looping line
January 12	1921	323	∞, lemniscatic planetary orbits
January 17	1921	323	lemniscatic rotation, Bessel
January 18	1921	323	∞
August 26	1921	324a	Q&A, Copernicus 3
October 8	1921	343	Copernicus 3
January 5	1923	220	Copernicus 3
May 5	1924	349	Copernicus 3

Various attempts have been made to unite Rudolf Steiner's scattered indications into a consistent interpretation but to date, no view has successfully encompassed all of them. For some of the more significant efforts, see (in chronological order) Locher [1942], Hagemann [1966], Kaiser [1966], Schmidt [1966], Vetter [1967], Van Bemmelen [1967], Unger [1981], Bauer [1981, 1988], Hemming / Pinkall [1983], Hardorp [1983], Junge [1983], Rudnicki [1984], Adams [1989] (Chapter 4), and Vanscheidt [1992].

[100]The mechanical interpretation of the solar system that has been

customary since Newton's time renders the assumption of a separate third Copernican movement "superfluous." That is, if the Earth is seen as an (almost) symmetrical top spinning in the Sun's gravitational field, then according to the law of the preservation of rotation, the direction L of the axis of rotation (Earth's axis) essentially remains fixed in space. This interpretation, derived from physics, of course, would have been foreign to Copernicus. Among his successors, only a very few authors lament the neglect of the third Copernican movement or even consider it a serious factor. On this subject, see C. L. Menzzer's informative note 36 on *De Revolutionibus*, volume 1, chapter 11, *"Beweis von der dreifachen Bewegung der Erde"* ("Proof of the Threefold Movement of the Earth") (Copernicus [1879], appendix, p. 28-31). In this context, Rudolf Steiner's lecture of September 25, 1919 (GA 300a), also mentions the works of the poet and author *Johannes Schlaf* (1862–1941). See Schlaf [1914] and [1919]; both were found in Steiner's library, and the first contains a handwritten dedication by the author to Rudolf Steiner.

[101]Elisabeth Vreede (1879–1943), mathematician and astronomer and, from 1924 on, the first head of the Section for Mathematics and Astronomy of the School of Spiritual Science at the Goetheanum in Dornach. During this conference, Dr. Vreede gave two lectures (on October 13 and 14, 1920) on "The Justification for, and Limits of, Mathematics in Astronomy" [1922].

[102]Vreede [1922], pp. 138ff and 160.

[103]*Carl Unger* (1878–1929), manufacturer, engineer, and philosopher. During this conference, he gave six lectures (october 11–16, 1920) on the subject of Rudolf Steiner's work [1921]. See also the report on these lectures by Willy Storrer in Unger [1921], especially sections III and IV.

[104]For more about the theory of relativity with regard to the passage that follows, see the question-and-answer session of March 7, 1920 and the corresponding notes and the question-and-answer sessions of March 31, 1920, and January 15, 1921.

[105]See the passage by Einstein quoted in Note 6 to the question-and-answer session of March 7, 1920. Steiner is referring here to a problem later known as the "paradox of the twins" or the "paradox of the clocks." Its interpretation, still controversial today, is related to the significance of the concept of time in physics, but more especially to the interpretation of a physical system's "own time" in the context of the theory of relativity. On this subject, see Gschwind [1986], for example, and the references listed there.

[106] According to Einstein [1917], §18, the special principle of relativity states that the universal natural laws of physics are formally identical for two systems of reference subject to uniform motion (inertial systems). Of course, this statement presupposes that inertial systems exist. Popular examples taken from elementary mechanics do not strictly satisfy most of the prerequisites, hence, such examples fail to correspond to reality even from the perspective of physics.

Thus, for example, the frame of reference "Earth" (like any rotating system) is an accelerated system, as is the frame of reference "car." Because it overcomes the resistance of friction, a uniformly moving car executes accelerated movement. Because of wear and tear, the car is not an unchanging system—the more so when it has a flat tire and its speed decreases. Similar considerations apply to the oft-cited example of the train and the railway embankment.

The only examples of relativistic behavior that the field of physics considers realistic occur on the atomic or subatomic level, as Einstein [1917] also points out in his lecture. According to Steiner, however, the full reality of the realm of such phenomena cannot be grasped without extending physics in keeping with anthroposophical spiritual science (see the lectures of the first and second scientific courses, GA 320 and GA 321).

[107] *Friedrich Wilhelm Bessel* (1784–1846), astronomer, geodesist, and mathematician in Königsberg. Bessel made fundamental contributions to the techniques and technology of astronomical observation, including improvements in the instruments, systematic analysis of errors due to instruments and faulty observation, and thorough reduction of observations. Both instrumental errors and the influence of the Earth's atmosphere (refraction) must be eliminated when the location of a star is measured. Furthermore, for the sake of an objective standard that can be compared with other measurements, such locations must be calculated in terms of a common point in time, taking the effects of the observation point and the Earth's movement into account. Doing this requires an exact knowledge of precession, nutation (slight oscillation of the Earth's axis caused by the moon), and daily, yearly, and long-term aberration (caused by the ultimate/finite speed of light and apparent changes in the location of stars due to the Earth's movement).

Bessel's analysis/utilization (reduction) of the positions of 3,222 stars obtained by *James Bradley* (1693–1762) of the Greenwich observatory became a milestone in astronomical observation because it made precisely reliable star positions available for the first time. Bessel published his results in the books *Fundamenta Astronomiae pro Anno 1755 Deducta ex Observationibus Viri*

Incomparabilis James Bradley in Specula Astronomica Grenovicensi per Annos 1750–1762 Instituti (Königsberg [1818]) and *Tabulae Regiomantanae Reductionum Observationum Astronomicum ab Anno 1750 usque ad Annum 1850 Computatae* (Königsberg [1830]).

Related studies by Bessel yielded improved methods of determining the independent movement of fixed stars and the first means of determining parallaxes of individual fixed stars. These parallaxes constituted the first astronomical proof of the yearly movement of the Earth (on this and other proofs of this movement, see Teichmann [1983], chapter 3.4). The so-called Bessel reduction formulas for star coordinates have to do with the yearly and long-term influences of precession and nutation. (For more on this subject, see Schmidt [1967], Wolf [1890–1893], §609 and §613; and astronomical yearbooks such as The *Astronomical Almanac*, 1981ff, p. §22 ff.)

[108]*Albert Steffen* (1884–1963), poet and, from 1924 on, the first head of the Section for Fine Arts/Arts and Letters of the School of Spiritual Science at the Goetheanum in Dornach. During this conference, Steffen gave two lectures (on october 14 and 15, 1920) on the subject of "Spiritual Science and Crisis in the Life of the Artist." Steffen published his own summary of these lectures in the collection *Die Krisis im Leben des Künstlers* ("Crisis in the Life of the Artist") [1922]. See especially the essay of the same title in part II, pp. 31ff.

[109]Set theory was founded almost single-handedly by the mathematician *Georg Cantor* (1845–1918). Cantor sent Rudolf Steiner a copy of his *Lehre vom Transfiniten* ("Theory of the Transfinite") [1890], complete with personal dedication and handwritten corrections. In a treatise dated 1884, Cantor gives this definition of a set: "In general I understand a "manifold" or "set" to be a group of multiple elements that can be thought of as a whole. It is the epitome of specific elements that can be lawfully united into a whole. I believe I have thus defined something related to the Platonic *eidos*, or idea … (Cantor [1932], footnote to p. 204).

Rudolf Steiner's remarks refer to Cantor's investigations of various levels of infinity. The basis for these studies is this definition, which Steiner paraphrases: "I understand the *prime or cardinal number* of a set S (which consists of distinct and conceptually separate elements s, s',… and is defined and delineated by them) to be the general or universal concept that we gain by abstracting from the set both the character of its elements and all relationships of these elements either to each other or to other objects, and especially the order that may prevail among the elements, and reflect only on what is common to all sets that are equivalent to *S*. I call two sets *S* and *T equivalent*, however, when each element of one can clearly be made to correspond to exactly one element of the other" (Cantor [1890], p. 23 ff. Or [1932] p. 387). See also the essay entitled *"Georg Cantor and Rudolf Steiner* ("Georg Cantor und Rudolf Steiner") in *Beiträge zur Rudolf Steiner Gesamtausgabe* ("Articles on the Complete Edition of Rudolf Steiner's Work"), No. 114/115, Dornach, 1995.

[110] Oswald Spengler (1880–1936), originally a mathematician, later a writer. "Form and Actuality," the first volume of Spengler's principal work *The Decline of the West*, appeared in its first edition in 1918, and by 1920 had appeared in 32 printings. The second volume, "Perspectives of World History," which appeared in 1922, did not have as wide a readership. *Decline of the West* was first published in the U.S. In 1926–28.

[111] The second law of thermodynamics is based on the concept of entropy, which was first formulated by *Rudolf Clausius* (1822–1888). This concept states that entropy strives toward a maximum in any real thermodynamic process that takes place in a self-contained physical system. In the context of physics, proof of this law is possible only on the basis of other unprovable assumptions or postulates. For example, in the statistic kinetic gas theory dating back to *James Clark Maxwell* (1831–1879) and *Ludwig Bolzmann* (1844–1906) this second law takes the form of a provable theorem (Boltzmann's so-called H theorem) based on the hypothesis of complete molecular chaos.

[112] *Count Hermann Keyserling* (1880–1946), philosopher, author, and cofounder and scientific head of the "School of Wisdom" (or "Society for Independent Philosophy") in Darmstadt. See his works, such as *Das Reisetagebuch eines Philosophen* ("A Philosopher's Travel Diary") [1919a], *Der Weg der Vollendung: Des Grafen Hermann Keyserling philosophischen Schaffen* ("The Path of Perfection: The Philosophical Activity of Count Hermann Keyserling") [1919b], and *Philosophie als Kunst* ("Philosophy as an Art") [1920].

[113] Keyserling, *Philosophie als Kunst* ("Philosophy as an Art") [1920], p. 293: "The School of Wisdom must become a third element alongside the church (taking the word in the broadest possible nondenominational sense) and the university. Like each of these other elements, its intent is to shape the whole human being and spiritualize the human soul. In addition, however, it aspires to a synthesis between human soul life and the independent, fully conscious spirit, so that neither faith nor abstract knowledge is the final authority, but faith, knowledge, and life become one

in a living, higher unity of consciousness crowned by the School of Wisdom, whose task would be to organically incorporate abstract academic knowledge into a living synthesis and to transform mere "knowing" into "being."

[114] Presumably Steiner is referring to the weekly magazine *Die Zukunft* ("The Future"), edited by Maximilian Harden (volumes 1–118, 1892–1922). To date, the essay by Hermann Keyserling that Steiner mentions has not been found.

[114] Presumably Steiner is referring to the weekly magazine *Die Zukunft* ("The Future"), edited by Maximilian Harden (volumes 1–118, 1892–1922). To date, the essay by Hermann Keyserling that Steiner mentions has not been found.

[115] See also the discussions about Keyserling in the periodical *Dreigliederung des sozialen Organismus* ("The Threefolding of the Social Organism"), volume 2, 1920/1921, nos. 20–25, especially the report by *Ernst Uehli* (1875–1959) on Rudolf Steiner's lecture of November 16, 1920, in nos. 21 and 22. Further comments about Keyserling can be found in Rudolf Steiner's lecture of August 26, 1921, published in the periodical *Gegenwart* ("The Present"), volume 15, 1953–1954, no. 2, pp. 49–64.

[116] To date, the source of this statement by Keyserling has not been discovered.

[117] Goethe, *Faust*, Part II, Act 2, Scene 2, in the laboratory, verses 6989ff. *Homunculus* says to Wagner, who remains behind:

Unfold the ancient parchments,

As bidden, collect life's elements and join them carefully to each other, considering the *What*, but more the *How*.

While I wander through a portion of the world, I will, no doubt, discover the dot upon the i.

[118] Question-and-answer session at the conclusion of four lectures to an academic audience on the relationships between spiritual science and individual specialized fields of science. The four lectures in this cycle, *Proben über die Beziehungen der Geisteswissenschaft zu den einzelnen Fachwissenschaften* ("Attempts at Formulating the Connections of Spiritual Science to Individual Specialized Fields of Science"), were held in Stuttgart

from January 11 to 15, 1921, and were first published in the following editions of the periodical *Gegenwart* ("The Present"), vol. 14 (1952–1953): January 11, 1921, no. 2, pp. 49–67, January 12, 1921, no. 3, pp. 97–118, January 15, 1921, no. 4/5, pp. 145-167, January 14, 1921, no. 6, pp. 225–236, and no. 7, pp. 257–268, question-and-answer session of January 15, 1921, no. 8, pp. 305–317. These lectures will be published in GA 73a. See also the report on this conference by *Eugen Kolisko* (1893–1939) in the periodical *Dreigliederung des sozialen Organismus* ("The Threefolding of the Social Organism"), vol. 2, 1920–1921, no. 31, pp. 4–5, no. 32, p. 5, and no. 33, p. 4.

[119]*Geisteswissenschaftliche Impulse zur Entwickelung der Physik: Zweiter Naturwissenschaftlicher Kurs. Wärmelehre* ("Spiritual Scientific Impulses for the Further Development of Physics: Second Scientific Course. Heat Theory") (GA 321), Stuttgart, March 1 to 14, 1920.

[120]*Rudolf Clausius* (1822–1888), physicist in Berlin, Zürich, Würzburg, and Bonn. Clausius, along with *Ludwig Boltzmann* (1844–1906) and *James Clark Maxwell* (1831–1879), is considered one of the founders of modern thermodynamics, which is based on kinetic gas theory and statistical mechanics.

Clausius's book *Die Mechanische Wärmetheorie* ("The Mechanical Theory of Heat") includes his treatises on heat theory [1876-1891]. See also Rudolf Steiner's lectures of March 1 and 11, 1920 (GA 321).

[121]The editors of Steiner's second scientific course (GA 321) point out that various authors expressed concern about efforts to explain thermodynamics on the basis of mechanics. (See the Note to p. 26 of the lecture of March 1, 1920, on pp. 222 ff.). We would like to add here that prior to the discovery of quantum mechanics and quantum statistics, it was not possible to reconcile completely various attempts to develop a mechanical model of the molecular structure of matter with experimental findings, especially those of spectroscopy. On this subject, see Harman [1982], chapters V and VI.

[122]The ether drift experiment conducted by Michelson and Morley beginning in 1881 was intended to determine the Earth's speed relative to the presumably stationary quasimaterial ether of physics. The outcome of this extremely precise experiment was negative and raised questions about the validity of all theories of light and electricity that were based on the assumption of an absolutely stationary ether. A theoretical explanation of these findings was developed by *Hendrik Antoon Lorentz* (1853–1928) and *George Francis Fitzgerald* (1851–1901), working independently of each

other. A short time later, *Albert Einstein* (1879–1955) derived the resulting formulas, such as Lorentz's contraction, from the basic assumptions of his special theory of relativity (the principle of relativity, the absolute constancy of the speed of light). Einstein used a series of experiments that exist only in thought to derive and illustrate his theory.

[123] On the formulas for conductive and radiant heat and on the explanations that follow here, see also Rudolf Steiner's lectures of March 12, 1920 (GA 321), and January 8, 1921 (GA 323). The relevant equations are discussed according to the methods of modern mathematics in Dustmann/Pinkall [1992].

[124] See, for example, the chapter in Rudolf Steiner's *Riddles of the Soul* (GA 21) entitled "Max Dessoir on Anthroposophy" and the discussions about Hermann Keyserling at the end of the previous question-and-answer session (october 15, 1920).

[125] Questions and answers (disputation) during the second anthroposophical conference at the Goetheanum in Dornach, April 3 to 10, 1921. Rudolf Steiner's lectures on "Anthroposophy and the Specialized Sciences" appeared, along with the question-and-answer sessions (disputations), in *Die befruchtende Wirkung der Anthroposophie auf die Fachwissenschaften* ("Anthroposophy's Positive Effect on the Specialized Sciences") (GA 76). Reports by Willy Stokar on this conference can be found in the periodical *Dreigliederung des sozialen Organismus* ("The Threefolding of the Social Organism"), vol. 2, (1920–1921), nos. 42 and 43. Eugen Kolisko's reports were published in *Die Drei* (The Three"), vol. 1 (1921–1922), pp. 471–478. See also the invitation to this conference and the detailed program in *Dreigliederung des sozialen Organismus*, vol. 2 (1920–1921), no. 36.

[126] *Metageometry* is an almost obsolete term encompassing various types of non-Euclidean geometry. In the second half of the nineteenth century, these non-Euclidean geometries included projective geometry, hyperbolic and elliptical geometry, the geometry of general curved spaces (Riemann's geometry), and the geometry of higher-dimensional spaces.

[127] Riemann: See Note 1, Lecture 1 (March 24, 1905).

[128] Gauss: See Note 1, Lecture 1 (March 24, 1905).

[129] "Riemann's metageometry" probably means either so-called elliptical geometry, which was first discovered and described by Riemann and is closely related to the geometry of a spherical surface, or the general theory —also based on Riemann's work—of curved spaces (manifolds with a Riemannian metric), of which elliptical geometry is only a special instance

(space with a constant positive curve).

[130] Kant did not distinguish between the mathematical or geometric view of the concept of space and the laws of perceived space. He interpreted the latter as necessary, subject-based prerequisites of sense perception. "Space is a necessary idea *a priori* and underlies all external views." (*Critique of Pure Reason* = CPR, B 38). "The apodictic certainty of all geometric theorems is based on this necessity *a priori*, and the possibility of their construction *a priori*" (CPR, A 24). Thus, "Geometry is a science that determines the properties of space synthetically and yet *a priori*" (CPR, B 40). "For example, space has only three dimensions, such statements, however, cannot constitute, and cannot be concluded on the basis of, empirical judgments" (CPR, B 41).

"How can the mind encompass an outer view that precedes the objects themselves and in which the concept of the latter can be determined *a priori*? Apparently only to the extent that it is affected by objects only in the subject, as the latter's formal constitution…that is, only as the form of the outer *sense* altogether." (CPR, B 41) Thus, "Space is nothing other than simply the form of all manifestations of outer senses, that is, the subjective condition of sensory nature, which alone makes our outer perception possible" (CPR, B 42).

Thus for Kant, the laws of perceived space coincide with geometric principles that can be thought. In Kant's time, ideas about non-Euclidean measurement and spaces with more than three dimensions had not yet appeared in mathematics. In particular, Kant lacked the clear distinction between topological and metric properties that dates back only to Riemann, so he saw no difference between the topological attribute of limitlessness and the metric attributes (that is, those pertaining to measured relationships) of infinity. Thus, in his explanations of the "antinomies of pure reason," where he proclaims the insolubility of certain problems that cannot be interpreted from his perspective, Kant says, The same is true of the dual answer to the question of the size of the cosmos, because if *it is infinite* and boundless, it is *too big* for all possible empirical concepts. *If it is finite* and limited, you are right to ask, What determines the limit?" (CPR, B 515). Kant's concept of space, which clings to three-dimensional Euclidean geometry, could no longer be reconciled with the various concepts of space that developed as mathematics continued to evolve. One of the first to point this out clearly from the perspectives of physics and physiology was *Hermann von Helmholtz* (1821–1894). On this subject, see Helmholtz's speech *Die Thatsachen in der Wahrnehmung* ("Facts in Perception") [1878].

[131] Kant's discussion of the paralogisms (deceptive or faulty conclusions)

and antinomies of pure reason constitute the major portion of the second volume, *Transcendental Dialectics, of The Critique of Pure Reason* [1787]. Kant intended his critique of the paralogisms of pure reason as a critique of the claims of the rational psychology of his day (including the problems of unchangeability, preexistence of the soul, etc.) rather than as a discussion of classic paralogisms.

"A logical paralogism is the formal falsehood of a rational conclusion, regardless of its content. A transcendental paralogism, however, has a transcendental reason for coming to a formally false conclusion. In this way, a faulty conclusion of this sort has its reasons in the nature of human reason itself and carries an inevitable if not insoluble illusion with it" (CPR, B 399). As he does later in his discussion of the antinomies of pure reason, Kant also attempts here in his discussion of paralogisms to demonstrate that they "dissolve" only when his own view is applied, namely, that we can know only the manifestations of "things as such" and that while our reason can order these manifestations according to regulative principles (such as the perceived forms of space and time), no direct insight into the constitution of things as such is possible. The problem of space plays only a peripheral role in Kant's discussion of the paralogisms of pure reason, namely, in the fourth paralogism about the soul's relationship "to possible objects in space" (CPR, B 402). In contrast, Kant's view of space is of fundamental importance in his discussion of the system of cosmological ideas in the section on the antinomies of pure reason.

> [132]Of course, three-dimensional Euclidean space was the historical point of departure and, initially, the foundation on which non-Euclidean concepts were developed in projective geometry and the geometries of curved and higher-dimensional space. To this extent, these new forms of space were derivative in nature, although they were not special instances of Euclidean space, they expanded the concept of space on the basis of fundamental Euclidean concepts. Steiner's reference to circular logic has to do with the fact that we achieve only an apparent generalization of the view of space as long as the relevant concepts depend essentially on a Euclidean point of departure.

The further evolution of mathematics has shown that we can dispense with the Euclidean foundation, that the laws of space can be developed step by step without presupposing the development of any specifically Euclidean concepts. We begin with a topological manifold that is defined as coordinate-free, supplement it with metrical and, if needed, differential geometric structures, arriving at Euclidean geometry as a special instance of a three-dimensional metric manifold. Seen systematically, there is no longer any circular logic involved in this process. When Steiner answered this question, these issues had not been clarified finally, even among mathematicians. See also Rudolf Steiner's handwritten notes and the corresponding footnotes in no. 114/115 of *Beiträge zur Rudolf Steiner Gesamtausgabe* ("Articles on Rudolf Steiner's Complete Works"), Dornach, 1995, p. 49. In any case, with regard to the structure of real space, mathematical concepts, which indicate only which spatial forms are possible, are indeed abstract and remote from reality in this sense, as long as their correspondence with reality has not been established.

[133] The concept of space that dates back to *Euclid* (ca. 320–260 B.C.) can be found in his comprehensive, thirteen-volume work *Elements*, especially in book XI and, to a lesser extent, in book I. This view of space focuses on the fundamentals of stereometry, that is, calculating the volumes of three-dimensional objects.

[134] On the relationship of Imagination, Inspiration, and Intuition to the dimensions of space, see Rudolf Steiner's lectures of August 19 and 26, 1923 (GA 227, pp. 39–41 and 161–163). See also his lectures of May 17, 1905 (GA 324a), September 16, 1907 (GA 101, pp. 189ff.), January 15, 1921 (GA 323, pp. 274–283), April 8, 1922 (GA 82), June 24, 1922 (GA 213), and the question-and-answer session of April 12, 1922 (GA 82 and 324a).

[135] See also Rudolf Steiner's lectures of April 9 and 10, 1920 (GA 201), March 17, 1921 (GA 324), December 26 and 27, 1922, and January 1, 1923 (GA 326). In the section on Goethe's concept of space in *Einleitungen zu Goethes Naturwissenschaftlichen Schriften* ("Introductions to Goethe's Scientific Works," GA 1, pp. 288–295), Steiner also develops the idea that the three dimensions are not interchangeable, but from a totally different perspective.

[136] Essentially, Euclid's three-dimensional geometry is still stereometry, that is, the study of the geometric properties of three-dimensional objects. Right angles and the concept of the perpendicular play an important role in Euclidean geometry, but Euclid placed no particular emphasis on the cube or on the related system of three perpendicular axes.

The implicit introduction of such axes as a reference system for the algebraic treatment of curves dates back to *Pierre de Fermat* (1601–1665) and *René Descartes* (1596–1650). Both of these mathematicians, however, often used obliqueangled axes, and in their work the coordinate system did not yet play a role as an independent structure that could be dissociated from the geometric object being discussed. Until the end of the eighteenth century, the same was true of developments in analytical geometry based on the work of these pioneers. The systematic application of two perpendicular or oblique directions as a reference system for coordinates and the discussion of algebraic curves occurs first in a treatise by *Isaac Newton* (1643–1727) entitled *Enumeratio Linearum Tertii Ordinis* (1676). Newton was also the first to use negative coordinates systematically and to draw curves in all four quadrants of the coordinate system. The analytical geometry of three-dimensional space and the corresponding use of a system of three perpendicular axes dates back to systematic studies of surfaces conducted by *Leonhard Euler* (1707–1783). Analytical geometry in the modern sense was definitively formulated in the late eighteenth and early nineteenth centuries by *Gaspard Monge* (1746–1818) and his pupil *François Lacroix* (1765–1843), who was one of the nineteenth century's most successful authors of mathematical textbooks. Previously, coordinate systems had been used primarily in connection with specific geometrical figures, but in the new analytical geometry, a preexisting coordinate system provided a framework for the study of geometric figures, their internal proportions, and their interrelationships. See the standard work on this subject by Boyer [1956].

[137] See the discussion of this problem in Note 8 above.

[138] See the question-and-answer session of March 7, 1920, and the corresponding notes, particularly Note 3.

[139] Questions and answers (open discussion) during the Summer Art Course at the Goetheanum, August 21 to 27, 1921. Rudolf Steiner's own summaries of his lectures during this conference were published in the *Nachrichten der Rudolf Steiner-Nachlassverwaltung* ("News from the Rudolf Steiner Archives"), no. 8, 1962, pp. 4–20. (Beginning with no. 29, 1970, the name of this publication was changed to *Beiträge zur Rudolf Steiner Gesamtausgabe* ["Articles on Rudolf Steiner's Complete Works"].) A detailed conference program was published in the journals *Dreigliederung des sozialen Organismus* ("The Threefolding of the Social organism"), vol. 3, no. 5, and *Das Goetheanum*, vol. 1, 1921–1922, no. 1. Transcripts of the lectures were first published in the periodical *Gegenwart* ("The Present"). The introductory lecture of August 21, 1921, appeared in vol. 14, 1952-1953, no. 9/10, pp. 353–363, the lecture of August 23, 1921, in vol. 14, no. 11, pp. 417–428; the lecture of August 24, 1921, in vol. 15, 1953–1954, no. 1, pp. 4–19; and the lecture of August 26, 1921, in vol. 15, no. 2, pp. 44–63. Publication of this lecture series is planned for GA 73a. The question-and-answer session appears here in print for the first time.

[140] Compare this and the following passages to the question-and-answer

session of october 15, 1920, and the relevant notes.

[141] See also Rudolf Steiner's lectures of May 2, 1920 (GA 201), and January 16, 1921 (GA 323).

[142] In this lecture, Rudolf Steiner lists these laws in the order given by Copernicus in chapter 11 of the first volume of his main work, *De Revolutionibus Orbium Coelestinum*. See also Notes 2 and 3 to the question-and-answer session of october 15, 1920.

[143] Presumably, Rudolf Steiner refers here to Bessel's reductions, which he mentions in the question-and-answer session of October 15, 1920.

[144] Question-and-answer session at the end of a series of lectures to university instructors in The Hague, April 7–12, 1922. These lectures were published in the volume entitled *Damit der Mensch ganz Mensch werde. Die Bedeutung der Anthroposophie im Geistesleben der Gegenwart* ("To Be Fully Human: The Significance of Anthroposophy in Modern Intellectual Life"), GA 82, Dornach, 1994.

[145] For more information on Hinton, see Note 1 to the lecture of March 31, 1905. on the tessaract, see the lecture of May 31, 1905, and the relevant notes.

[146] See Notes 10 and 11 and the corresponding passages in the question-and-answer session of April 7, 1921.

[147] See Rudolf Steiner's lectures of April 8, 9, and 10, 1922.

[148] See the similar passages at the end of Rudolf Steiner's lecture of January 10, 1921 (GA 323, pp. 199–200) and at the beginning of the lecture of January 18, 1921 (GA 323, pp. 318–320).

[149] Presumably Rudolf Steiner refers here to the lecture he gave to the Mathematical Society in Basel during the winter semester of 1920-1921. For more about this lecture, see the essay *Über einen mathematischen Vortrag Rudolf Steiners in Basel* ("on a Mathematical Lecture by Rudolf Steiner in Basel") in *Beiträge zur Rudolf Steiner Gesamtausgabe* ("Articles on Rudolf Steiner's Complete Works"), no. 114/115, Dornach, 1995.

[150] See the parallel passages in the lectures of January 11, 1921 (published in *Gegenwart* ["The Present"], vol. 14, pp. 49–67, especially p. 65) and April 5, 1921 (GA 76).

[151] See the question-and-answer session of March 7, 1920, and the relevant notes.

[152] For more on this subject, see the lectures of October 28, 1909, and February 10, 1910, in Rudolf Steiner's *Metamorphosen des Seelenlebens*

("The Metamorphoses of Soul Life") and *Pfade der Seelenerlebnisse* ("The Paths of Soul Experience"), GA 58 and 59.

[153]*Friedrich Wilhelm Ostwald* (1853–1932), chemist, color theorist, and scientific philosopher. In his lecture *Die Überwindung des wissenschaftlichen Materialismus* ("overcoming Scientific Materialism) of September 20, 1895, which included a plea for his own energetics-based worldview and consciously contrasted it to the mechanistic worldview of *Emil du Bois-Reymond* (1818–1896), Ostwald said:

While efforts to interpret the familiar phenomena of physics in mechanical terms may seem in vain, having ultimately failed in every single serious attempt, the conclusion is unavoidable that success is even less likely with regard to the incomparably more complex phenomena of organic life. The same principled contradictions apply here, too, and the claim that all natural phenomena essentially can be traced back to mechanical phenomena cannot even be considered a usable working hypothesis, it is a simple error. This error becomes most apparent when we confront the following fact. A feature of all mechanical equations is that they permit changing the sign of the unit of time. That is, theoretically perfect mechanical processes can run backward as well as forward. In a purely mechanical world, therefore, there would be no earlier and later as we know them in our world. A tree could revert to the seed stage, a butterfly could be transformed back into a caterpillar, and an elderly person into an adult. The mechanistic worldview cannot explain why this does not occur, and because of the above-mentioned feature of mechanical equations, no such explanation is possible. Thus, the non-reversibility of true natural phenomena proves the existence of processes that cannot be described by mechanical equations and pronounces judgment on scientific materialism ([1895], p. 20).

[154]Steiner means that a projective straight line must be visualized as having only one (rather than two) infinitely distant points.

[155]The founder of modern perspective was *Filippo Brunelleschi* (1377–1446), the architect and builder of the cupola of the cathedral in Florence. The new theory of perspective was first promoted by the architect and scholar *Leon Battista Alberti* (1401–1472) and the painter and mathematician *Piero della Francesca* (1416–1492). A work by *Albrecht Dürer* (1471–1528), *Underweysung der messung mit dem zirckel und richtscheyt in linien, ebnen, und gantzen corporen* ("Instruction in Measuring with Compass and Straightedge in Lines, Planes, and Solid

Bodies," 1525) had a decisive influence on the cultural region north of the Alps.

[156] On color perspective, see Rudolf Steiner's lectures of June 2, 1923 (GA 291), and April 19, 1922 (GA 304, p. 208), and the question and answer session of March 11, 1920.

[157] Rudolf Steiner's additional comments during the lecture cycle *Der Enstehungsmoment der Naturwissenschaft in der Weltgeschichte und ihre seitherige Entwickelung* ("The Emergence of the Natural Sciences in World History and Their Subsequent Development"), GA 326. Comments on the discussion following a lecture by *Ernst Blümel* (1884–1952) on "Die vier Raumdimensionen im Lichte der Anthroposophie" ("The Four Dimensions of Space in the Light of Anthroposophy"). To date, no transcript of Blümel's lecture has been found.

[158] my *lectures*: The lectures given on December 26–28, 1922 (GA 326). On tactile and visual space, see Rudolf Steiner's lectures of March 17, 1921 (GA 324), and January 1, 1923 (GA 326).

[159] Rudolf Steiner points to the transition from a sphere to a plane or a circle to a straight line in many different places. See the parallel passages in this volume in the lecture of March 24, 1905, and in the questions and answers of September 2, 1906; July 28, 1908, and November 25, 1912.

[160] For more about "apprehending reality" through projective geometry, see Rudolf Steiner's lectures of January 11, 1921 (published in *Gegenwart* ["The Present"], vol. 14, 1952, no. 2, pp. 49–67, planned for publication in GA 73a); April 5, 1921 (GA 76); and the question-and-answer session of April 12, 1922 (GA 324a and 82).

[161] Today inevitable movements are understood as movements possessing only one degree of movement, that is, movements that are so restricted that only one free parameter for movement exists. Presumably, however, what Steiner means here is the very general problem of movement subject to secondary conditions. The Newtonian formulation of mechanics proves unwieldy in calculating movements subject to secondary conditions. Furthermore, this formulation made it difficult to introduce standard, non-rectilinear coordinates for movement. The *LaGrange equations*, which are based on a principle of mechanical variation, offer elegant solutions to both problems.

[162] See Rudolf Steiner's lecture of December 27, 1922 (GA 326).

[163] On negative gravitation, see Rudolf Steiner's lectures of January 7 and 8, 1921 (GA 323).

[164]*LaGrange equations. Joseph-Louis LaGrange* (1736–1813), mathematician, physicist, and astronomer in Turin, Berlin, and Paris. The derivation, discussion, and application of the equations later named after LaGrange constitute the majority of his book *Mécanique Analitique* (Paris, 1788). On the LaGrange equations, see Note 159.

[165]*Phylogenetics*: See Rudolf Steiner's lecture of December 28, 1922 (GA 326).

Milton Keynes UK
Ingram Content Group UK Ltd.
UKHW052214050923
428087UK00014B/928